Elite Sport Development

Elite Sport Development addresses important questions in contemporary sports development, providing detailed analysis of the emergence and current status of elite sport policy and practice in the UK, Australia and Canada.

The authors consider the problems faced by governments and national governing bodies in establishing a successful elite sport infrastructure and examine in detail the particular issues associated with provision of facilities, coaching, sports science and competition. The lives and needs of full-time athletes are studied and tensions generated by competition for resources between elite sport, schools and community provision are explored. The book includes discussion of:

- Why do governments invest heavily in elite sport?
- What are the relationships between governments and NGBs?
- How does elite sport investment affect 'Sport for All'?
- How are individual sports selected for priority funding?

Elite Sport Development will be of interest to students, researchers and professionals working in sports development and policy.

Mick Green is a lecturer in Sport and Leisure Policy and Management and **Barrie Houlihan** is Professor of Sport Policy, both at the Institute of Sport and Leisure Policy, School of Sport and Exercise Sciences, Loughborough University, UK.

Elite Sport Development

Policy learning and political priorities

Mick Green and Barrie Houlihan

 Routledge
Taylor & Francis Group

LONDON AND NEW YORK

First published 2005
by Routledge
2 Park Square, Milton Park, Abingdon, Oxon OX14 4RN

Simultaneously published in the USA and Canada
by Taylor & Francis Inc.
270 Madison Ave, New York, NY 10016

Routledge is an imprint of the Taylor & Francis Group

© 2005 Mick Green and Barrie Houlihan

Typeset in Goudy by
HWA Text and Data Management, Tunbridge Wells
Printed and bound in Great Britain by
MPG Books Ltd, Bodmin

Every effort has been made to ensure that the advice and information in
this book is true and accurate at the time of going to press. However,
neither the publisher nor the authors can accept any legal responsibility
or liability for any errors or omissions that may be made. In the case of
drug administration, any medical procedure or the use of technical
equipment mentioned within this book, you are strongly advised to
consult the manufacturer's guidelines.

British Library Cataloguing in Publication Data
A catalogue record for this book is available from the British Library

Library of Congress Cataloging in Publication Data
A catalog record for this book has been requested

ISBN 0–415–33182–X (hbk)
ISBN 0–415–33183–8 (pbk)

To Judy

Contents

Figures and tables

Figures

Tables

Acknowledgements

Although we take full responsibility for this work, it has not been achieved without incurring a number of debts. Our largest debt is to the officials in the nine national sporting organisations/national governing bodies of sport, the Australian Sports Commission, Sport Canada and UK Sport and the academic and sporting analysts who willingly gave up their time for interviews. Their readiness to talk through the issues raised provided a rich vein of information upon which much of the study was based. In addition, we are also especially grateful to Gene Schembri at the Australian Sports Commission, Professor Peter Donnelly of the University of Toronto, and Professor Anita White, formerly of the English Sports Council, for taking the time to listen to our research interests and for facilitating access to many of the organisations and people who have helped with our study. We would also like to thank staff at Loughborough University's Institute of Sport and Leisure Policy for their advice and support, and for engendering a sustained research ethos upon which studies such as this are, in many ways, reliant. Last but not least, the success of our investigations in the three countries was also heavily reliant on the willingness of librarians to help uncover the vital and often elusive documentary evidence that underpinned our study. We are especially grateful in this respect to the library staff at Loughborough University and the University of Ottawa, and to Greg Blood at the Australian Sports Commission's National Sport Information Centre.

Abbreviations

AAA	Amateur Athletics Association
AAI	Athletics Australia Incorporated
AAP	Athlete Assistance Programme
AC	Athletics Canada
ACC	Australian Coaching Council
ACF	Advocacy Coalition Framework
AIS	Australian Institute of Sport
AOC	Australian Olympic Committee
APA	Athlete Personal Award
ASA	Amateur Swimming Association
ASC	Australian Sports Commission
ASFGB	Amateur Swimming Federation of Great Britain
ASI	Australian Swimming Incorporated
ASCTA	Australian Swimming Coaches and Teachers Association
AT&FCA	Australian Track and Field Coaches Association
AYFI	Australian Yachting Federation Incorporated
BAAB	British Amateur Athletic Board
BAF	British Athletic Federation
BOA	British Olympic Association
CAC	Coaching Association of Canada
CBET	Competency-Based Education and Training
CCPR	Central Council of Physical Recreation
COA	Canadian Olympic Association
COC	Canadian Olympic Committee
CSC	Canadian Sport Centre
CTFA	Canadian Track and Field Association
CYA	Canadian Yachting Association
DAS	Direct Athlete Support
DASET	Department for the Arts, Sport, the Environment and Territories
DASETT	Department for the Arts, Sport, the Environment, Tourism and the Territories

DCITA	Department for Communication, Information Technology and the Arts
DCMS	Department for Culture, Media and Sport
DEST	Department for the Environment, Sports and Territories
DISR	Department of Industry, Science and Resources
DNH	Department of National Heritage
FINA	Fédération Internationale de Natation Amateur
GDR	German Democratic Republic
IAAF	International Association of Athletics Federations
IOC	International Olympic Committee
MoU	Memorandum of Understanding
MYA	Member Yachting Association
NCAA	National Collegiate Athletic Association
NCAS	National Coaching Accreditation Scheme
NCCP	National Coaching Certification Programme
NCF	National Coaching Foundation
NGB	National Governing Body (of Sport)
NSO	National Sporting Organisation
OAP	Olympic Athlete Programme
OSG	Olympic Steering Group
P/TSO	Provincial/Territorial Sporting Organisation
QPP	Quadrennial Planning Process
RYA	Royal Yachting Association
SFAF	Sport Funding and Accountability Framework
SNC	Swimming/Natation Canada
SSC	Specialist Sports College
TSPGP	Targeted Sports Participation Growth Programme
UKA	UK Athletics
UKSI	United Kingdom Sports Institute
USSR	Union of Soviet Socialist Republics
YRA	Yacht Racing Association

1   Investigating elite sport policy processes and policy change

Over the last 40 years at least there has been an increasing awareness among governments of the value of elite sporting success. More often than not elite success has been seen as a resource valuable for its malleability and its capacity to help achieve a wide range of non-sporting objectives. For the USA, USSR and the European communist countries sport was a tool for demonstrating ideological superiority and for East Germany it had the additional utility of aiding the country's claim to sovereignty. More recently, international sporting success has been variously valued for the national 'feel good' factor that it generates, for its capacity to deliver economic benefits through the hosting of major events, and for its general diplomatic utility. Needless to say, governments soon recognised that if they were to maximise some or all of these benefits they had to be able to guarantee that they had a squad of elite athletes capable of winning medals.

For a number of years it was possible to be confident that the key structural factors of economic prosperity and a large population would be sufficient to ensure medal success at the Olympic Games. As Stamm and Lemprecht (2001) noted, between 1964 and 1980 half the variation in the success of countries at the Olympics could be explained by three variables: population size; duration of International Olympic Committee (IOC) membership (as an indicator of depth of sporting tradition); and the level of economic development. A fourth variable, a communist government, was a further significant indicator. Since 1956, the most successful 10 per cent of countries at the Olympic Games have accounted for between 64 per cent and 83 per cent of all medals. In the Sydney Games 20 countries accounted for 72 per cent of all medals. The picture is similar for the winter Olympics. In 1956, the most successful 10 per cent of countries won 47 per cent of all medals. By the Salt Lake City Games of 2002, the figure had risen to 67 per cent. Over this period the composition of the 10 per cent most successful countries has changed little in both the summer and winter Games. In the 2000 and 2002 Games the most successful countries fell into one of two groups. With the exception of Ethiopia they were either rich industrial countries or former/current communist countries.

Despite the consistency with which the rich and populous countries dominate the medal tables, there is a constant need for their governments to ensure the continued availability of the resource – the athletes – that allows them to exploit to their advantage their position in the medal tables or to bid successfully to host the Games. Although 'big and rich countries are still at a considerable advantage when it comes to international sport' (Stamm and Lemprecht 2001: 135) these traditional sports powers have increasingly sought to maintain their relative advantage by adopting more systematic, professional and science-based approaches to elite athlete development (cf. Green and Oakley 2001a; Whitson 1998). Governments have shown a considerable willingness to devote significant sums of public or government controlled money (e.g. national lotteries) to the maintenance or improvement of elite sporting success. The United Kingdom (UK), for example, spent around £120 million establishing a regional network of elite sports institutes as well as approximately £100 million in the four years prior to the Sydney Olympics supporting approximately 600 athletes. Other countries have invested similar sums. Hogan and Norton (2000) calculated that between 1980 and 1996 the Australian government spent $AUS0.918 billion and won 25 Gold medals and a total of 115 Olympic medals at an average cost of $AUS37 million for each Gold medal and $AUS8 million for each general medal.

The achievement of international, and especially Olympic, sporting success is increasingly important to a growing number of countries. In recent years governments have become more willing to intervene directly in the elite development process requiring substantial changes on the part of national sporting organisations (NSOs) and national governing bodies (NGBs) of sport (professional management, high quality coaching, and talent identification programmes for example) as a condition of grant aid. This book provides an analysis of the shifts in elite policy in Australia, Canada and the UK in three sports – swimming, athletics and sailing/yachting.[1]

In Australia, the establishment of the Australian Institute of Sport (AIS) in 1981 and the creation of the federal government agency – the Australian Sports Commission (ASC) – in 1985 have, arguably, been the clearest manifestations of the country's desire to reverse its 'slide in international sporting competitions' (Adair and Vamplew 1997: 93). Importantly, a large degree of political consensus across the country's two main political parties underpinned these developments. What has emerged in the intervening years is a systematic, planned and increasingly scientific approach to developing the country's elite athletes. Yet, a recurrent and significant theme in the development of Australian sport policy is the discourse surrounding the relative funding allocations for mass participation initiatives and those for elite sport programmes. Indeed, an examination of Australian public policy since 1975 reveals an apparent reluctance to address both sport policy goals with equal commitment (Armstrong 1997; Booth 1995; Nauright 1996). In short, as Hogan and Norton note, funding has been targeted towards 'the skill development of talented athletes in the continuum of elite athlete "production"' (2000: 215–16). In Chapter 4, we draw out some of the key consequences of this policy approach for the sports of swimming, athletics and sailing.

In Canada, beginning in the 1970s, the federal government was responsible for the construction of a policy framework that underpinned the establishment of a cadre of elite athletes capable of achieving medal-winning success at major international sporting events, most notably at the Olympic Games[2] (cf. Macintosh and Whitson 1990). The unintended consequences of this drive for sporting excellence in Canada were brought into sharp relief with the Ben Johnson drugs affair at the 1988 Seoul Olympic Games. What followed, was a number of inquiries into the values and belief systems underpinning Canadian sport, in general, and Canadian high performance sport, in particular (cf. Blackhurst *et al.* 1991; Canada 1992; Dubin 1990). The subsequent debate over the values/belief systems underpinning the country's 'sport delivery system' (cf. Thibault and Harvey 1997) resulted in the changing emphases evident in the new Canadian Sport Policy (Canadian Heritage 2002) and subsequent legislation, *An Act to Promote Physical Activity and Sport* – Bill C-12 (House of Commons of Canada 2002). In short, in Canada there is evidence of a significant shift in policy direction and emphasis at the federal level, the ramifications of which are dealt with in more depth in Chapter 5.

With regard to the UK, policy priorities towards developing a framework of support systems for elite level athletes have, traditionally, been rather more ambiguous. Yet, two factors in particular are central to the changing direction and emphasis of sport policy in the UK since the mid-1990s. First, in 1994, the National Lottery was introduced with sport being one of five 'good causes' to benefit from the monies raised. The significance of Lottery monies for the emergence of a more systematic approach to developing the country's elite athletes cannot be underestimated. In 2001–2, for example, '£22,550,608 was allocated from the World Class Performance[3] programme to 33 UK/GB[4] sports, representing a total of 762 athletes' (UK Sport 2002c: 7). The significance of Lottery monies is clear if we consider that, in the same year, UK Sport distributed (just) £5,817,768 of Treasury funding to UK/GB NGBs and other partner organisations to support, largely, their non-elite activities (UK Sport 2002c). Second, in 1995 the Conservative Government published *Sport: Raising the Game* (Department of National Heritage [DNH] 1995), the first government policy statement on sport in 20 years. The two key strands of *Sport: Raising the Game* – youth sport and excellence – were sustained in the Labour Party's sport policy document, *A Sporting Future for All* (Department for Culture, Media and Sport [DCMS] 2000). A further instructive aspect of this document is the emphasis put on the modernisation of NGBs, to be achieved, in large part, by meeting objectives set at DCMS/UK Sport/Home Country Sport Council levels. Therefore, an important aspect of the discussion in Chapter 6 centres on assessing the significance of the changing pattern of resource dependency and the government prioritisation of elite success for policy at the elite levels of swimming, athletics and sailing.

In order to analyse the process of elite sport policy change in the three countries we draw on insights provided by a prominent meso-level theoretical approach – the advocacy coalition framework (ACF) – and provide an account of the emergence of sport policy in general and an explanation of the development of elite sport policy in particular, in Australia, Canada and the UK; an evaluation of the utility of the meso-level ACF in relation to its application to elite sport policy change; and an analysis of the process of policy change within the sport development policy subsystem.

Research methodology

Our research methodology draws on Marsh *et al.*'s (1999) identification of seven requirements necessary for a 'satisfactory account' of political and policy change over time. In this respect, a satisfactory account:

> i   should have a strong historical perspective, being theoretically informed but empirically grounded;
>
> ii needs a sophisticated, rather than a simplistic, conception of change;
>
> iii should recognise the importance of political, economic and ideological factors in any explanation of change, rather than exclusively emphasising one of them;
>
> iv must recognise that any explanation has to take account of the international as well as the domestic context within which change occurs;
>
> v   needs to be underpinned by a stated and developed epistemological position;
>
> vi must utilise a dialectical approach to structure and agency, rather than giving priority to either; and
>
> vii must acknowledge that the relationship between the material and the ideational is crucial and, again, dialectical.
>
> (Marsh *et al.* 1999: 1–2)

It is argued that by drawing upon the meso-level ACF the first four of these seven requirements can be addressed. The final three requirements identified above by Marsh *et al.* are addressed in the following sections of this chapter, and further consideration is given to the fourth requirement by way of using examples related to the notion of globalisation processes in order to illustrate key issues throughout the following discussion.

Although an in-depth discussion of ontology and epistemology would be inappropriate, it is important to note that this study is premised upon a set of ontological and epistemological assumptions closely associated with critical realism (cf. Archer *et al.* 1998; Bhaskar 1975). Drawing on this body of work, Sayer argues that 'the explanation of social phenomena entails that we critically evaluate them … [and] their associated practices and the material structures which they produce and which in turn help to sustain those practices' (1992: 40). From this perspective, theory helps to identify and explain underlying structural relationships in policy networks, communities and advocacy coalitions, for example (Hay 1995, 2002; Marsh and Smith 2000, 2001). In short, this study is premised on what can be termed an 'anti-foundationalist' ontology (that is, not all social phenomena are directly observable, structures exist that cannot be observed empirically and those that can may not present the social/political world as it actually is) and an 'interpretivist' epistemology (Grix 2002: 183). Using the phenomenon of globalisation as an example, and one that cannot be ignored in this comparative study, it is evident that there are both real processes going on, yet it is the discursive construction of these processes that, to some extent, shapes and mediates policy-making processes (Marsh *et al.* 1999). For example, with regard to our focus on elite sport, there has been an increase in the ease of global communication (e.g. knowledge-based epistemic communities involved in elite sport), the global role of the media and the increasing influence of multinational corporations (e.g. elite sport sponsorship).

These developments have political/policy consequences. For example, both state and non-state actors and electorates are now more aware of the policy problems faced, and the solutions adopted, by other countries. This is reflected in the increasing interest in issues surrounding policy transfer (cf. Dolowitz and Marsh 2000; Evans and Davies 1999; Marsh and Stoker 1995). Clearly, there are significant arguments about the extent of such globalisation processes but there is little doubt of their existence (Marsh *et al.* 1999). At the same time, however, the ways in which globalisation processes impact upon national policy-making are mediated by its discursive construction. Questions are thus raised with respect to how state and non-state actors in the UK, for example, have discursively constructed knowledge gained from other countries, such as Australia, with regard to elite sport policy.

In order to understand better the nature of (elite) sport policy processes and policy change, the methodology adopted takes account of the three dialectical relationships highlighted by Marsh and Smith (2000). Drawing on Marsh and Smith's work on policy networks, we can extend their analysis to policy subsystems. The three dialectical relationships are those between structure and agency; subsystem and context; and subsystem and outcome. In short, a theoretical framework that makes it possible to acknowledge both the influence of actors on the development of policies in subsystems and the impact of the structural context in which actors operate (cf. Goverde and van Tatenhove 2000). Our argument, then, is that this dialectical standpoint has significant implications for the interpretation of changes in elite sport.

First, the emphasis is on analysis that considers (policy) change over a considerable time period. As a dialectical approach calls for a longitudinal analysis partial snapshots of a brief period of time are rarely instructive. Thus, this study provides a review of sport policy developments over a period of 30 years, as well as a more detailed analysis of elite sport policy change over the past 10 to 15 years. In the UK, for example, such an approach requires an evaluation of 'structural' factors, such as the relatively enduring (political/policy) relationships embodied in government–civil society interaction, and those between the central government department for sport – currently the Department for Culture, Media and Sport (DCMS) – and Sports Councils on the one hand, and actors/organisations within specific sport policy subsystems on the other. The analysis also takes account of 'agency' factors. An instructive example in this sense is the important catalytic role played by Prime Minister John Major in placing sporting issues higher on the political agenda in the early 1990s. Second, this view emphasises the need to adopt an analysis that takes account of the interaction between economic, political and ideological factors. It is argued that the ACF is particularly valuable in this respect because it emphasises the requirement of a long-term approach (usually over a decade or more) to the analysis of policy change and because it requires that analysis takes account of both exogenous factors – 'relatively stable parameters' and 'external (system) events' – *and* endogenous factors – the role of negotiating actors in policy subsystem coalitions (Sabatier and Jenkins-Smith 1999: 149).

Conceptualising power relations

The conceptualisation of power relations, in the initiation of policy, in influencing policy outcomes, and in setting policy agendas, for example, are central to an understanding of the policy process. It is important, therefore, to clarify how power is conceptualised in our analysis (cf. Hay 1995, 1997, 2002; Layder 1985; Lukes 1974, 1986). In adopting the epistemological and methodological assumptions outlined above, which incorporate a dialectical dimension, power is viewed as the capacity of agents as well as a relational and structural phenomenon (Goverde and van Tatenhove 2000). This formulation invokes the need for a *relational* conception of both structure and agency. As Hay argues, 'one person's agency is another person's structure. Attributing agency is therefore attributing power (both causal and actual)' (1995: 191). Indeed, with regard to the analysis of policy networks and policy outcomes, Marsh and Smith observe that 'By examining networks we are looking at the institutionalisation of power relations both within the network and within the broader socio-economic and political context' (2000: 6). Agency, as manifest here, is evident in a tight policy community, in Marsh and Rhodes' (1992a) terms, or in an advocacy coalition (cf. Sabatier and Jenkins-Smith 1999). In an advocacy coalition, for example, actors share a set of fundamental beliefs (policy goals, plus causal and other perceptions), and aim to influence rules, budgets and governmental personnel in order to achieve these goals over time (Jenkins-Smith and Sabatier 1993b). In line with this position, Marsh and Smith (2000: 6) draw attention to structural aspects of power in arguing that such 'shared values and ideology will privilege certain policy outcomes', thereby reflecting Lukes' (1974) seminal argument regarding the 'three dimensions of power'[5], and the third dimension of power in particular.

Lukes' analysis of the third dimension of power involves 'the exercise of power to shape people's preferences' (Ham and Hill 1993: 70) in order that a deeper account of the ways in which the socio-economic structure shapes the nature of people's wants, expectations and overt interests might be explored. In this model, conscious policy decisions and expectations are only one aspect of the wider political phenomenon to be investigated and a more complete picture might be gained through an analysis of unconscious values, overt manipulation and covert preferences (McLennan 1990). Our view of power relations also has resonance with more recent work by Hay (1997, 2002), a key aspect of which is the argument that power can be conceived of as 'context-shaping' (Hay 2002: 185). To define power in this way, Hay argues, is to emphasise power relations in which structures, organisations and institutions are shaped by actors such that the parameters of subsequent action are altered. In short, this is 'an *indirect* form of power in which power is mediated by, and instantiated in, structures' (Hay 1997: 51). Policy subsystems can thus be conceived of as involving 'the institutionalisation of beliefs, values, cultures and particular forms of behaviour' (Marsh and Smith 2000: 6).

In sum, this conceptualisation of power relations moves beyond that inherent in conventional pluralist approaches; thus reinforcing the earlier argument for adopting the assumptions of a critical realist epistemology and a dialectical approach to the meso-level analysis of elite sport policy processes. At the meso-level of analysis, these observations are reinforced by Marsh and Smith, who argue that certain groups occupy privileged positions, which:

> give them access to important policy networks [or subsystems] and membership of these networks is a key resource that gives them greater opportunities to affect outcomes. In order to understand or explain outcomes, we need to recognise and *explain* that structured privilege.
>
> (Marsh and Smith 2001: 537)

Identifying interests and the groups that coalesce around them; specifying the range of resources available to interest groups; and charting the strategies developed for their deployment are the central concerns of this study. In sum, it is argued that, in adopting the epistemological and methodological assumptions underlying critical realism, and in giving primacy to the ACF as a meso-level theoretical lens, together with the insights generated by the above discussion of power relations, a more complete picture of elite sport policy processes and policy change can be accomplished.

Research methods

The two key research methods employed in this study were semi-structured interviews and document analysis. The semi-structured interview, based on an interview guide, with open-ended questions and informal probing to facilitate a discussion of issues, was the key qualitative method used here. Such intensive interviewing allows people to talk freely and to offer their interpretation of events. Indeed, if individual agency is deemed important in aiding the understanding of policy-making, then the 'assumptive worlds' (Young 1977) of key actors need to be explored. In short, the rationale for adopting semi-structured interviews in this study was based on the following line of reasoning. Semi-structured interviews were used in order to: (i) gain a more (agent-) informed understanding of historically-developed processes and developments relating to elite sport policy direction; (ii) allow distinctions to be made between the 'rhetoric' provided in policy documents and the 'reality' of an agent's insights into her/his perspective on a particular issue or policy; and (iii) attempt to discern the normative values and belief systems underlying the agent's perspective as well as her/his perception of the constraining/facilitating structural context within which she/he operates.

In order to elicit data on policy change, interviewees within the NSOs/NGBs were selected on the basis that they had been involved at a senior strategic level of decision-making and, where possible, in order to map *changing* policy decisions, that they had been involved over a number of years. In order to map the nature of relationships between the NSOs/NGBs and the Australian Sports Commission, Sport Canada and UK Sport (the lead elite sport agencies in each country), it was imperative to gain access to actors who had some knowledge of each sport within these organisations. In order to maintain anonymity, we refer to the above interviewees as 'senior officials' or 'senior officers' in Chapters 4, 5 and 6. In addition, contributions were sought from actors who were either formerly involved with a specific sport and/or quasi-governmental sporting organisation in a strategic capacity, or had contributed to the analysis of elite sport policy processes, either in general, or in respect of particular sports.

The criteria for the selection of the three sports in this study were: first, that they were all prominent Olympic sports; second, that they have major World Championships; and third, that their NSOs/NGBs have responsibility for a number of sub-disciplines, all of which (potentially) compete for resources and attention of influential actors in the policy-making process. Other sports could have been selected but it was considered that these sports provided ample opportunity to investigate issues such as: (a) resource allocation decisions by government and quasi-governmental organisations; (b) the impact of government policy on the strategic direction of NSOs/NGBs; and (c) the nature of power relationships, within the sports, between sports, and between individual sports and their funding partners.

The second key method used in the study was the analysis of policy-related documents, what May refers to as the 'sedimentations of social and political practices' (1997: 157). Our analysis of policy-related documents therefore goes beyond what Altheide (1996: 15) has termed 'qualitative content analysis' and is closer to his description of 'qualitative document analysis'. This technique is used in order to understand how different discourses structure the activities of actors and how they 'are *produced*, how they *function*, and how they are *changed*' (Howarth 1995: 115). In sum, by utilising both semi-structured, in-depth interviews and qualitative document analysis it has been possible to triangulate data gained from interviews with key actors involved in elite sport policy developments with an analysis of, for example, policy documents relating to (elite) sport policy processes.

Comparative analysis

Reflecting the study's interest in aspects of policy learning/transfer, a key component of comparative research is 'the careful analysis of the conditions under which certain foreign practices deliver desirable results, followed by consideration of ways to adapt those practices to conditions found at home' (Noah 1984: 558). Furthermore, Heidenheimer *et al.* (1990) argue that a comparative approach is needed which can span levels of government and public/private sectors as, in recent years, policy burdens have shifted to local jurisdictions and semi-public groups. Thus, by drawing on insights provided by the ACF, which prompts interest in the interactions between actors from different levels of government, as well as interest groups, researchers and journalists – this study reflects Heidenheimer *et al.*'s argument that, 'Perhaps more than ever before, public policy has become a mosaic pieced together by government authorities at different levels and by private sector actors with public policy responsibilities' (1990: 4–5).

The research design incorporates a 'focused comparisons' (Hague *et al.* 1998: 280) or 'multiple-case' (Yin 1994: 44) approach. Using this design, Hague *et al.* note that research focuses on an 'intensive comparison of a few instances'. Thus, detailed description of a specific topic is provided and, while significance beyond the case may be useful, the focus is on how variables interact and evolve in a particular setting. The emphasis, then, in a multiple-case design is on the comparison at least as much as on specific cases. The usefulness of the focused comparisons method, as well as the utility of analysing policy processes over a decade or more is supported by Hague *et al.*'s argument that 'Focused comparisons work particularly well when a few countries are compared over time, examining how they vary in their response to common problems' (1998: 280). For this study, the common (policy) problem can be conceived of as the development of sporting excellence.

These observations lead on to the question of how countries should be selected for a focused comparison. Przeworski and Teune (1970) suggest that such a selection involves either a 'most similar' or a 'most different' approach. With regard to the latter, Peters (1998) argues that this approach proceeds on the assumption that the phenomenon/issue being explained resides at a sub-systemic level, for example, the development of, and changes to, elite sport policy. In essence, the 'most different' approach assumes that there are only a limited number of different types of political issue (for example, distributive, redistributive, regulatory) and that the nature of the issue necessarily involves particular interests and imposes constraints on the policy options available; thus generating broadly similar policy (Houlihan 1997). Houlihan also notes that this approach 'assumes that the political systems selected for study are as different from each other as possible except for the phenomenon to be explained' (1997: 8). In short, the aim is to 'force analysts to distil out of this diversity a set of common elements that prove to have great explanatory power' (Collier 1993: 112). However, the 'most similar systems' design is generally the preferred method when undertaking comparative policy analysis (Peters 1998; but see Hopkin 2002).

Within the most similar design, countries are selected that appear to be similar in as many ways as possible in order to control for extraneous variations. Advocates of the most similar approach argue that 'a comparison between "relatively similar" countries sets out to neutralise certain differences in order to permit a better analysis of others' (Dogan and Pelassy 1990: 133). In other words, a most similar design takes similar countries for comparison on the assumption that 'the more similar the units being compared, the more possible it should be to isolate the factors responsible for differences between them' (Lipset 1990: xiii). Moreover, as policy transfer may be an important variable, Antal's following comments are instructive, 'Research that focuses on differences is less likely to unearth similarities and to teach lessons worth learning in a new setting. Projects designed to discover similarities are more likely to find them and to propose transferring experiences' (1987: 513). However, caution is also advised when adopting this approach. Peters (1998), for example, notes that, although the most similar systems design may eliminate a number of possible explanations, it also acknowledges that it cannot address them all. The key issue here is that it may not be possible to identify all the relevant factors that can produce variations amongst systems. With these cautionary caveats in mind, the similar cases method is the preferred approach and Australia, Canada and the UK share the following characteristics: sport is a significant cultural element; a concentration on elite sport is evident or emerging; democracy is well-established and stable; interest group activity is a major feature of democratic politics; and their economies are mature (Houlihan 1997). This is not to argue that each country does not have its own distinctive characteristics. Rather, the assumption is that each country's distinctive characteristics are outweighed by the degree of overall similarity.

2 Theorising sport policy

This chapter provides the theoretical and conceptual context for the study. We begin by outlining the importance of the role of the state and how it relates to the power structure of a society as a whole at a macro-level. We then present a more detailed account of the salience, for this investigation, of the meso-level advocacy coalition framework. The final section of the chapter draws attention to the ways in which we might begin to think about conceptualising elite sport development models. Here, examples of the systematic and planned approaches to developing elite athletes in two former Eastern bloc countries are reviewed, with a brief account of how Australia, to a large degree, 'borrowed' many of the key principles underpinning these systematic approaches.

Macro-level analysis

Role of the state

In respect of the importance of the role of the state in public policy processes, Hill, for example, argues that 'Policy is the product of the exercise of political influence, determining what the state does and setting limits to what it does' (1997b: 41). For Hay, 'The contemporary state is something of a paradox' (1996: xii), while Connell notes that 'Drawing boundaries around "the state" is not easy' (1990: 509). It is generally agreed then that the state is not unified. Conflicts can arise between elected politicians and non-elected civil servants over policy direction, between different departments or units of the state and between politicians at different levels of the state over policy and resources. Therefore, as Smith argues, 'it is very difficult to identify the state's interests because various parts of the state can have conflicting interests' (1993: 2).

A further problem arises from the ill-defined term, 'public policy'. The ambiguity surrounding the term is clear in Hill's suggestion that 'The definitional problems posed by the concept of policy suggest that it is difficult to treat it as a very specific and concrete phenomenon' (1997a: 7). A number of potential routes through this definitional quandary have been suggested. Heclo, for example, emphasises action in arguing that 'A policy may usefully be considered as a course of action or inaction rather than specific decisions' (1972: 85). Heclo's reference to 'inaction' is particularly apposite with respect to policy-making and relations of power. A rather more concrete definition is provided by Jenkins, who suggests that public policy can be conceived of as a set of interrelated

> decisions taken by a political actor or group of actors concerning the selection of goals and the means of achieving them within a specified situation where these decisions should, in principle, be within the power of these actors to achieve.
>
> (Jenkins 1997: 30)

Although it would be wise to qualify Jenkins' definition by adding 'non-decisions', his definition usefully draws attention to two important 'attributes' of policy relevant to this study. First, there is an emphasis on the interrelatedness of decisions, suggesting that policies cannot be viewed in isolation but as part of a sequence or cluster of decisions. Second, the reference to 'political actors' signals issues of power and policy influence and 'alerts us to the assumptions of pluralist politics where power and resource control are not monopolised by holders of formal offices' (Houlihan 1997: 4). In line with these arguments, while we acknowledge the important contributions of various Marxist interpretations, corporatism and elitism (cf. Dunleavy and O'Leary 1987; Held 1996), this study adopts a broadly neo-pluralist perspective at this macro-level of analysis. A brief outline of this perspective helps to substantiate our argument.

Neo-pluralism

Given the conceptual and empirical problems (cf. Crenson 1971; Held 1996; Lukes 1974) associated with what we might term, the 'classic pluralist' perspective, a number of 'competing schools and tendencies' (Held 1996: 214) have evolved; one of the most notable being the 'neo-pluralist' position. Neo-pluralism acknowledges that business interests are often in a stronger position than other groups and enjoy certain advantages over the consumer and the market (Dunleavy and O'Leary 1987). Lindblom (1977) has been a key proponent of the neo-pluralist position, arguing that policy-making is constrained by the workings of capitalism, particularly business interests and market forces. Smith provides a useful summation of this position:

> The importance of business to the government means that the government will respond automatically to business's interests. Power is structural rather than observable. Lindblom's position is closer to some Marxists than it is to pluralists. He acknowledges that power can be exercised in an unobservable way through structures, anticipated reaction and ideology.
>
> (Smith 1995: 223–4)

It could be argued that the disproportionate influence of business has important implications for elite sport policy processes – for example, in the increasing significance/role of multinational corporations, particularly in the realm of sponsorship deals (cf. Horne *et al.* 1999). There are two further aspects to neo-pluralist developments which can be signposted here: (i) the significance given to the use of 'policy analysis' (Dunleavy and O'Leary 1987: 280–3; Parsons 1995: 428); and (ii) the acknowledgement that 'the modern extended state has grown chiefly as a decentralised network of multiple agencies' (Dunleavy and O'Leary 1987: 306). The significance of these aspects is evaluated in the ensuing evaluation of the advocacy coalition framework.

Meso-level analysis

Our concern with meso-level theorising focuses on those developments that address aspects of stability and change in the policy-making process. These developments include, stages models (cf. deLeon 1999), varieties of institution-alism or neo-institutionalism (cf. Ostrom 1999), policy networks (cf. Marsh and Rhodes 1992b), multiple streams (cf. Kingdon 1995), punctuated equilibrium theory (cf. True *et al.* 1999) and the advocacy coalition framework (ACF) (cf. Sabatier and Jenkins-Smith 1993b, 1999). These developments vary across a number of dimensions where, broadly speaking, differences exist: in the relative significance granted to political processes as against rational/technocratic approaches; the emphasis placed on government as opposed to governance; on structure versus agency; on policy stability or change; and on whether interests or ideas are of greater importance. They also vary in the extent to which they have been applied, empirically, to concrete cases. Our preferred approach is to adopt the ACF which has been subject to increasing scholarly interest in the USA and Europe (cf. Fischer 2003). However, to date, the ACF has not been applied to any significant degree to the area of sport policy (for exceptions, see Green 2003; Green and Houlihan 2004; Parrish 2003). This relative lacuna in the literature thus affords an opportunity for an analysis of the ACF's explanatory value in respect of its application to the process of elite sport policy change.

The advocacy coalition framework

While the advocacy coalition framework (ACF) 'has much in common with the policy network school' (John 1998: 169) John suggests that the ACF 'is a broader set of processes than that evoked by the network metaphor' (1998: 169) and, in exploring this 'broader set of processes', the ACF's appeal as a persuasive approach for this study can be set out. An 'advocacy coalition' has been defined as:

> people from a variety of positions (elected and agency officials, interest group leaders, researchers) who (1) share a particular belief system – i.e. a set of basic values, causal assumptions, and problem perceptions – and who (2) show a non-trivial degree of co-ordination over time.
>
> (Sabatier and Jenkins-Smith 1999: 138)

The initial version of the ACF (1987–8) emerged out of a search for an alternative to the stages models that were then dominating policy studies; a desire to blend the key features of the 'top-down' and 'bottom-up' approaches to policy implementation; and a commitment to give technical knowledge a more central role in theories of the policy process (Sabatier 1998). A key feature of the ACF, therefore, is its focus on the policy process as a whole. Indeed, Sabatier suggests that 'Its goal was to provide a coherent understanding of the major factors and processes affecting the overall policy process – including problem definition, policy formulation, implementation, and revision in a specific policy domain – over periods of a decade or more' (1998: 98). The reference to a time span 'of a decade or more' comes directly from findings concerning the significance of the 'enlightenment function' (Weiss 1977) of policy research, and is relevant to the ACF's focus on policy-oriented learning. As Weiss argues, 'As new concepts and data emerge, their gradual cumulative effect can be to change the conventions policymakers abide by and to reorder the goals and priorities of the practical policy world' (1977: 544).

It should be noted that the ACF has undergone a number of revisions since the initial version was developed in the late 1980s and it is not the intention to review all these developments here (for more detail, see Sabatier and Jenkins-Smith 1999). The intention is to evaluate the ACF against the criteria outlined earlier as crucial to this study. Thus, according to the logic of the ACF, policy change over time is a function of three sets of processes (see Figure 2.1).

The first of these processes concerns the (endogenous) interaction of competing advocacy coalitions within a policy subsystem. It is important here to clarify how the term 'subsystem' is used in this study given the terminological ambiguity implicit in the use of the term in the literature (cf. Coleman and Perl 1999). For ACF purposes, a subsystem consists of 'those actors from a variety of public and private organisations who are actively concerned with a policy problem or issue … and who regularly seek to influence public policy in that domain' (Sabatier and Jenkins-Smith 1999: 119). Such actors share a set of fundamental beliefs (policy goals plus causal and other perceptions) and aim to influence rules, budgets and governmental personnel in order to achieve these goals over time (Jenkins-Smith and Sabatier 1993b). Thus, within the subsystem, the ACF assumes that a number of discrete coalitions will emerge. From the above, and following the line adopted by Marsh and Rhodes (1992a) in their work on policy networks, a policy subsystem can be likened to an 'issue network', with its broad membership and open access, while the shared world view and interests of an advocacy coalition are analogous to a 'policy community' (Bulkeley 2000: 732).

The second set of processes, *exogenous* to the subsystem, are concerned with the (relatively) 'stable system parameters' – such as social structure and constitutional rules – that constrain the various subsystem actors. The third set of processes concern changes that are also exogenous to the subsystem, and the ACF assumes that these are more susceptible (than the first set of exogenous

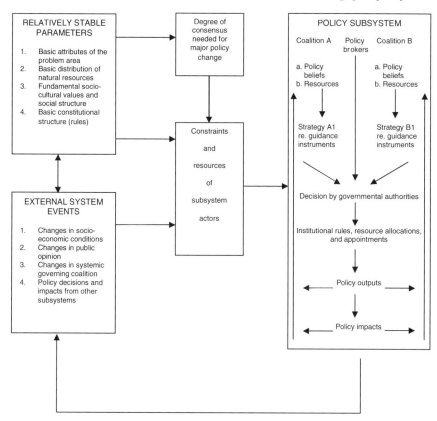

Figure 2.1 Structure of the advocacy coalition framework (adapted from Sabatier and Jenkins-Smith 1999: 149)

processes) to change over a decade or more and are a critical prerequisite for major policy change. These processes relate to changes in:

• socio-economic conditions and technology – in the area of elite sport, these might be a realignment of funding allocations for sport and contemporary developments in sports science/medicine;
• the systemic governing coalition or 'elections that produce changes in chief executives and key legislators' (Sabatier and Jenkins-Smith 1993a: 223). In the UK, for example, the change in Prime Minister from Margaret Thatcher to John Major in 1990 has been widely acknowledged as significant with regard to changing governmental approaches to sport in general and for elite sport in particular;
• public opinion – in the UK, for example, UK Sport has established a longitudinal survey of the general public's 'sporting preferences'. Of particular

interest here, is the desire to track public opinion in relation to which sports should be funded at the elite level (UK Sport 2002d) and;

- policy decisions and impacts from other subsystems that provide opportunities and obstacles to the competing coalitions – for example, in Australia and Canada, educational policy (and thus school sport) is the responsibility of the States, Territories and Provinces.

A defining feature of an advocacy coalition is its organisation around a tripartite hierarchy of beliefs, namely, 'deep core', 'policy core' and 'secondary aspects' (Sabatier and Jenkins-Smith 1999: 133). Deep core beliefs include basic ontological and normative beliefs, for example, the relative valuation of individual freedom versus social equality. At the next level, policy core beliefs represent a coalition's basic normative commitments and causal perceptions across a policy subsystem, that is, fundamental value priorities and the identification of groups whose welfare is of greatest concern. For example, the emphasis put on Sport for All initiatives relative to programmes for elite level sport. Finally, secondary aspects comprise a large set of narrower (less than subsystem-wide) beliefs concerning, for example, the seriousness of a problem or the relative significance of various causal factors in specific settings, or specific policy preferences regarding funding allocations. It is assumed that these structural categories of belief systems offer decreasing resistance to change, with deep core (normative) beliefs offering the greatest and secondary aspects the least, resistance (cf. Kübler 2001: 624).

The ACF thus takes account of the 'interplay', or dialectical relationship, between the exogenous and endogenous factors discussed above (and see Figure 2.1); a relationship that has been persuasively endorsed by Hay and others (cf. Hay 2002; Marsh 1998; Marsh and Smith 2000, Marsh *et al.* 1999). Indeed, for Sabatier and Jenkins-Smith, a fundamental premise of the ACF is that 'although policy-oriented learning often alters aspects of a coalition's belief system, changes in the policy core aspects of a governmental programme require a perturbation in noncognitive factors external to the sub-system' (1999: 123). Following, Heclo (1974), Jenkins-Smith and Sabatier conceptualise policy-oriented learning as 'an ongoing process of search and adaptation motivated by the desire to realise core policy beliefs' (1993a: 44). The ACF hypotheses that change in policy core beliefs requires an accumulation of evidence over a decade or more, encompassing the enlightenment function referred to earlier. The strength of this argument, in relation to realising policy objectives regarding elite sport, is one that is further explored in Chapters 4, 5 and 6.

In addition, the concept of the policy broker is significant for the sport policy sector 'where the level of organisational complexity alone suggests the need for such a role' (Houlihan 2000b: 9). Within the ACF, the policy broker has a major role to play. As Sabatier and Jenkins-Smith suggest, 'Conflicting strategies from various coalitions may be mediated by a third group of actors, here termed policy brokers, whose principal concern is to find some reasonable compromise that will reduce intense conflict' (1999: 122). In the area of elite sport, examples of policy brokers in the UK might be Patrick Carter, currently Chair of Sport England, who was brought in to mediate an intense and often debilitating conflict surrounding the redevelopment of Wembley Stadium, and Sue Campbell, currently acting as Reform Chair at UK Sport and cross-departmental government advisor on sport and education policy. In Canada, the role of Denis Coderre, the former Secretary of State (Amateur Sport) has been highlighted as crucial in initiating the wide-ranging policy deliberations underpinning the new Canadian Sport Policy – most notably in his ability to garner collaborative support at, and between, federal-provincial/territorial levels.

The concept of policy broker is significant in other ways given the argument that the sport policy sector can be characterised as a relatively new and often marginal area of public policy concern (Houlihan 2000b). Jenkins-Smith and Sabatier provide an apposite example here by way of discussing the process of policy-oriented learning and the ways in which 'problems' are advocated between coalitions; a process usually mediated by policy brokers who are interested in keeping the conflict within acceptable limits:

> In *a new* policy area, knowledge about the seriousness of the problem and the validity of various causal assumptions is normally sufficiently uncertain and the political resources of those challenging the status quo sufficiently modest that the *initial* governmental programme involves a significant research component but little coercion.
>
> (Jenkins-Smith and Sabatier 1993a: 47, emphasis added)

With regard to the exhortations by Daugbjerg and Marsh (1998) and Marsh and Stoker (1995) to integrate theoretical perspectives and levels of analysis, it is argued that the ACF can be conceived of as a meso-level concept which can accommodate a micro-level analysis of the 'model of the individual' (cf. Sabatier and Jenkins-Smith 1999: 130), as well as an analysis located within the assumptions of neo-pluralism at the macro-level. Thus, the notion of a policy subsystem within ACF assumptions is pertinent to Dunleavy and O'Leary's discussion of neo-pluralism (at the macro-level) and policy communities (at the meso-level). With respect to these two levels of analysis, it is argued that:

> Wherever policy-making is split between different agencies or tiers of government, complicated systems of inter-governmental or inter-agency relations evolve. These systems create 'policy communities' [or advocacy coalitions] where rational debate and education about issues can take place … They are networks of personal contacts, or more formalised channels for ideas and communication between diverse agencies.
>
> (Dunleavy and O'Leary 1987: 306)

One final point is worthy of note. As mentioned above, given that the sport policy sector has been characterised as a relatively new and often marginal area of public policy concern, an interesting aspect of such coalition-forming in

Australian, Canadian and UK sporting contexts is the ACF's focus on groups of people and/or organisations interacting regularly over a period of a decade or more. Such observations have important implications for the study's empirical investigation into three sports. It is important, for example, to explore the conditions pertaining to a 'nascent' and a 'mature' policy subsystem within which coalitions might evolve. The former is one that is in the process of forming, whereas the latter is one that has 'sought to influence public policy for a fairly long period of time' – seven to ten years is suggested by Sabatier and Jenkins-Smith (1999: 136). Research utilising the ACF (cf. Kübler 2001; Mawhinney 1993) suggests that actors tend to coalesce into discrete coalitions within the subsystem around some watershed event(s) that clarifies underlying conflicts regarding the particular (policy) issue in question.

In Australia, the federal government gave substantial support to elite sport development following the disappointing results at the 1976 Montreal Olympics, leading in 1981 to the creation of the Australian Institute of Sport (AIS). In Canada, beginning in the 1970s, the federal government was responsible for the construction of a policy framework that underpinned the establishment of a cadre of elite athletes capable of achieving medal-winning success at global sporting events (cf. Macintosh and Whitson 1990). With respect to the UK, Houlihan and White suggest that sport development is 'a sub-area primarily, but not exclusively, within the broader area of sport policy which itself has only been acknowledged as a legitimate and regular focus for government expenditure and policy for just over thirty-five years' (2002: 1). From an ACF perspective, then, it is clear that in all three countries we have evidence of public policy involvement of over 10 years: the ACF's requirement. Following the logic of the ACF, a key objective of the investigation is to discern whether a number of coalitions have emerged around different aspects (of potential conflict) within the sport development policy subsystem. Taking the logic one stage further, how might these coalitions be implicated in policy change?

Conceptualising elite sport development models

The first part of this section provides an understanding of the key principles of organisation and administration underlying 'models' of elite sport development in two former Eastern bloc countries – the Union of Soviet Socialist Republics (USSR/Soviet Union) and the German Democratic Republic (GDR) – that achieved considerable success at major global sporting events. We then highlight briefly how Australia's elite sport development model emerged, mirroring, in large part, these former Eastern bloc approaches. Thus, a further aim is to identify the degree of similarity in elite sport development models. In relation to this, Houlihan raises an interesting point of departure for this study in suggesting that Australia has:

> adopted policies of elite squad development which are very close to the Soviet model in a number of key respects including the systematic sifting of

school-age children as a means of identifying the potential elite, the development of specialist training academies, the subordination of domestic governing bodies to government policy and the use of public money to support elite athletes.

(Houlihan 1997: 6)

This suggested pattern of policy similarity draws attention to the potential salience of policy transfer in explaining policy outputs and outcomes. Although Dolowitz and Marsh acknowledge that policy transfer is not the sole explanation of any, let alone most, policy development, they do suggest that 'an increasing amount of policy development, and particularly policy change, in contemporary polities is affected by policy transfer' (2000: 21).

Before considering each country in turn, some brief comments on the rationale for selecting the three countries is required. The selection of the Soviet Union is justified first by its outstanding success at the Olympic Games between the period 1952–88 and second, by its explicit attempt to identify and develop sporting talent systematically. As the President of the International Association of the Theory and Methodology of Training in Elite Sport notes:

The main methodological concepts of the modern sports training system were established in the early fifties by Russian coaches who were faced with the problem of preparing Soviet athletes for the XV Olympic Games (Helsinki 1952) and for other major international competitions.

(Verkhoshansky 1998: 9)

With regard to the GDR, its 'dominance' in major international sports events over a similar period has led Volkwein and Haag to suggest that the country's state-controlled apparatus 'regulated the sphere of sports into such a state of perfection that the successes of the GDR seemed almost miraculous' (1994: 184). Both the Soviet Union and the GDR, then, were renowned for their highly structured approaches to developing elite performers, which have, arguably, provided a 'template' for the subsequent development of elite sport models in Western nations (cf. Green and Oakley 2001a, 2001b; Oakley and Green 2001a). The selection of Australia is justified by its decision to establish the AIS in 1981, which signalled a significant shift in emphasis towards a systematically managed approach to elite sport. The selection is also justified by the clear commonality between Australia's emerging model and the former Eastern bloc countries' systematic approach to developing elite athletes which led Magdalinski to observe that 'the popular image of a "monster" eastern European sports network, intent on seeking and selecting future star athletes, no longer had currency as Australia increasingly and whole-heartedly adopted so-called "communist" training and managerial techniques' (2000: 317). The final justification is that from the creation of the AIS in 1981, Australian elite athletes have steadily increased their medal-winning performances at the Olympic Games.

Systematic and asystematic models

A central theme running through the evolution of 'successful' elite sport development models is the notion of a strategic, planned and co-ordinated approach. As a former Director of the AIS has argued, 'Passion alone is not enough any more. You need to have the infrastructure, the support and the strategic approach at the national level to achieve results' (de Castella 1994). It should be noted that, for the purpose of this discussion of elite sport development models, we focus on those models funded primarily through public sector bodies; therefore excluding the more commercial or 'market models' of elite athlete development such as the youth academy schemes common in professional soccer and rugby union in the UK. It is acknowledged, however, that the dividing line between such models is becoming increasingly blurred. For example, youth soccer development in England is now part-funded by Sport England, a quasi-public sector organisation.

Fisher and Borms (1990) argue that, although many countries have discovered the benefits which accrue from encouraging high levels of sporting achievement, the trends in performance levels probably mean that success in Olympic or world events will become increasingly unlikely unless the emergence of talent becomes more organised. Two key components of any elite sport development model are talent selection/identification and talent development and, according to Fisher and Borms, it is important that they are recognised as complementary and interdependent (see also Abbott *et al.* 2002). Fisher and Borms (1990: 37) identify what might be termed a 'dualism' of talent selection and development: the 'Systematic' and 'Asystematic' models. In the latter, a talented young person might emerge and demonstrate potential for sport at an elite level but the structure and organisation for sport is inadequate to help develop this potential. The suggestion is that this model is typical of the situation in many developing countries where issues such as basic nutrition and health care exacerbate the difficulties involved in developing elite athletes. With regard to the Systematic model, this is further sub-divided into (a) 'System-related' models, where private or state organisations actively search for talent in an organised, systematic manner through testing or competitive procedures, and (b) 'Person-related' models, where talented individuals emerge from a mass base premised on, for example, Sport for All principles, with structures available to then nurture the talented athlete. Fisher and Borms suggest that, to a greater or lesser extent, the Person-related model has been dominant in many countries in their development of young sporting talent.

Eastern bloc approaches to elite sport development

It is important to note that the notion of 'Eastern bloc approaches' is not used to imply homogeneity. As Anthony (1978: 5) observes, 'there are many common factors and shared principles ... [but] there are also big differences' to account for in any study of these former communist countries. While the USSR utilised sport as a means of changing society, and integrated sport into 'a gigantic effort to take a backward and poor country from near-feudalism to modernity in sixty years' (1978: 5), a somewhat different rationale underpinned the approach to sport in the GDR, which was 'born of a divided and beaten Reich and reared in the heat of the Cold war, adapting the scientific systematisation of pre-war Germany to a Marxist–Leninist philosophy' (1978: 5).

Union of Soviet Socialist Republics

The early Soviet sporting philosophy was radically at variance with that in Western states in that it echoed Marxist conceptions of the interdependence of the physical and mental states of human beings, for both the all-round development of the individual and, ultimately, for the health of communist society (Riordan 1999). A significant turning point for the direction and shape of (elite) sport in the USSR occurred under Stalin's leadership. The foundation of Stalinist sport had been the promotion of competition as a socially useful way of life. The official turn toward sport 'productivity' came in 1936, with a Party-endorsed shift of emphasis from purely physical culture to physical culture combined with competitive sport as a means of socialising the population to the new prevailing norms. The emphasis was on sport's utilitarian, 'applied' functions in preparing the population for labour and defence (Hoberman 1984; see also Riordan 1978). As Hoberman observes, 'The cloud that had hung over the word "sport" (implying competition) since the early 1920s was now officially lifted' (1984: 192).

Soviet athletes competed at the 1952 Olympic Games for the first time, signalling a new era in the development of competitive amateur sport. From 1952, until the demise of communism in the Soviet Union and GDR in the late 1980s, competition at global events such as the Olympic Games was more than just about achieving sporting excellence. As Morton observes in respect of the USSR in the early 1980s, 'At home foreign sports triumphs, officially presented as proof of socialism's superiority over capitalism, are primarily used to stimulate feelings of national pride and Soviet patriotism to aid in preserving national unity in a polyglot society' (1982: 210). Table 2.1 summarises the key principles and main features of the USSR's systematic approach to developing its elite performers.

Despite the public rhetoric of a balance between Sport for All and elite sport, the former was often sacrificed to the latter (cf. Riordan 1993; Shneidman 1978) with, for example, all the specialist sports schools catering primarily for Olympic sports (except for chess) (Riordan 1986a). Indeed, to many ordinary Soviet citizens, the worst aspect of this system was 'the misplaced priorities, the gap between the living standards and ordinary sports facilities on the one hand, and the funds lavished on elite sport and stars on the other' (Peppard and Riordan 1993: 133). Moreover, following the collapse of communism in the late 1980s, a strong anti-elite sport (i.e. anti-Olympic) sentiment emerged with revelations of state-sponsored production, testing, monitoring and administering of

Table 2.1 Key principles and main features of the USSR's elite sport development model

Key principles	Main features
Normative programmes	'*Gotov k trudu i oborne*' (Ready for labour and defence) – viewed as the horizontal development of mass sport initiatives from which potential 'stars' could be drawn. The 'Unified All-Union Sport Classification' – viewed as the vertical development of Soviet elite sport, and based on a set of standards/norms according to which athletes were awarded ranks/titles in different sports according to results. Programmes linked to Soviet sports schools system.
Central state funding	Ostensibly directed at the so-called 'human base' of Soviet athletics. Also channelled through the para-military Dinamo society and the Central Army Sports Clubs. Difficult to ascertain with any confidence the amounts of funding involved.
Sports schools	Six-stage hierarchy of sports schools, with Sports boarding schools at the apex – focused on Olympic sports. Republican school games important as a scouting venue for talented youngsters. Para-military Dinamo society and Central Army Sports Clubs played important financing/administration role.
Talent identification and development	Planned system of selection and elimination over a period of several years utilising a three-stage approach. Information on several parameters was included, in particular, performance at various ages, the rate of progress and the ideal physical profile in relation to specific events. Critics suggest that the system lacked rigour and was not based on a nationwide programme of strictly uniform tests and norms.
Well-qualified coaches	Imperative to Soviet success at elite level. Of 25,000 coaches working in 'Children and young people's sport schools' in 1967, some 80% were qualified. In 1967, of 42,130 full-time instructors/coaches, over half were employed in elite-oriented schools – in stark contrast to the situation in the West at the time, where such qualifications were not deemed essential.
Sports physicians	Key role centred on assessing, through medical indicators, athlete's functional capabilities at elite level. Worked closely with both coaches and athletes in an interdependent system. Educational/professional level of coaches complemented role of physicians and other specialists. Early experimentation with performance-enhancing drugs.

Source: Adapted from Goldman and Katz (1992); Jarver (1981); Kane (1986); Kondratyeva and Taborko (1979); Riordan (1978, 1986b, 1991, 193); Shneidman (1978)

performance-enhancing drugs with regard to young children. Doubts have also been voiced in respect of the Soviet's so-called 'scientifically rigorous' approach to talent identification and development. Indeed, Riordan argues that 'Many tests would certainly seem relatively primitive to Western coaches. Most tests in the early selection stages are simple field tests, and the coach's or PE teacher's eye often provides the most ready information' (1986b: 228). Yet, if we put aside the above caveats for a moment, it is clear that the Soviet approach to elite sport development achieved outstanding results, dominating both summer and winter Olympic Games, with only a few exceptions, from 1952. In relation to Fisher and Borms' (1990) typology, the Soviet approach was a clear example of the System-related, Systematic model.

German Democratic Republic

Childs points to some of the key principles that were to underpin the subsequent development of sport in the nascent GDR: 'The attempt to improve sporting performance by the application of science and medicine was in line with the importance given to science in German society generally. Both these features distinguished German sport from that in Britain' (1978: 75). Moreover, the East German sports system did not develop in a historico-political vacuum and a number of factors need to be borne in mind in respect of its development. First, the sports system was one element of an all-encompassing social system; second, it was used as a means of establishing the nation as the equal of the Federal Republic; thirdly, the importance put upon achieving influence within the Warsaw Pact group was significant; and, finally, it should be viewed as a medium through which the country could achieve sporting status and political recognition on a global stage (cf. Childs 1978; Riordan 1999; Sutcliffe 1988).

Two historico-political factors, in particular, are instructive. First, Walter Ulbricht, the dominant political figure in the GDR until his retirement in 1971, had a personal interest in sport and its capacity as a vehicle for demonstrating the political superiority of socialism (Hoberman 1984). Second, if Ulbricht was the key individual behind the advancement of East German sport, the Soviet Union was its 'doctrinal mentor', most notably in its influence on the evolution of the GDR's educational programme (Hoberman 1984: 203). For example, in 1952, the official organ of the Socialist Unity Party (SED) published an article entitled, *Learn from the Scientific Physical Education in the Soviet Union*. The article reflected Stalin's influence with regard to sport 'productivity', with future developments in East German sport signalled in references to 'managing the emotions of the athlete scientifically', 'the importance of high performance', and of the Soviet coach 'who is both pedagogue and political educator' (Hoberman 1984: 204). The key principles and main features of the GDR's sports system are identified in Table 2.2, which indicates clearly the meticulous approach to the development of its elite level athletes.

It is clear from Table 2.2 that the GDR's sports system comprised a highly-centralised apparatus which proved to be an impressive 'recipe for success', at

Table 2.2 Key principles and main features of the GDR's elite sport development model

Key principles	Main features
One-party control	Sport was enshrined in the GDR's constitution. *Deutscher Sportausschuss* (German Sports Committee – DSA) established (in 1951) as the 'supreme organ' in all fields of sport/culture. *Das Staatliche Komitee für Körperkultur und Sport* (State Committee for Physical Culture and Sport) officially designated (in 1952) as the highest sports authority. *Der Deutsche Turn- und Sports-bund* (German Gymnastics and Sports Association – DTSB) replaced the DSA in 1957 and had total power for planning/funding of both elite and mass participation sport at youth/adult levels.
Central state funding	Vital feature but, as in USSR, accurate figures are difficult to ascertain – it has been suggested that some US$2 billion was allocated to sport annually and in contrast to $US70 million per year in the Federal German Republic. Despite official ideological rhetoric of Sport for All, the focus was clearly on the elite level.
Talent identification and development	Conducted in sports boarding schools, which were a key aspect of the GDR's sports system and usually aligned to a sports club focusing on selected disciplines. Also used in schools, in general, in sports co-operatives (Dynamo and Forwards of the police and army), and at the *Spartakiaden* – sports competitions for scouting talented youngsters. System based around a similar three-stage approach as in the USSR.
Well-qualified coaches	*Deutsche Hochschule für Körperkultur* (German University for Physical Culture – DHfK) in Leipzig played a central role in training coaches, PE teachers and sports officials. Unofficial data suggest approx. 10,000 coaches were employed in the GDR. Integrated system contrasts to the fragmented situation in Britain at the time.
Sports science/sports medicine	*Forschungsinstitut für Körperkultur und Sport* (Research Institute for Physical Culture and Sport – FKS) employed approx. 600 staff in top secret sports science research. Post-1989, FKS became infamous for its role in the ideological indoctrination of athletes and for experiments with performance-enhancing drugs.

Source: Adapted from Childs (1978); Dick (1990); Kozel (1996); Lahmy (1985); Sutcliffe (1988); Volkwein and Haag (1994)

least at the elite level (Merkel 1995: 100). Many of the key organisational and administrative principles underpinning the GDR's well-planned approach to elite sport development reflected those found in the Soviet Union; not an unexpected outcome given the shared ideological doctrine of communism. Elite sport development in the GDR can thus be conceptualised (as for the USSR) as reflecting Fisher and Borms' (1990) System-related, Systematic model. Although it will be argued below that many aspects of the Eastern bloc models discussed here have been adopted in some form in a number of Western countries, there may also be 'negative lessons' (Rose 1991) to be learnt from both Soviet and East German models of elite sport development. First, and arguably most importantly, sport was used overtly as a political tool to promote a particular (communist) ideology. This is not to suggest that sport has not been used as a political and ideological tool by Western nations (for Canadian and UK/England examples, see Kidd 1988a, 1988b, 1995; McDonald 2000). Rather, it is to point to the characteristics of modern liberal democracies, which do not allow for the degree of political and ideological control exerted under socialist/communist regimes (cf. Coghlan and Webb 1990).

Second, the elite athlete in the GDR was treated as 'a dehumanised tool within the sport system and was respected only if successful' (Volkwein and Haag 1994: 191; see also Hoberman 1992). Third, and clearly related to the first two points, the now well-documented use of performance-enhancing drugs in the GDR's sports system has to be accounted for in any analysis of elite sport in the twenty-first century. Clearly, the use of performance-enhancing drugs was (and is) not confined solely to the GDR (cf. Houlihan 2002). However, the GDR's doping experiments displayed an unusual lack of respect towards both their athletes and the ethos of sport. As Volkwein and Haag observe with respect to sports science/medicine research in the GDR, 'The protocols of the research documents read like the ones found in some of the most inhumane experiments of the SS or other doctors of the Third Reich' (1994: 191).

Fourth, concerns remain in relation to the nature of talent identification and selection techniques employed in the GDR. Krüger provides an instructive insight into the rationalisation and scientisation processes underlying the nature of such techniques, in arguing that 'talent selection based on genetic tests was the basis for the athletic success of the small German Democratic Republic after 1968 – using the same anthropometric procedures developed by the racial scientists prior to 1945' (1999: 44). The final concern centres on the debate regarding the balancing of provision for Sport for All policies and those for elite sport development; clearly, in both the Soviet Union and the GDR, the focus was on the latter. The point being made here is that the concerns raised above can be viewed as negative lessons to be learnt by Western nations seeking to emulate the 'success' of Eastern bloc approaches to elite sport. Interestingly, observations from Kidd (1988a, 1988b, 1995) and McDonald (2000), in Canada and England respectively, suggest that such lessons may not have been learnt.

The Australian approach to elite sport development

The Australian example is instructive not only because it includes many of the key principles underlying former Eastern bloc approaches but also because it demonstrates that such an approach has delivered improved elite success. Broom (1996) suggests that the period of Eastern bloc dominance (1952–88) at the Olympic Games, in particular, signified a transfer of international sporting power and acted as a catalyst to other nations to strive to emulate them. Moreover, Broom's comments below give some credence to the proposition that the characteristics/nature of the objective (elite success) to some extent determines, or at least limits, the possible policy responses by both state and non-state actors in different countries. Broom has argued that:

> Common to former socialist 'development of excellence systems', and mirrored in the more recent state-supported models in other countries, are systematic co-ordinated plans of development from foundation to elite performance levels, in which principles of organisational structure and administration have a distinctive part to play.
>
> (Broom 1996: 1)

However, Western approaches, in general, have been characterised by a more fragmented organisational and administrative structure, and by competing (and often contradictory) aims and ideologies of the various actors and institutions involved. This view is reflected in Adair and Vamplew's observation that, in Australia, 'government sports policy up to the 1970s was characterised by a rather incoherent mixture of limited financial involvement at the national level and infrastructure support at the local level' (1997: 41). Although a Labor administration created a Federal Ministry of Tourism and Recreation, whose programmes reflected the government's primary commitment to fostering mass participation, at this time the development of elite performers was a secondary concern. As the Minister for Tourism and Recreation observed in 1972:

> we have no intention of imitating some countries which regard success in sport as some sort of proof of the superiority of their way of life, ideology and race. Our task lies clearly elsewhere, in meeting more basic needs, in catering for masses, not just a small elite.
>
> (quoted in Semotiuk 1986: 162)

Arguably, the defining moment for the emergence of a more systematic policy framework for developing medal-winning elites in Australia was the establishment of the AIS in 1981. The creation of the AIS is interesting on a number of levels. First, on a political/philosophical level, the delay in implementing recommendations from two reports in the 1970s (Bloomfield 1973; Coles 1975) regarding the development of an elite sports institute was indicative of the Liberal-Country Coalition Party's reluctance to intervene in the sport policy domain. Yet, the cross-party support for the AIS (and thus elite level sport) was a clear manifestation of increasing policy convergence between the two major political parties during the 1980s. Second, on a political/symbolic level, the federal government, cognisant of the public outcry over the poor performances of Australian athletes at the 1976 Olympic Games, saw potential political capital in supporting the development of an elite sports institute (Paddick 1997). Third, on an individual (agent) level, the role of Bob Ellicott, the minister responsible for sport from 1978 to 1980, was instrumental in operationalising plans for the institute after the announcement that the government would proceed with the idea. In short, the establishment of the AIS 'was seen by the government as a crucial policy innovation designed to enhance Australian prospects in international competition' (Houlihan 1997: 70).

Following a period (1975–83) of Liberal-Country Party rule, which sanctioned the abolition of the Department of Tourism and Recreation, the incoming Labor Government re-established a senior department that included a Sport portfolio – the Department of Sport, Recreation and Tourism – and oversaw the creation of the Australian Sports Commission (ASC) in 1985 – see Table 2.3. Operating under the Australian Sports Commission Act 1989, the ASC is in receipt of federal government funding and, although the ASC's twin objectives cross-cut the usual mass participation/elite development spectrum, the commitment to balance these twin objectives continues to invite sceptical interpretations. Booth, for example, notes that 'Notwithstanding initiatives to improve participation among "ordinary" Australians ("Life Be In It"), children ("Aussie Sports") and women (public awareness campaigns), elite sport remains the Commission's priority' (1995: 7). In sum, the establishment of the AIS and the ASC in the 1980s signalled federal government (financial) support that would continue and further strengthen into the 1990s, especially following the award of the 2000 Olympic Games to Sydney. Finally, as was the case for the former Eastern bloc countries, developments in Australia's elite sport model can be conceptualised in terms of Fisher and Borms' (1990) Systematic, System-related model.

Conclusion

Selecting an appropriate framework for the analysis of public policy is far from easy. A wide variety of meso-level analytical frameworks and models are currently competing for attention (John 1998; Sabatier 1999). These frameworks/models differ, *inter alia*, in the weight they give to structure as opposed to agency, the degree to which they seek to explain both policy stability and change, and in the extent to which they have been elaborated with sufficient clarity to enable application. While the ACF has been selected as the framework of analysis for this study of elite sport policy it has been done so partly because of its heuristic value, that is its capacity to direct analysis to potentially revealing aspects of the policy process. In other words, the attraction of the ACF is its capacity to take account of structure and agency and to offer explanations of both stability

Table 2.3 Key principles and main features of Australia's elite sport development model

Key principles	Main features
'Sporting culture'	The importance of the Australian 'sporting culture' cannot be underestimated in the development of the country's elite athletes. While the Soviet Union and GDR exploited the overarching doctrine of communism in order to establish a systematic and scientific approach to elite sport development, Australia was able to draw upon a deeply-rooted cultural predisposition to sport as a defining element of Australian national identity.
Federal funding	From the inception of the AIS in 1981, Australia's leading political parties have continued to support the development of medal-winning elite athletes. More recently, the publication of, *Backing Australia's Sporting Ability: A More Active Australia* by the Department of Industry, Science and Resources, reveals that federal funding support for elite level sport remains relatively high: over the four year period from 2001–2, the 'Sporting Excellence' theme of this federal sport policy document, reveals that some $AUS408 million is to be allocated to the elite level – over 80% of total federal monies for sport, in general, over this period.
Elite sports institute	The creation of the AIS, together with the establishment of the ASC in 1985, has provided the organisational and administrative framework within which elite sport developed over the past two decades.
Talent identification and development	The early selection of talented athletes is a vital element of Australia's elite sport model. Recent technological developments have led to the adoption of a talent software programme – Talent Search – in the country's drive for sporting excellence.
Well-qualified coaches	The National Coaching Council was established in 1978 (renamed the Australian Coaching Council (ACC) in 1979) and some 200,000 coaches have been accredited in 90 sports over the past 25 years. The ACC emulated earlier developments in this field by adopting the tenets of Canada's National Coaching Certification Programme which provided coaching education at five hierarchical levels.
Sports science/sports medicine	Early pioneering work in the late 1940s and early 1950s by Professor Frank Cotton and his protégé, swimming coach, Forbes Carlile, provided a relatively early (for Western countries) acknowledgement of, and thus foundation for, the continued development of these disciplines in academic institutions, the AIS, and State/Territory academies/institutes of sport.

Source: Adapted from Adair and Vamplew (1997); Cashman (1995); Department of Industry, Science and Resources (2001); Magdalinski (2000); Phillips (2000); Vamplew *et al.* (1997)

and change. The framework is also valuable because its extensive application across a range of policy areas has generated a substantial number of empirical studies which can prompt further lines of enquiry in relation to elite sport policy.

The policy development undertaken by the pioneers of government supported elite sport development, the USSR and the GDR, provides an important benchmark against which the more recent experiences and policy innovations of Australia, Canada and the UK can be assessed and compared. Of particular importance is the extent to which countries that have prioritised elite sport achievement as a goal of public policy have been able to develop models that differ from the systematic approach developed by the USSR and refined by the GDR. In addition, it will also be important to determine whether the three countries covered in this study have been able to meet the extensive resource demands of elite development and also maintain and develop an infrastructure of sport facilities and opportunities for the mass of the population.

3 Development of sport policy in Australia, Canada and the United Kingdom

This chapter provides a brief account of the wider historical and socio-political context for sport in general from the 1960s onwards and, more specifically, traces the key aspects of policy developments at the elite levels of sport in Australia, Canada and the UK. A key issue here surrounds the extent to which the three countries have come to terms with the assumed requirements of modern elite international sport which suggest that 'an athlete must now train full-time and must be supported by a retinue of coaches, trainers, logistical staff, and others ... [and] that Olympic and other international success requires an expensive, bureaucratic, and highly technical elite athlete delivery system' (Franks *et al.* 1988: 680). A second key issue for consideration is how the three countries balance the often conflicting pressures to meet the needs of elite athletes and to provide and develop grass roots sport and mass participation programmes.

Australia

Sport in Australia

As in other developed nations before the Second World War the federal government's involvement regarding sport policy was ad hoc and limited to a concern with the fitness of the population for military service (cf. Armstrong 1997; Booth 1995): the 1941 *National Fitness Act* reflected such concerns. Indeed, when compared to other industrial nations, Baka contends that, 'Australia definitely exhibited a late entry into the field of governmental involvement in sport' (1986: 27).

1970s

A defining moment for Australian sport, generally, and an acknowledgement that sport was a significant policy area for federal intervention, in particular, was the election of the Whitlam Labor Government in late 1972 (cf. Adair and Vamplew 1997) – see Table 3.1. The Labor Government created a Federal Ministry of Tourism and Recreation whose programmes reflected the government's primary

Table 3.1 Australian sport policy: 1970s

Key political/ policy event	Organisational and administrative implications	Funding implications	Implications for elite sport development
1972: Labor Party elected	Department of Tourism and Recreation established; sport linked to wider planning concerns at urban level through Sports and Capital Assistance programmes	First real commitment to funding sport from federal level	Initial focus on mass programmes, not elite level
1973: Bloomfield Report, *The Role, Scope and Development of Recreation in Australia*	Argued that success at international level would promote greater participation at lower levels	9 of 12 recommendations on direct financial support were aimed at the national and international levels; not reflected in actual allocations	Institute of sport recommended; evidence of policy transfer – Bloomfield had visited major European sports institutes
1975: Liberal-Country Coalition Party elected	Department of Tourism and Recreation abolished; limited support for Sports and Capital Assistance programmes	Reduced public spending; federal sport expenditure reduced from $AUS11.4m in 1975–6 to $AUS5.8m in 1978–9	Similar reluctance to support elite sport
1975: Coles Report, *Report of the Australian Sports Institute Study Group*	Not implemented until 1980; indicative of reluctance at the time to support sport at federal level		Drawing on Bloomfield Report, a national institute of sport was recommended
1976: Confederation of Australian Sport established; Montreal Olympics	The Confederation's aim was to bring together a fragmented sporting community		Poor performance at Montreal, just five medals won – acted as catalyst for Australian Institute of Sport
1978–80: Role played by Bob Ellicott, minister responsible for sport	Important shift in priorities during this time, from a relative balance between mass/elite, to a focus on elite level		Ellicott instrumental in the establishment of a national elite sports institute

Source: Adapted from ASC (1998); Booth (1995); Houlihan (1997); Jacques and Pavia (1976); Westerbeek (1995)

commitment to fostering mass participation, with the development of elite performers a secondary concern. As described in Chapter 2, the primacy of mass participation over elite development, and an implicit denunciation of Eastern bloc approaches to sport, was apparent in statements from the Minister for Tourism and Recreation in 1972 (Semotiuk 1986).

Whitlam's Labor Government placed sport policy firmly on the planning agenda, linking the development of sport and recreation facilities to the regeneration of urban areas, funded primarily through the Sports Assistance and Capital Assistance Programmes (cf. Baka 1986; Semotiuk 1986). The first tangible evidence of a planned approach to elite sport development also occurred during this period. John Bloomfield was commissioned by the federal government to prepare a sports plan (see Table 3.1), with the subsequent report (Bloomfield 1973) revealing suggestions of policy learning as it was based on studies of major sports institutes in Europe. The upshot of the Bloomfield Report was the establishment of a Task Force, under Dr Allan Coles, to report on the feasibility of an elite sports institute in Australia. Yet, despite recommendations within the Bloomfield Report for financial support at the elite level, only 11 per cent of the Department of Tourism and Recreation's expenditure in 1974 was for 'direct assistance to national and international sport' (Jacques and Pavia 1976: 152).

The election of Malcolm Fraser's Liberal-led Coalition party in late 1975 resulted in a further change of direction in Australian sport policy. The Department of Tourism and Recreation was abolished; the Sports Assistance Programme was discontinued, although later reinstated, and the Capital Assistance Programme was sustained only insofar as it honoured commitments previously given by the Labor Government (Semotiuk 1986). Interestingly, Semotiuk also notes that the change in government illustrated 'the profound difference in philosophical approach to sport between the present Liberal-Country Party government and the Australian Labor Party opposition' (1986: 163). These observations are instructive for this study given the ACF's premise that values and belief systems, together with non-cognitive events such as 'changes in the systemic governing coalition' (Sabatier and Jenkins-Smith 1999: 120), are central to stimulating policy change.

Although the Liberal-Country Coalition's philosophy resulted in sport being pushed down the policy agenda, Houlihan (1997) notes that this downgrading was tempered by four key factors (and see Table 3.1): (i) the establishment in 1976 of the Confederation of Australian Sport, which aimed to bring together what was then perceived to be a fragmented sporting community (Westerbeek 1995); (ii) a recognition that sport and recreation provision was popular with the electorate; (iii) the commitment of Bob Ellicott, minister responsible for sport from 1978 to 1980; and (iv) the poor performance of the Australian team at the 1976 Montreal Olympic Games (cf. Armstrong 1997). Of especial note, however, was the abandonment of a balance between elite development and provision for mass participation, a shift, moreover, that was indicative of increasing federal support for elite sport during the 1980s.

1980s

Arguably, the key defining moment for sport in Australia during the 1980s was the establishment in 1981 of the Australian Institute of Sport (AIS) (see Table 3.2). The AIS was established in Canberra and, from the beginning, was dubbed the, 'gold medal factory', indicating its primary function in the Australian sporting environment (Magdalinski 2000: 317). However, due to criticisms surrounding the narrow range of sports located at the Canberra site, and the overly centralised nature of its operation, the AIS subsequently decentralised. Although Canberra continued to house the AIS, a network of eight State/Territory institutes and academies of sport was developed, incorporating some 25 sports (ASC 1998; Pyke and Norris 2001). The shift in government sport policy priorities towards elite development in the early 1980s is clear in Armstrong's observations that the Liberal-Country Coalition Party 'regarded the AIS as the primary responsibility of its sports policy' (1997: 189–90).

The 1983 election saw the Labor Party return to power with a strong commitment to sport reflected in a doubling, to $AUS50 million, of federal funding. The Labor Government's commitment to sport was also indicated by the establishment of a senior department incorporating responsibility for sport, the Department of Sport, Recreation and Tourism, and by the establishment of the Australian Sports Commission (ASC) in 1985. Although the ASC's objectives cross-cut the usual mass participation/elite development divide, the federal commitment to balance these twin objectives continued to invite sceptical interpretations (cf. Commonwealth of Australia 1999). Armstrong, for, example notes that Labor's 'election promise of seventy-five community leisure centres ... was quietly abandoned' (1997: 190). The establishment of the AIS and the ASC in the 1980s was a clear indication of the federal government's primary concern and of its determination that Australia would 'return to glory' (Magdalinski 2000: 317). Interestingly, Magdalinski also suggests that:

> The growing financial backing of elite sport, the foundation of the AIS and the increasingly centralised organisation of sport throughout the 1980s were tied to the recognition that Australian sport could not match the successes of communist nations without adopting the organisational strategies and the more professional and scientific approach to 'producing' athletes that had underscored the success of the Eastern Bloc athletes.
>
> (Magdalinski 2000: 317)

These observations thus give further credence to the suggestion that the characteristics/nature of the objective to some extent determines the possible policy responses by both state and non-state actors in different countries. It could be argued, however, that what differentiates various countries' elite sport models is not the organisational and administrative principles underpinning the 'developed' model but the social, political and ideological context within which the model is developed (cf. Digel 2002). In short, at the end of the 1980s, sport

Table 3.2 Australian sport policy: 1980s

Key political/policy event	Organisational and administrative implications	Funding implications	Implications for elite sport development
1981: Australian Institute of Sport (AIS) established	Initially established as a centralised institution in Canberra – decentralised operations during the 1980s	Funded by federal government, although private sector sponsorship for specific projects	Confirmation of federal policy shift towards elite level
1983: Labor Party elected	Re-established department incorporating sport portfolio – Department of Sport, Recreation and Tourism; increasing consensus between political parties on support for elite sport	Despite funding of $AUS50m overall for sport, commitment to establish 75 community leisure centres abandoned	Recommendation for an Australian Sports Commission
1985: Australian Sports Commission (ASC) established	Stated priorities of both mass (e.g. 'Aussie Sport') and elite programmes; increasingly centralised organisation of sport	$AUS0.8m allocated to ASC in 1984–5; by 1989–90, increased to $AUS42.5m, which included AIS funding	Despite rhetoric, elite level sport increasingly the focus of ASC
1989: ASC restructured	Relationship with government altered to give it greater independence	ASC was federally-funded; thus, despite quasi-autonomous status, ASC policies reflected federal concerns	ASC amalgamated with AIS, further emphasising elite focus
1989: Going for Gold, Parliamentary inquiry into sports funding and administration	Wide-ranging report that focused on the elite level	Recommended increased funding for sport; increased accountability for how monies spent also a priority	Indicates increased federal interest in providing a robust platform for elite success; recommended targeting specific sports and creation of talent development programmes
1989: Federal government sport strategy, The Australian Sports Kit (Next Step)	Central aim was to increase participation in sport to create a larger 'talent pool'	Pledged additional $AUS100m-plus for sport and recreation over following four years	Additional $AUS51.7m pledged for elite development over following four years

Performances at the three Olympic Games in the 1980s were variable: Moscow (1980), nine medals; Los Angeles (1984), 24 medals (four of which were Gold); and in Seoul (1988), 14 medals.

Source: Adapted from Adair and Vamplew (1997); Court (1997); DASETT (1989); Hogan and Norton (2000); Houlihan (2000); Parliament of the Commonwealth of Australia (1989); Wallechinsky (2000)

policy developments in Australia were increasingly framed in the context and language of elite sport performance (cf. Department for the Arts, Sport, the Environment, Tourism and Territories [DASETT] 1989; Parliament of the Commonwealth of Australia 1989).

1990–2002

Arguably, *the* defining catalyst for Australian sport in the 1990s was the 1993 decision by the International Olympic Committee (IOC) to award the 2000 Olympic Games to Sydney (see Table 3.3). This decision had a profound effect on the pace and direction of federal sport policy administration and funding allocations; a decision, moreover, which further strengthened the elite sport lobby in Australia. In relation to these comments, four points are worthy of note. First, the approach to sport in general in the 1990s can be characterised by an increasingly centralised, federal government funded administrative structure. Second, the ASC and AIS were at the heart of this administrative structure. In principle, the ASC/AIS amalgamation in 1989 was established with the primary aim of neutralising perennial arguments surrounding the balancing of the twin objectives relating to mass participation and elite sport. Questions remained, however, as to the relative emphasis put on each of these policy strands. For example, the regionalisation of sports institutes and academies in Australia has decentralised resources and provided some opportunities for collaborative use of facilities at a community level. Yet, as mentioned in Chapter 1, these facilities, and coaching and sports science expertise, have been focused on skill development of talented athletes in the continuum of elite athlete production.

The third point reflecting the increasing focus on the elite level was the establishment in 1993 of the National Elite Sports Council (NESC), the primary purpose of which was to facilitate greater co-ordination across all bodies involved in the development of elite-focused programmes (cf. Pyke and Norris 2001). The fourth point relates to funding allocations for sport where, since 1975, there has been an apparent reluctance to demonstrate the same commitment to fostering mass participation as has been shown to improving elite performance (cf. Booth 1995; Hogan and Norton 2000; Nauright 1996). Of note here is Sydney's successful bid for the 2000 Olympic Games, which provided the catalyst for a six-year elite development programme with a combined funding allocation of $AUS418 million (Nauright 1996: 20), including additional monies for elite athletes under the Olympic Athlete Programme (OAP) – see Table 3.3.

The approach adopted by Australia had much in common with elite development practices in the former Eastern bloc countries. For example, the AIS adopted a computerised model of talent identification and development ('Talent Search'), which broadly reflected the 'stages approach' developed in the Eastern bloc (cf. AIS 2001; Hoare 1996). In addition, the OAP provided funds for a national talent identification programme involving a range of organisations, for example, schools, the AIS and State/Territory institutes/academies of sport, as well as national and State/Territory sporting organisations (Hoare 1996). The

Table 3.3 Australian sport policy: 1990–2002

Key political/policy event	Organisational and administrative implications	Funding implications	Implications for elite sport development
1990: *Can Sport be Bought?*, Parliamentary inquiry into sports funding and administration	Recommended ASC provide results of efficiency reviews and how it meets twin objectives set out in ASC Act; revealed inadequate data re. mass sport objectives	Led to confirmation that increased funding for elite sport is associated with greater international success	Further justification for elite sport support at federal level
1991: Labor Party re-elected	Federal Minister for Sport maintains rhetoric of increased participation despite increasing emphasis on elite level	Overall sports budget continues to rise, although disproportionately skewed to elite level	Prime Minister, Paul Keating, uses 2000 Olympic bid as platform for an Australian republic (see 1993 below)
1992: *Maintain the Momentum*, Australian Government Sports Policy 1992–6	Consolidation of the 'Next Step' programme; identified seven 'key priorities' across the sporting spectrum	Overall commitment to sport and recreation of $AUS293m	Aim was to build a 'national approach' to elite athlete development
1993: Sydney awarded 2000 Olympic Games; National Elite Sports Council (NESC) established	Sydney 2000 Games raised wider questions regarding disproportionate skew towards elite level at the expense of social-equity goals; invoked national pride theme	See OAP below	Development of AIS elite programmes; increasingly scientific approach adopted, e.g. talent identification; establishment of NESC further centralises co-ordination at elite level
1994: *Olympic Athlete Programme* (OAP) established	Emphasis on support for a co-ordinated approach across all States/Territories and institutes/academies of sport	Pledged additional $AUS135 over six years with specific aim of supporting the Australian Olympic team	Explicit support for elite athletes with the aim of increased medal counts at Sydney 2000; Talent Search programme created

Key political/policy event	Organisational and administrative implications	Funding implications	Implications for elite sport development
1996: Liberal-led Coalition Party elected	Funding reductions to a range of sports and sporting bodies; number of 'minor sports' affected	Budget for Sydney 2000 remained immune from public expenditure cuts; renewed support in 1998 for OAP	See 'Funding implications'
1999: *Shaping Up* (Sport 2000 Task Force), Report to the Federal Government	Recommended a 'major change in government priorities' to achieve further economic, health and social benefits from sport and recreation	Recommended that new 'off-budget' funding sources be found	Separate high performance sport agency recommended – not realised; acknowledged that emphasis on elite sport had overshadowed mass participation objectives
2000: Hosted Sydney Olympic Games	Australia basks in the general acknowledgement of a successfully managed Games	Post-Sydney debates centre on termination of OAP funding and cuts to community sport	Australian elite athletes win 58 (16 Gold) medals – best ever performance
2001: Federal government sport policy, *Backing Australia's Sporting Ability: A More Active Australia*	Stated 'centrepiece' of policy: to increase community participation in sport; rhetoric does not match funding allocations	Additional $AUS161.6m for sport over four-year period beginning 2001–2; brings total funding to record level of $AUS547m; yet total funding allocations reveal mass participation strand awarded just 20% of that allocated to elite level	Extra federal funding for elite level of $AUS122.2m; total funding for 'Sports Excellence' strand approx. $AUS408m over this four-year period

Source: Adapted from Australian Labor Party (2001a, 2001b); Booth (1995); Commonwealth of Australia (1999); Department for the Arts, Sport, the Environment and Territories [DASET] (1992); Department for the Environment, Sport and Territories [DEST] (1994); Department of Industry, Science and Resources (2001); Hogan and Norton (2000); Houlihan (1997); Parliament of the Commonwealth of Australia (1990)

identification and development of talented athletes requires specialist coaching; thus, a further aspect of the Australian model found in other systemic approaches was the value placed upon trained coaches. Although the significance of the coach in Australian sport was acknowledged as long ago as the 1950s, it was not until 1979 that a National Coaching Accreditation Scheme was implemented (Adair and Vamplew 1997; see also Phillips 2000). In 1994, the OAP initiative provided 14 new national head coaches in Olympic sports, with a further 20 specialist coaches appointed at the AIS. In addition, 10 designated sports received funding for international expertise and 35 intensive-training centre coaches were appointed from OAP funds (Nauright 1996).

The primacy of sports science and sports medicine expertise is also a key principle underlying the contemporary development of Australia's elite sport model. The increasing significance of this type of expertise has led Adair and Vamplew (1997) to suggest that the development of elite athletic performance in Australia is becoming more of a team effort than just a partnership between athlete and coach – thus reflecting the observations in Chapter 2 regarding the integrated approach to elite sport established in the Eastern bloc, most notably at the German University for Physical Culture (DHfK) in Leipzig. The AIS and the network of State/Territory institutes/academies of sport are the cornerstone of this integrated approach to sports medicine, sports science and the related disciplines of sports physiology and biomechanics (Schembri 2000).

Policy change and conclusions

Throughout the 1970s and early 1980s Liberal-led Coalition and Labor administrations exhibited somewhat divergent philosophies towards sport as a policy sector, with the former generally adopting a more non-interventionist approach than the Labor Party. The evidence presented here, however, suggests that, from the inception of the AIS in 1981 and the ASC in 1985, the policies of Australia's two dominant political parties converged in the prioritisation of international sporting success. It is here that the advocacy coalition framework (cf. Sabatier and Jenkins-Smith 1999) is instructive in drawing attention to the values and belief systems of key actors situated within strategically significant sporting organisations and agencies in Australia, which have, arguably, stimulated this trend towards policy convergence around elite sport. Of particular interest is the way in which these key actors, using the language of rationality and technocracy, increasingly frame the construction of the elite sport policy discourse (cf. Haas 1992).

In relation to these observations, a recurrent and significant theme in the development of Australian sport policy is the discourse surrounding relative funding allocations for mass participation initiatives and those for elite level programmes. We have already noted that any examination of Australian public policy since the mid-1970s shows an apparent reluctance to address both policy goals with equal commitment. In other words, the political rhetoric of support for mass participation has not been matched with funding comparable to that allocated to elite sport. Hogan and Norton (2000) substantiate this argument in suggesting that the ASC (in conjunction with the AIS) has clearly adopted what they term, a 'top-down' approach to the stated twin objectives of excellence in elite sport performances and increased participation in sport and sport activities for all. In short, this top-down approach targets funding towards producing excellence in sport by those already identified as being talented. The expectation is that by providing the optimum training facilities, coaching and science expertise, and international competition through targeted grants and scholarships, 'there is a greater probability that world-class Australian performers will follow' (Hogan and Norton 2000: 205). Moreover, the expectation is that other benefits will follow, for example, increased Australian pride, sporting interest and mass partici-pation in sport and physical activity – termed the 'trickle-down' or 'demonstration' effect (ASC 1993a, 1993b). The analysis in Chapter 4 therefore centres on probing the ways in which this emergent discourse was (and is) constructed to define the field, articulate positions and thus subtly set limits to the possibilities of policy change.

Canada

Sport in Canada

1961–79

The selection of 1961 as a starting point for this review reflects the federal govern-ment's relatively early (compared to Australia and the UK) involvement in sport through the 1961 Bill C-131, *An Act to Encourage Fitness and Amateur Sport*. Before 1961, federal government involvement in sport, beyond control and prohibitive legislation, was limited (Macintosh and Whitson 1990: 1). The 1961 Act was prompted by two key concerns: first, the low level of physical fitness among the nation's population; and second, the country's failure (and Soviet success) in international ice hockey competitions and the summer Olympic events (cf. Macintosh *et al.* 1987; Semotiuk 1996). A key thread running through the federal government's increasing influence during this period was the instrumental use of sport to promote a 'Canadian' identity. Macintosh and Whitson, for example, note that, in a campaign speech in 1968, Prime Minister, Pierre Trudeau argued that sport 'could serve as a powerful force for national unity' (1990: 4), a theme that was clearly evident in both the *Report of the Task Force on Sport for Canadians* (Canada 1969) and the subsequent White Paper, *A Proposed Sport Policy for Canadians* (Canada 1970) – see Table 3.4. The Task Force Report and White Paper were also important in establishing the organisational and administrative framework within which changes occurred in Canadian sport policy over the next decade.

Of note for elite sport development during this period was the establishment of the National Sports and Recreation Centre in Ottawa, which provided a central location for the country's national sporting organisations (NSOs), and the creation

Table 3.4 Canadian sport policy: 1961–79

Key political/policy event	Organisational and administrative implications	Funding implications	Implications for elite sport development
1961: Bill C-131, *Fitness and Amateur Sport Act*	National Fitness and Amateur Sports Advisory Council established – no executive power; Fitness and Amateur Sport Directorate established	$CAN5m per annum allocated for national programme of fitness and amateur sport	First recognition of support for elite sport programmes
1967: Inaugural Canada Games	Major facilities programme; invoked 'Unity through Sport' theme	Federal government shared costs with provinces and municipalities	All levels of government became involved with facilities for elite sport
1969: *Report of the Task Force on Sport for Canadians*	Proposed an independent body for elite sport – not realised; highlighted inadequate coach training; elite focus led to *Ross Report* on mass participation programmes	Recommended public/private sector co-operation in creating a structure for sport	Legitimation of federal involvement; first indications of a rational approach to sport planning; 'National Unity' theme again linked to elite achievement
1970: White Paper, *A Proposed Sports Policy for Canadians*	Sport Canada (elite) and Recreation Canada (mass) established in the Fitness and Amateur Sport Directorate; National Sports and Recreation Centre founded; a number of arm's length agencies created	Fitness and Amateur sport budget approx. $CAN6m in 1971–2, 11m in 1972–3, 17m in 1975–6 and 25m in 1976–7; COA's Game Plan '76 established in 1972	Mass participation rhetoric, but programmes focused on elite sport; 'National Unity' theme prominent; reiterated rational approach to sport

Key political/policy event	Organisational and administrative implications	Funding implications	Implications for elite sport development
1976: Iona Campagnolo appointed first Minister of State for sport and fitness; hosted Montreal Olympics	Montreal focus pushes other areas of sport into background; construction of elite facilities for Montreal Olympics	Further support promised for amateur sport and fitness programmes; during 1975–6, $CAN3.7m federal funding allocated to Game Plan '76	Campagnolo stated elite sport was priority; 11 Olympic medals won (but no Gold medals)
1977: Green Paper, *Toward a National Policy on Amateur Sport*	During 1977–8 Recreation Canada re-designated as Fitness and Recreation Canada	Period of economic austerity in Canada; pressure on funding allocations for sport	Focus on elite sport and poor performances in international competitions
1978: Hosted Edmonton Commonwealth Games	Facilities constructed for Edmonton Games	Federal funding of $CAN21m for the Games	Federal policy bears fruit – 1st in unofficial rankings
1979: White Paper, *Partners in Pursuit of Excellence: A National Policy on Amateur Sport*	Advocated a partnership of shared-sector responsibilities; renewed calls for autonomous Sport Canada rejected; Fitness and Recreation Canada divided	NSO grants increasingly tied to specific goals to be achieved in elite sport; reliance on sports lottery monies	'National Unity' theme prominent; emerging technical and bureaucratic approach to elite sport

Source: Adapted from Campagnolo (1979); Canada (1969, 1970); Hinings *et al.* (1996); Macintosh (1996); Macintosh and Whitson (1990); Macintosh *et al.* (1987); Morrow *et al.* (1989); Redmond (1985)

of two new divisions within the Fitness and Amateur Sport Directorate – Recreation Canada (Fitness Canada from 1980) and Sport Canada, the latter charged with responsibility for promoting high performance sport. It was thus becoming increasingly apparent that elite sport was the primary focus for federal intervention, with responsibility for recreation and mass participation programmes left to the provinces, territories and municipalities. The termination, in 1969, of federal-provincial cost sharing agreements for sport and physical education was indicative of this changing policy direction (cf. Macintosh *et al.* 1987). Although the publication of the White Paper, *Partners in Pursuit of Excellence: A National Policy on Amateur Sport* (Campagnolo 1979) maintained the theme of national unity, this was undermined by the extent to which the provinces, especially Quebec, were developing their own elite sport agenda (Harvey 1999). As Macintosh has argued more generally:

> In the rush to get on the high-performance band-wagon provincial governments abandoned their previously strongly held position as champions of mass sport … and commenced to compete with the federal government for the attention and glamour associated with international events.
>
> (Macintosh 1991: 271)

A further important trend in the late 1970s was the increasing emphasis put upon the technical and bureaucratic approach to elite sport (see Table 3.4), one manifestation of which was the federal government's insistence on a more objective and accountable method of allocating federal expenditures to NSOs, with grants increasingly linked to specific goals in high performance sport (cf. Macintosh *et al.* 1987).

1980s

In 1981 the recently elected Liberal Government published a further White Paper, *A Challenge to the Nation: Fitness and Amateur Sport in the '80s* (Canada 1981) that largely ignored the 1979 White Paper's recommendations for a quasi-independent sports council and for shared responsibilities between government and the private sector (see Table 3.5).

Elite sport development during the 1980s was thus firmly under the control of the federal government (Macintosh *et al.* 1987). A defining moment during this decade was the approval, in 1982, of the 'Best Ever' campaign for the 1988 Calgary winter Olympics. The federal government committed $CAN25 million for 10 winter Olympic sport organisations to ensure that Canada would have a 'Best Ever' performance in 1988. However, this financial commitment had a caveat. The 10 NSOs were required to develop four-year plans 'to improve their technical and administrative capacities to produce better high-performance athletes' (Macintosh 1996: 54). These four-year plans, known as the Quadrennial Planning Process (QPP), required NSOs to identify performance targets and to specify the material and technical support systems (from training camps and centres of

Table 3.5 Canadian sport policy: 1980s

Key political/policy event	Organisational and administrative implications	Funding implications	Implications for elite sport development
1981: White Paper, *A Challenge to the Nation: Fitness and Amateur Sport in the '80s*	Fitness and Recreation amalgamated under Fitness Canada in 1980–1; elite national training centres recommended	Priority funding for sports committed to excellence; Athlete Assistance Programme introduced	Rhetoric regarding shared responsibilities and quasi-independent sport council ignored; thus, elite sport in 'control' of federal government; conceded need for greater emphasis on social-equity issues
1982: Approval of 'Best Ever' programme for 1988 Calgary winter Olympics	Four-year plans required from sports involved – the QPP	$CAN25m budget for 'Best Ever' programme	Confirmation of support for elite sport; strengthening of bureaucratic approach
1983: Sponsorship controversy	Continuing pressure on NSOs to seek private sector sponsorship leads to conflict	Indicative of federal policy in the late 1970s for NSOs to seek funding from private sector; however, Sport Canada's budget increased from $CAN26.4m to $CAN50.6m between 1980–1 and 1986–7	Threats to cut off funding to NSOs with sponsorship from tobacco/alcohol companies
1984: 'Best Ever' extended to summer Olympics in 1988	Pressure on NSOs to relocate to NSRC in Ottawa	$CAN38m committed over four years to 'Best Ever' – not part of Sport Canada's base budget; Sport Recognition System introduced in 1985 to guide funding levels	QPP and increasing bureaucratisation/professionalisation leads to disquiet amongst NSO volunteers; 44 medals won at Los Angeles Olympics

(continued …)

Table 3.5 Canadian sport policy: 1980s (continued)

Key political/policy event	Organisational and administrative implications	Funding implications	Implications for elite sport development
1988: Hosted Calgary winter Olympics; Ben Johnson drugs affair at Seoul summer Olympics	Major facilities constructed for Calgary but later criticised for elite focus	Approx. $CAN300m overall federal commitment for Calgary, in addition to 'Best Ever' funding for both Games	Calgary performances perceived a success; Ben Johnson drugs affair leads to calls for re-evaluation of priorities in elite sport; just 10 medals won in Seoul
1988: Task Force Report, *Toward 2000: Building Canada's Sport System*	Called for a 'coherent Canadian Sport System'; rhetoric addressed both elite and social-equity goals; scepticism remained regarding the perceived link between elite goals and programmes in schools/ universities	Reiterated earlier goal for NSOs to contribute 50% of funding; this goal and threats to reduce funding not realised	Further focus on elite sport; criticised for ignoring drugs and ethical issues; reaffirmed professionalisation at elite level

Source: Adapted from Canada (1981, 1988); Hinings *et al.* (1996); Macintosh (1996); Macintosh and Whitson (1990); Macintosh *et al.* (1987); Redmond (1985)

excellence to coaching and paramedical arrangements and research programmes) necessary for the achievement of each set of targets. Moreover, this increasing growth in federal grant-aid to NSOs also included monies direct to elite athletes through the Athlete Assistance Programme (AAP), which was managed by Sport Canada and which further marginalised the National Fitness and Advisory Council and with it an independent voice for sport (Houlihan 1997; see also Beamish and Borowy 1987). The argument being developed here is that the Best Ever campaign, and the QPP, brought to the surface three issues that were to influence the subsequent development of elite sport in Canada.

First, a significant consequence of increasing federal involvement in elite sport was the declining autonomy of NSOs; dependence on government for financial support was central to this decline. For example, in a survey of 66 NSOs, Macintosh and Whitson found that '15 relied on the federal government for more than 85 per cent of their total revenues and 35 for between 50 and 85 per cent' (1990: 20–1). The resulting imbalance of power in the relationship between the federal government and NSOs was seen as an inherent weakness in the organisation and administration of elite sport – due primarily to the interests and concerns of the sports organisations not being actively represented. Moreover, attempts to redress this imbalance failed. For example, efforts to unify the NSOs and the important multi-sport organisations, such as the Canadian Olympic Association (COA – now Canadian Olympic Committee – COC) and the Canadian Inter-University Athletic Union (renamed Canadian Interuniversity Sport in 2001) did not materialise, largely due to internecine conflicts over which body would assume overall control (Macintosh and Whitson 1990). Alongside the failed attempts to unify elite sport organisations, there were also protestations from other interest groups (for example, those representing disabled people and native Canadians) who objected to the federal government's focus on the elite level (Whitson and Macintosh 1988).

The second issue highlighted by the QPP surrounds disparities of roles, values, power and expertise between the full-time professional staff and many volunteer executive members within NSOs. These tensions were especially acute between the full-time professional staff, the NSOs and Sport Canada on the one hand and the volunteer executive members who represented various regional bodies of NSOs on the other. The third issue draws attention to a dilemma in Canadian sport present from the inception of the 1961 *Fitness and Amateur Sport Act*, namely, the federal government's struggle to balance competing claims of elite sport and those for mass participation programmes. The balancing of elite/mass programmes at NSO level is further developed in Chapter 5.

1990–2002

The early to mid-1990s has been characterised as a period of confusion, turmoil and introspection for the Canadian sporting community (cf. Macintosh 1996). Indeed, this period can be viewed as a nadir in Canadian sport that had much to do with the ramifications of the 1988 Seoul Olympics where the Ben Johnson drugs affair blighted the Games and Canada won just 10 Olympic medals. The upshot of the drugs affair was an inquiry by Charles Dubin, who declared that there was a moral crisis in high performance sport in Canada (Dubin 1990) – see Table 3.6.

The Dubin Inquiry not only had significant repercussions for anti-doping policy, it also stimulated a wider reflection on the fundamental values underpinning Canada's sport delivery system. The federal government's response came in the form of a Task Force on Federal Government Sport Policy, *Sport: The Way Ahead*, (Canada 1992 – known as the Best Report) that reflected Dubin's criticisms regarding the manipulation of, and over-concentration on, elite sport by the federal government. The Best Report criticised Sport Canada for 'exercising excessive day-to-day control and direction over sport organisations' (Canada 1992: 192) through its administration of federal policies and programmes. Moreover, the Best Report argued, *inter alia*, for a more wide-ranging re-evaluation of how elite sport should be supported and posed a cluster of questions that included, 'Why do we support high-performance sport at all? [and] Do we appreciate the difference between "being the best you can be" and "being the best?"' (1992: 26). Such questions characterise debates surrounding competing philosophies, values and belief systems of key actors in the Canadian sporting community and the role that such values and belief systems might play in contributing to elite sport policy change. What is clearly underlined here is that the issue is not just about funding allocations; rather it is also one of priorities and political will.

Developments in sport policy during the early to mid-1990s also need to be placed within the broader context of recent Canadian politics. For example, developments such as the 1995 referendum in Québec, which resulted in a close decision against Québec separation from Canada (Harvey 1999); the weakness of the economy; and the election of the cost-cutting government of Liberal Prime Minister Jean Chrétien. In short, sport during this period was forced down the policy agenda and federal funding for sport was reduced by some 17 per cent between 1990–1 and 1996–7 (Houlihan 1997). Indeed, Sport Canada's budget for 1998–9 was $CAN52 million, still some way short of the $CAN86 million in 1986–7 (Canadian Heritage 1998). This period thus witnessed a number of important shifts in federal sport policy. However, although funding was cut, elite sport remained a priority for, as Houlihan noted, the government largely ignored 'the thrust of the Best Report and its argument for a less elitist approach to sport, and confirmed the priority of elite success by making it clear that federal funding would be used primarily to fund elite athletes' (1997: 83).

The introduction, in 1995, of a new funding framework for NSOs – the Sport Funding and Accountability Framework (SFAF) – was intended to help realise elite sport policy objectives. The government had not only been criticised for spreading its funding across too many sports (Canada 1992), but the QPP (and the Sport Recognition System) as a vehicle for distributing funding had also been a major source of conflict between the government and NSOs. One reading of the SFAF suggests that it was proposed to help implement Sport Canada's objectives and to increase the accountability of NSOs in the use of federal funding. On the

Table 3.6 Canadian sport policy: 1990–2002

Key political/policy event	Organisational and administrative implications	Funding implications	Implications for elite sport development
1990: Dubin Inquiry	Major implications for anti-doping policy; recommended a re-evaluation of sporting structures and processes	Critical of federal funding controlling 'the entire sports system'	Suggested there was a 'moral crisis' in high performance sport; criticised federal focus on elite level
1992: Task Force Report on Federal Sport Policy, *Sport: The Way Ahead* (Best Report)	Wide-ranging recommendations – many ignored – in particular, those relating to broader social goals	Recommended reduction in nos. of sports funded; early 1990s period of financial constraint in Canada – approx. 25% cut in allocations to NSOs	Recommended less emphasis on elite sport; medal targets should not be primary criterion of success
1993: Ministry of State for Fitness and Amateur Sport abolished by Conservative Government	Fitness Canada portfolio moved to the ministry responsible for health and Sport Canada to newly created, Dept of Canadian Heritage	One aspect of general cutbacks in government spending	Some viewed this change as a decrease in importance attributed to amateur sport; others believed government would now be less directly involved in this area
1995: Sport Funding and Accountability Framework (SFAF) introduced	Attempt to encompass wider social goals in funding process to NSOs	Aim was to ensure that federal funds allocated to NSOs contributed directly to federal sport objectives and priorities	Rhetoric suggested a move away from QPP, Sport Recognition System and elite focus
1998: Mills Sub-Committee Report, *Sport in Canada: Everybody's Business*	Wide-ranging examination into the 'industry of sport' in Canada; led to creation of Secretary of State (Amateur Sport) position	Recommended federal government continue its policy and funding support for amateur sport generally	Recommended increase in number of NSOs to be funded; more funding for coach training; increased scope for funding to 'carded' athletes
1998: Sport Canada Strategic Plan 1998–2001	Basis for consultation with the sport community on future policies and programmes; outlined four 'Strategic Directions'	Federal funding focused predominantly on elite sport; $CAN10m extra federal funding allocated	Goal at elite level: to enhance the ability of athletes to excel at highest international level through fair and ethical means

(continued ...)

Table 3.6 Canadian sport policy: 1990–2002 (continued)

Key political/policy event	Organisational and administrative implications	Funding implications	Implications for elite sport development
2000: A response to the Mills Report (news release from Dept of Canadian Heritage)	Included a commitment to create a 'real national policy on sport'; six regional conferences to be held	Additional $CAN7.5m funding for amateur sport	Beneficiaries: Athlete Assistance Programme, National Sports Centres, and agencies involved in fight against doping
2001: Towards a Canadian Sport Policy: Report on the National Summit on Sport	One outcome of Mills Report consultations; focus on three 'policy pillars' – Participation, Excellence, Building Capacity	Recommended additional $CAN650m over the period 2001–8 for sport generally	Recommended funding excellence as: 'spending per result'; public-private partnerships again encouraged
2002: The Canadian Sport Policy	Outcome of two years' deliberations across federal-provincial-territorial forums; a fourth policy pillar – 'Interaction' – added to those identified in Towards a Canadian Sport Policy; emphasis on stronger links between sport/health policy	No specific policy guidelines on future funding allocations	No initial extra funding for high performance sport; focus at NSO level remains primarily on high performance objectives, despite policy rhetoric
2002: Bill C-54, (now Bill C-12) An Act to Promote Physical Activity and Sport	Updates 1961 Act (Bill C-131); emphasis on participation, physical activity issues, hosting policy and an 'alternative dispute resolution' for sport	See above	Evidence of significant shift in federal focus away from high performance sport

⌐ At the summer Olympic Games during this period, across all events, Canada won 18 medals in Barcelona 1992 (6 Gold), 22 medals in Atlanta in 1996 (3 Gold) and 14 medals in Sydney 2000 (3 Gold). ⌐

Source: Adapted from Canada (1992, 1998); Canadian Heritage (1998, 2000a, 2000b, 2002); Hinings et al. (1996); House of Commons of Canada (2002); Macintosh (1996); Macintosh and Whitson (1990)

other hand, despite the recommendations of the Dubin Inquiry and Best Report for a less elitist focus, the SFAF criteria were heavily weighted towards elite success, with far less weight given to broader social objectives (cf. Houlihan 1997).

More recent examples of the unresolved tensions between sports funding priorities included the allocation of an extra $CAN7.5 million for amateur sport in March 2000 (Canadian Heritage 2000a); in part, a response to the report by Dennis Mills – *Sport in Canada: Everybody's Business* – (Canada 1998, known as the Mills Report). Significantly, a substantial proportion of this extra funding – $CAN6.9 million – was directed towards elite level 'carded' athletes and national sports centres. A second example was the announcement, in July 2001, that Canada's top Olympic athletes were to benefit from an extra $CAN1.2 million for the 2002 winter Games in Salt Lake City – an initiative known as Podium 2002. As Denis Coderre, Secretary of State for Amateur Sport at the time, stated, 'Following the Sydney Games [where Canada won just 14 medals], the need was identified for a funding programme focused on high performance sport with the specific objective of achieving medal-winning results' (quoted in Canadian Heritage 2001). Coderre's statement is in stark contrast to the Best Report's recommendation that 'it is inappropriate to target medals/medal counts as goals or policy determinants for the federal government' (Canada 1992: 210). Two further points are worthy of note regarding the tensions permeating funding priorities for sport.

First, in the wake of perceived poor performances at the Sydney Olympics, it was argued that still more funding was required in order for the Canadian elite sport development model to compete with countries such as Australia (cf. Morse 2002; Scammell 2001). Second, and in contrast to the first point, in the 2001 policy document, *Towards a Canadian Sport Policy: Report on the National Summit on Sport*, there is a partial attempt to reduce the emphasis on the elite level. *Towards a Canadian Sport Policy* outlined three 'policy pillars' upon which a new national sport policy should be built, namely Participation, Building Capacity and Excellence (Canadian Heritage 2001). Of specific interest, however, within the Excellence section, is the suggestion by Marion Lay, President of the Board of Directors of Greater Vancouver's National Sports Centre, that 'we must look at excellence in a different way – "spending per result"' (quoted in Canadian Heritage 2001). Lay's statement not only contradicts the Best Report's recommendation that elite level sport is not just about medal counts but also, unwittingly, draws attention to comments in the same report from Bruce Kidd. In the introduction to the Building Capacity section, Kidd argues that:

> The National Summit on Sport is one of those special moments that provide opportunity in time of crisis. The crisis is that what we have called the Canadian sport system is, frankly, on its last legs. The opportunity is that never before have we had such strong winds in our sails for progressive change.
> (quoted in Canadian Heritage 2001)

Notwithstanding the above observations, the Canadian federal government has created a centrally-planned and bureaucratic elite sport development model which reflects many of the 'rational' organisational and administrative principles evident in the Eastern bloc models discussed in Chapter 2. The suggestion that the characteristics/nature of the problem determines, or at least limits, the possible policy responses by both state and non-state actors in different countries is, therefore, given further support. In sum, Canada's elite sport development model is underpinned by the following organisational and administrative principles: a centralised national sports administration centre – Sport Canada; a relatively sophisticated cluster of sports science, sports medicine, and physical therapy services for elite athletes; a well-developed national coaching certificate programme (cf. Macintosh and Whitson 1990); a number of specialist sports schools for the identification and development of young athletes (cf. Bales 1996; Treadwell 1987); a financial support system for elite athletes – in particular, the AAP (cf. Canada 1992) – as well as for coaches, and technical and administrative staff; and a country-wide network of multi-sport training centres (cf. Canadian Heritage 1999b).

Policy change and conclusions

Three key themes emerge from this review: (i) increasing federal government intervention legitimised, initially at least, by an emphasis on 'national unity'; (ii) tension between the competing claims of mass participation and elite sport programmes; and (iii) an increasing emphasis on the discursive construction of sport policy around a technical and bureaucratic approach to high performance sport programmes. Moreover, the emergence of these themes has been against a background of a significant shift in the prevailing political economy of Canadian society and, as Cavanagh argued in the late 1980s:

> As the economic commitment of the state to elite sport reaches its most significant level through Best Ever, so too does the organisation of amateur sport work as a remarkable pedestal upon which structures of power work to produce and reproduce dominant features of ideology and consensus, and in doing so, work to reproduce themselves.
>
> (Cavanagh 1988: 131–2)

Cavanagh's observations are instructive not only with regard to the increasingly bureaucratic organisation and administration of elite sport but also in respect of the related issue of the increasing 'professionalisation of the Canadian high performance sport system' (Macintosh and Whitson 1990: 26). Of specific interest here is the legitimisation of sports science research that developed in higher education institutions in Canada following the federal government's decision in the early 1970s to promote sport and, in particular, high performance sport. For Whitson and Macintosh, this 'bureaucratic rationalisation of sport is entirely consistent with values that most of the new sport bureaucrats will have been initiated into in their undergraduate and graduate programmes in sport science

and management' (1988: 93–4). The effect of which, as Haber
argued, is to redefine issues so that normative questions are present
ones, thereby disqualifying the views of lay people.

With regard to the emergence of dominant belief systems, rese
values and organisational structure of Canadian NSOs has idea
'indicators' that summarise the values and belief systems driving the
amateur sport system throughout the 1980s and into the 1990s: (i) ...gn performance emphasis; (ii) government involvement; (iii) organisational rationalisation;
(iv) professionalism; (v) planning; (vi) corporate involvement; and (vii)
quadrennial plans (Hinings *et al.* 1996: 897). These observations are useful in
guiding our analysis with regard to how such values and belief systems might be
operationalised in an investigation of elite sport policy change in Australia, Canada
and the UK in swimming, athletics and sailing/yachting. In relation to this, Kikulis
and Slack argued that:

> within NSOs, dominant coalitions and interest groups (e.g. professional staff,
> regional interest groups, the volunteer executive), *in concert* with the
> institutional pressures created by Sport Canada, have helped bring about the
> type of changes that have occurred in the Canadian sport delivery system
> and the structural arrangements that characterise its organisations.
>
> (Kikulis and Slack 1995: 140)

Kikulis and Slack's assessment is close to Hay's (1997, 2002) *context-shaping*
conceptualisation of power which emphasises the capacity of actors to redefine
the parameters of what is socially, politically and economically possible for others.
These observations raise questions as to the role (and thus power) of expert
knowledge, language and technical information in the high performance sport
policy-making process. It is possible to argue that the application of scientific
expertise to public policy issues, and the restructuring of policy-making processes
so that expert opinion is afforded greater weight, promises more informed policies.
However, it can also be argued that the assumed need for scientific/technical
advice and expertise in defining sport issues helps to depoliticise the prioritisation
of elite sport at the expense of gender, class and regional inequalities in Canadian
sport, as well as those related to mass participation programmes.

United Kingdom

Sport in the United Kingdom

From the nineteenth century, and into the first half of the twentieth century, the
development of sport, and the government's role in that development, can be
characterised as haphazard and ad hoc (Coghlan and Webb 1990; Houlihan 1997;
Roche 1993). A piecemeal and reactive approach to sport and recreation at central
government level continued until the early 1960s. Government intervention was
prompted and shaped by three factors: (i) the role of sport in alleviating the

ₐroblem of (adolescent) urban disorder; (ii) increasing electoral pressure for an expansion of sport and recreation facilities; and (iii) the realisation that state-funded sport could help to improve Britain's international sporting achievements. The latter is of particular interest and, as Houlihan notes:

> What was also emerging in the 1950s and early 1960s was a growing interest in the pursuit of excellence partly due to Britain's 'decline' in international competition, and partly due to the early sporting successes for the 'systematic planning' of East Germany and the Soviet Union.
>
> (Houlihan 1991: 27)

The establishment of an Advisory Sports Council in 1965 was the first indication of a planned and co-ordinated approach to sport and recreation. Interestingly, although the Advisory Sports Council had been concerned to encourage and assist local authorities to increase public provision, the then Director stated that 'We were into excellence ... initially a lot of funds went into elitist sport' (quoted in Coalter et al. 1988: 58). There were also intimations of future policy direction in the allocation of funds to governing bodies. The receipt of grant-aid depended on the ability of the various organisations to comply with criteria formulated by the Advisory Sports Council. Thus, as Coalter et al. note, 'via the use of economic power, the ASC [Advisory Sports Council] was directly involved in rationalising and modernising the elite sector' (1988: 58).

1970s

The shift towards increasing central government intervention and away from what has been termed, a 'voluntarist' approach to sport (cf. Coalter et al. 1988; Henry 1993) became more pronounced in 1972 (see Table 3.7). The Advisory Sports Council was granted executive powers through a Royal Charter and became known as the Great Britain (GB) Sports Council (subsequently, Sports Councils were established in Scotland, Wales and Northern Ireland). At this time, although a stated aim of the GB Sports Council was 'To raise standards of performance in sport and physical recreation' (quoted in Coghlan and Webb 1990: 67), the focus was primarily on encouraging participation and improving the provision of new sports facilities for the wider community. Out of these aims emerged the Sports Council's Sport for All programme in 1972, six years after the government's endorsement of the Council of Europe's Sport for All campaign and a year before the Cobham Report (1973) – Sport and Leisure – which argued for a more concerted policy towards mass sport programmes. Houlihan notes that, at this time, 'There was little discernible tension between the interests of the elite and of the mass, as there was a consensus ... that an increase in facilities was the first priority' (1991: 98–9). It is also worth noting that it has been suggested that the Sport for All campaign was never more than a slogan and that the government increasingly directed the GB Sports Council to target its resources towards specific groups in society (cf. Coalter et al. 1988; Henry 1993, 2001). Thus, the notion of 'sport for

Table 3.7 UK sport policy: 1970s

Key political/policy event	Organisational and administrative implications	Funding implications	Implications for elite sport development
1972: GB Sports Council established	Ostensibly created as a 'buffer' between NGBs, voluntary organisations and government; key objective was mass participation and facility building	Grant-aid to NGBs rose considerably – from £3.6m in 1972 to £15.2m in 1979	Despite rhetoric of Sport for All, critics condemned funding to NGBs as elitist
1973: House of Lords Report, *Sport and Leisure* (Cobham Report)	Set the agenda for subsequent debates regarding links between social policies and sport	Funding should be focused less on 'identified demand' and more on 'latent demand'	Emphasised broader category of 'recreation' as against narrower conception of 'sport'
1975: White Paper, *Sport and Recreation*	Confirmed sport and recreation as a legitimate element of the welfare state – 'recreational welfare'; however, policies increasingly targeted at specific groups in society – 'recreation as welfare'	Funding increasingly diverted to areas of deprivation, principally, inner cities	Many references made to elite sport and national centres of excellence
1977: White Paper, *A Policy for the Inner Cities*	A background of increasing economic decline and unemployment sees sport and leisure used as a means to an end, rather than an end in itself	Growing congruence between government and Sports Council policies, e.g. Urban Programme objectives	No direct impact, but funding allocations increasingly directed at wider social objectives
1979: 'New Right' Conservative Party elected, with Margaret Thatcher as Prime Minister	Thatcher Government emphasised greater degree of accountability and corporate planning from sports organisations/agencies	Sports Council increasingly directed by government to account for use of funds by NGBs	See 'Funding implications' in respect of NGBs; Thatcher supported total boycott of 1980 Olympic Games – not realised

Source: Adapted from Coalter *et al.* (1988); Coghlan and Webb (1990); Henry (1993, 2001); Horne *et al.* (1999); Houlihan (1991, 1997); Roche (1993)

all' became 'sport for the disadvantaged' and 'sport for inner city youth' (Houlihan 1991: 99).

As can be seen from Table 3.7 the focus of sport policy in the 1970s (at least until 1979) sat comfortably within the broader political consensus surrounding the maturation of the welfare state, the ideological pre-eminence of social democracy, an economic context of growing affluence and an increasingly politicised, professional and bureaucratised approach to sport, as manifest, for example, in the creation of the Sports Councils. Table 3.7 also indicates that, despite the many references to 'diverting resources to those who are gifted in sport' (Department of the Environment 1975: 18) in the 1975 White Paper, government funding to the GB Sports Council was generally directed at wider social objectives shaped by the social and political background of growing civil unrest and unemployment in the late 1970s, particularly in inner city areas.

1980–94

The GB Sports Council strategy document of the early 1980s – *Sport in the Community: The Next Ten Years* (Sports Council 1982) – can be categorised as a key political/policy event (see Table 3.8) given the growing congruence described above between government policy (with regard to urban deprivation objectives, in particular) and that of the GB Sports Council. However, *Sport in the Community* also had implications for elite sport. As Coalter *et al.* (1988) note, despite the increasing emphasis on schemes for the recreationally deprived, the unemployed and the socially deprived, the GB Sports Council's largest funding commitment remained at the elite level. Moreover, the organisational and administrative framework for sport during the 1980s and into the early 1990s has been characterised by Roche (1993) as one of continuing fragmentation and disharmony between the various bodies involved in lobbying for sport's interests. A central theme running through such observations is that the organisation and administration of sport policy in the UK has been bedevilled by the lack of a coherent 'voice' for sport, exemplified by the almost constant friction between a statutory Sports Council and the two main voluntary bodies in sport, the Central Council of Physical Recreation (CCPR), which acts as the main forum for the many national governing bodies of sport and the British Olympic Association (BOA) (for more detail see, for example, Coghlan and Webb 1990; Horne *et al.* 1999; Pickup 1996; Roche 1993).

This description of the incoherent nature of sport's organisation and administration led to a number of reviews of the role and function of the Sports Councils (cf. Oakley and Green 2001b). Moreover, a recurring concern in discussions regarding the role of the GB Sports Council was that the structure of sport was seen as hindering developments at the elite level. As a former Director-General of the GB Sports Council argued:

> it is here on the cusp between casual participation and the quest for improved performance, that the efficiency of a nation's administrative structure for

Table 3.8 UK sport policy: 1980–94

Key political/policy event	Organisational and administrative implications	Funding implications	Implications for elite sport development
1982: GB Sports Council strategy, *Sport in the Community: The Next Ten Years*	Wide-ranging strategy reflected changes in late 1970s towards increased accountability, specific target groups and increasing links with government policy, e.g. Action Sport	Acknowledged that, despite growing rhetoric of welfarism, grant-in-aid had been weighted towards elitism	Elite sector – administrative and coaching grants to NGBs, centres of excellence and sports science – still in receipt of major proportion of Sports Council funding
1986: Rossi Committee Report	Examined the basis of, and justification for, the GB Sports Council's existence	Debates regarding funding centred on how grant monies were to be used	Representing NGB interests, the CCPR argued for more influence as to how funding allocations were spent
1986 and 1987: Treasury White Papers, *The Government's Expenditure Plans*	Confirmed links between sport, recreation and government policy in inner cities and other 'stress areas'	White Paper expenditure plans frequently stressed how funds should be used	No direct implications; funding concentrated on broader social policy objectives
1988: GB Sports Council strategy, *Sport in the Community: Into the '90s*	Major focus on women and young people (primarily the 13-24 age group) as target groups	Dismissive of East European model of making NGBs dependent on government	Aim was to help NGBs 'develop and implement their own strategies'
1990: John Major replaced Margaret Thatcher as leader of Conservative Party and Prime Minister	Major's appointment heralded a change in government's approach to sport	Major supported a National Lottery; sport one of five good causes to benefit	Major was also supportive of debates to improve performances at international level; linked to issues of national identity
1992: Department of National Heritage established	Reflected personal commitment of John Major; attempt to bring together a fragmented policy area	Further centralised control of funding allocations to sport	Raised status of sport at Cabinet level
1994: National Lottery introduced	Crucial impact on sport and recreation, largely for capital projects in early years	Sport to benefit from estimated additional £200m to £250m per annum by 1999	Arguably the single most important factor in the UK's development of an elite sport model

GB/NI athletes performed well at the four summer Olympic Games between 1980-94: In Moscow (1980) 21 medals; Los Angeles (1984) 37 medals (22 were Bronze); Seoul (1988) 24 medals; and Barcelona (1992) 20 medals.

Source: Adapted from Coalter et al. (1988); Henry (1993, 2001); Houlihan (1991, 1997); Roche (1993); Sports Council 1982, 1988); Wallechinsky (2000)

sport really matters ... At more modest levels of participation, plurality is an undoubted virtue. When, however, the provision of crucial support services such as top level coaching; elite training facilities; including access to consistent medical and scientific advice; or of opportunities for competitive experience are seen to be uncoordinated, inconsistent in quality and financially wasteful, it is time to take seriously the need for reform.

(Pickup 1996: 172–3)

Sport's organisational and administrative fragmentation was also due, in part, to the fact that the sport portfolio had been moved between a number of different government departments over the past 30 years. Indeed, it was not until the establishment of the Department for Culture, Media and Sport (DCMS) in 1997, under a new Labour administration, that 'sport' was included in the title of a government department (cf. Horne *et al.* 1999). The types of reform called for by the GB Sports Council's Director-General above are instructive given the policy responses in the early 1990s, due largely to the influence of the Prime Minister, John Major (see Table 3.8), which signalled an undoubted change in the government's approach to sport. Two key changes here were the raising of sport's status within government through the creation of the Department of National Heritage (DNH), and the establishment of a National Lottery in 1994.

1995–2002

In 1995, the Conservative Government published a comprehensive policy statement, *Sport: Raising the Game* (DNH 1995), which indicated the withdrawal of central government and the Sports Councils from the provision of opportunities for mass participation and focused, *inter alia*, on: (i) the development of elite performers and an elite sports academy/institute; (ii) developing the role of higher education institutions in the fostering of elite athletes; and (iii) funding allocations to governing bodies, which would now be conditional on the explicit support for government objectives. Arguably, for the first time in its relatively short history, 'sport' was considered a discrete domain for government intervention, with an emerging organisational, administrative and funding framework at the elite level. Moreover, it has been argued that the publication of *Sport: Raising the Game* abandoned any pretence of an integrated and multi-dimensional approach to sports development as conceived in the late 1980s by the GB Sports Council around the sports development continuum of four tightly integrated elements: foundation, participation, performance and excellence (Houlihan 2000a). Two prominent and interrelated themes are at work here: (i) an increasing preoccupation with elite sport development; and (ii) the ongoing retreat from support for community recreation. As Lentell argued in the early 1990s, 'It seems that the [GB Sports] Council is ending its "dangerous liaison" with the world of "Community" to rejoin the more comfortable world of "Sport"' (1993: 147).

Against this background, the Labour Government (elected in 1997) published its own strategy for sport, *A Sporting Future for All* (DCMS 2000) – see Table 3.9.

Table 3.9 UK sport policy: 1995–2002

Key political/policy event	Organisational and administrative implications	Funding implications	Implications for elite sport development
1995: Conservative Government policy statement, *Sport: Raising the Game*	Two key themes: (i) development of elite athletes and establishment of an elite training centre; (ii) youth sport and schools	Grants to NGBs now conditional upon support for government objectives	Substantial support for elite level, although funding implications were a concern
1996: Atlanta Olympic Games	Performances in Atlanta increased pressure to implement recommendations for an elite sport academy/institute	The World Class Programme introduced in 1997 (using Lottery monies) as part of strategy to improve elite performances	Low medal count (15 in total and just one Gold); leads to increased pressure for an elite sports academy/institute
1997: 'New' Labour administration elected	Introduction of 'Best Value' initiative aimed at modernising local government services, including sport and leisure; social inclusion becomes key policy direction; DNH renamed as DCMS	Increasing policy rhetoric linked sport funding to social inclusion objectives	Continued support for elite sports institute – network of centres (known as UKSI) operating from 1999; UK Sport Council created as part of reorganisation of Sports Councils – and distributor of Lottery funding from 1999
1999: Sport England strategy document, *Lottery Fund Strategy, 1999–2009*	Twin objectives – local projects for all and to improve medal-winning chances at international level	Two key strands: Community Projects Fund (£150m) and World Class Fund (£50m)	Further confirmation of support for elite level
2000: Labour Government policy statement, *A Sporting Future for All*	Reiterated much of rhetoric in *Sport: Raising the Game*; linked to Best Value objectives; Specialist Sports Colleges to be created	NGB funding now directly linked to performance targets	NGBs required to produce national talent performance plans identifying pathways from grass roots to international level

(continued …)

Table 3.9 UK sport policy: 1995–2002 (continued)

Key political/policy event	Organisational and administrative implications	Funding implications	Implications for elite sport development
2000: Sydney Olympic Games	In lead-up to the Games critics argued that there was too much emphasis on elite (Olympic) sports at expense of other (minor) sports	Lottery monies (World Class Fund) highlighted as major factor in improved performances in Sydney	Greatly improved performance by GB/NI team – 28 medals won (11 Gold); helped to legitimise central government support
2001: Elite Sports Funding Review	Called for increased co-operation between UK Sport and Home Country Sports Councils; and that NGBs produce just one integrated Performance plan	Recommended rationalisation of three-tiered World Class funding programmes; called for extra £10m Exchequer funding for World Class Performance level	Three-tiered World Class programmes to be rationalised into one; greater focus on coaching/coach education; more effort to be placed on talent identification and development systems
2002: The Coaching Task Force: Final Report	Recommended the professionalisation of coaching; coach development, employment and deployment require major revisions; the role of Sports Coach UK to be reviewed	Extra funding to be allocated to develop, train, educate and employ more full-time coaches	A more structured approach to elite sport recommended, with the provision of more full-time coaches working with elite performers
2002: Game Plan: A Strategy for Delivering Government's Sport and Physical Activity Objectives	Major government review of all levels, structures and financing of sport; symbiotic links between sport, education and health policy emphasised	Recommendations included 'simplifying the fragmented funding arrangements' for sport	Further prioritisation of funding to NGBs recommended, based on a 'twin-track' approach, incorporating likely medal-winning success as well as popularity of the sport

Source: Adapted from DNH (1995); DCMS (2000, 2001, 2002); DCMS/Strategy Unit (2002); Oakley and Green (2001b); Houlihan (1997); McDonald (2000); Sport England (1999a, 1999b); UK Sport (2000a, 2000b, 2002d);

Although the Labour strategy and *Sport: Raising the Game* are from different sides of the political spectrum, they demonstrate a striking note of unity on the twin emphases of school (youth) sport and elite development. However, as Houlihan notes, since 1997, the Labour Government 'has begun to make good its policy commitments in the area of sport, but it is notable that there has been far greater progress in addressing the issues associated with the elite end of the sports continuum' (2000a: 175).

It should be acknowledged, however, that the Labour Government introduced a new social policy agenda that had significant implications for the promotion and development of sporting provision and opportunities in the UK. Although the Labour Government eschews the use of politically-laden terms such as 'ideology', the so-called 'Third Way' (cf. Giddens 1998) is a philosophy that has permeated much of its recent policy discourse (cf. Oakley and Green 2001b). Related to this is the 'Best Value' initiative that emerged out of a wider modernisation agenda, and one of the contemporary public policy themes affecting sport. According to Sport England, a priority for sport is 'the modernisation of local government including the duty of Best Value; a duty to secure continuous improvement in the delivery of services with regard to economy, efficiency and effectiveness' (Sport England 1999a: 7). In short, the new public policy language of professionalism and modernisation was seen as a key vehicle for achieving welfare goals such as social inclusion and widening access for all.

However, the expectation that these welfare goals should permeate all public services has to be reconciled with the existence of entrenched service specific policy priorities. For example, the quest for Olympic medals may take priority over (or at least moderate) social inclusion goals to the extent that a disproportionate representation of social classes A and B in elite squads/teams will be accepted if it realises Olympic or other international sporting success (Houlihan 2000a). Indeed, an English Sports Council survey, *The Development of Sporting Talent 1997*, investigated 12 sports and found that 'the chance of becoming an elite performer were two times greater for individuals from professional classes than they were for those from manual classes, all else being equal' (English Sports Council 1998: 3).

Despite the above caveats, some of the most prominent sport policy commitments in the late 1990s were elite-related, for example, the development of an elite sports institute network (cf. Theodoraki 1999) and the establishment of a three-tier (Performance, Potential and Start) World Class Lottery Fund to support elite athletes at different levels of development. The UK Sports Council (UK Sport) became the distributor of Lottery funding for elite-focused programmes in 1999 and, during its first year (July 1999–March 2000), distributed £17 million to 24 sports at a UK level (UK Sport 2000a). Thus, two key elements underlying the UK's emergent elite sport development model are the UK Sports Institute (UKSI), based on the Australian decentralised institute network, and National Lottery funding. The latter, in particular was cited by many of the successful athletes at the Sydney 2000 Olympics as a key contributory factor in their success (UK Sport 2001). Lottery funding is also largely responsible for the construction of new facilities as part of the UKSI's network development. Mackay noted that the final phase (from April 2000) of this development would lead to 'a more systematic approach to performance support which will require significant investment, such as a national programme for elite coach and athlete identification' (1998b: 5). With regard to coaching, *The Coaching Task Force: Final Report* (DCMS 2002) emphasised the requirement for more full-time coaches which should be underpinned by the professionalisation of coach education and training.

Talent identification and development of young people is a further important element of the UK's recent support for the elite level. UK Sport requires that NGBs have a talent identification and development strategy, part of which involves the construction of 'pathways' to higher levels of competition especially between school and clubs (Hoey 2000: 14). In addition, the government is funding the establishment of up to 400 Specialist Sports Colleges (SSCs) (DfES/DCMS 2003), which have, among their various functions, the responsibility to act as the first rung on the talent development ladder and thus form an important part of a planned, co-ordinated and integrated organisational and administrative model of elite sport development.

The emphasis developed in the 1990s on elite sport success was reinforced in the most recent government strategy, *Game Plan* (DCMS/Strategy Unit 2002), which reiterated the government's commitment to elite success, and the need for a results-driven and evidence-based approach to the achievement of strategic aims. In sum, although the UK is at a relatively early stage of developing a coherent model/system for elite sport development, an organisational, administrative and funding framework is clearly emerging. This framework includes: (i) the establishment of the UKSI and its attendant support services associated with coaching programmes, sports science/medicine, physiology, psychology and bio-mechanics; (ii) Lottery funding for programmes such as the elite athlete-focused World Class Performance programme; (iii) talent identification and development techniques and systems; and (iv) the establishment of Specialist Sports Colleges.

Policy change and conclusions

From the 1960s, until the publication of *Sport: Raising the Game* in 1995, the approach to sport generally in the UK was characterised by its fragmented nature and disharmony between many of the key sporting bodies regarding organisational, administrative and funding matters. Government intervention was limited until the establishment of the executive Sports Councils in the early 1970s, which signalled an interest in improving the organisational and administrative structure of sport and recreation, primarily through the building of facilities and the adoption of a Sport for All programme to increase participation in sport and physical activities. This is not to argue that fragmentation and disharmony have been eradicated (cf. DCMS/Strategy Unit 2002). Rather, it is to suggest that, from the mid-1990s, there has been a concerted attempt by central government to provide some form of strategic guidance for the sport sector. Moreover, both Conservative and Labour administrations have shown an increasing willingness to not only support sport at the elite level, but also to construct a supportive policy discourse.

The perennial debates surrounding the mass/elite divide that have characterised sport policy rhetoric in the UK over the past 30 years also remain and permeate recent sport policy debates. Of particular note here, however, is the contention that changes at the elite level of sport policy-making have led to the strengthening of the elite sport policy community in relation to other sport policy concerns during the 1990s. These observations can be conceptualised in terms of the advocacy coalition framework (ACF).

First, within the ACF, 'policy-oriented learning' is conceptualised as an endogenous factor which can lead a dominant coalition to refine and adapt its belief system in order to realise its goals more efficiently. Second, the strengthening of the elite sport policy community has, in part, been due to 'sympathetic ministers and prime ministers and an upsurge in popular sentiment' (Houlihan 2000a: 179). The ACF conceptualises such factors as 'external system events' or exogenous factors, which shift the power distribution among subsystem actors by changing resource and constraint patterns. Since 'deep core' and 'policy core beliefs' are assumed to have a high level of resistance to change, the ACF argues that policy-oriented learning is most likely to concern only 'secondary aspects' of a belief system. The policy core is assumed to remain intact, and thus able to bring about only minor policy change. As a corollary, major policy change, namely a change in policy cores, is thought to be unlikely in the absence of non-cognitive events external to the subsystem (cf. Sabatier and Jenkins-Smith 1999). By way of summing up, a recent example helps to illustrate how actors' values and belief systems might be implicated in change within the sport development policy subsystem in the UK. Houlihan (2000a) points to three distinct groupings involved with the development of Specialist Sports Colleges (SSCs) – educational interests, community sports development and elite sport development. This is an instructive finding, given the insights generated by the ACF. One example from Houlihan's study of SSCs helps to illustrate the significance of this perspective.

With regard to SSCs and the policy issue of identification and development of talented youngsters, it can be hypothesised that actors within the three distinct groups (or coalitions in ACF terminology) noted above will reveal differing perceptions, values and belief systems on this issue. Educationalists have a primary concern with, *inter alia*, the educational needs of all children and the development of lifelong learning: in other words, a well-rounded and holistic education. The second group is that of a 'broader coalition concerned with a set of sports/community development interests' (Houlihan 2000a: 183). For this coalition, the SSC is seen as a resource for 'their local families of schools and their communities ... [and] will form a focal point for revitalising education in areas of socio-economic disadvantage' (Department for Education and Employment 1998: 1). The national governing bodies of sport are key members of the third potential coalition and their concerns are primarily with talent identification and developmental progress to the elite level. Indeed, the DCMS (2000: 8) states that SSCs 'will have an explicit focus on elite sport'. Thus, in contrast to the first two groupings, actors within the elite sport development coalition 'perceive young people as the seed-corn for future elite squads' (Houlihan 2000a: 179).

In ACF terms, such observations suggest that the sport development policy subsystem contains (at least) three coalitions of actors/organisations actively concerned with a policy issue – in this case, the SSCs and talent identification and development – and who regularly seek to influence public policy related to it. The policy subsystem, and advocacy coalitions therein, can be further analysed through the ACF's threefold hierarchy of belief systems (cf. Sabatier and Jenkins-Smith 1999). At the level of deep core beliefs, concerns surround fundamental normative and ontological axioms that define a vision of the individual, society and the world. At this level, and for this example, it could be hypothesised that elite sport development advocates (e.g. NGBs) would emphasise individual autonomy and achievement striving. In other words, relative to other groups in society, more emphasis would be put on the 'self'. At the next level, policy core beliefs revolve around causal perceptions, basic strategies and policy positions for achieving deep core beliefs. This would translate into policies that frame the 'problem', or policy issue; for example, the allocation of resources for sport. Thus, the elite-focused coalition would seek to frame the problem in terms that provide a conducive environment for the elite performer over, for example, social inclusion initiatives and/or sport/physical activity opportunities at grass roots levels.

At the final level, for the ACF, there is a set of secondary aspects, comprising instrumental considerations on ways in which to implement the policy core. In the case of the SSCs, the elite sport coalition would adopt particular strategies in an effort to realise its policy objectives; strategies that emphasise, for example, talent identification techniques that lead to development through identifiable pathways to the elite level. The ACF assumes that these structural categories of belief systems show decreasing resistance to change, with the deep core beliefs displaying the most, and secondary aspects the least, resistance (cf. Kübler 2001). Clearly, these observations are hypothetical and have been used here to illustrate the salience of the ACF's logic for our investigation of NSOs/NGBs in the following chapters.

Conclusion

Three key themes emerge from this review and analysis: (i) central/federal government involvement; (ii) perennial debates regarding mass participation versus elite sport programmes; and (iii) the discursive construction of sport policy discourse around the language of rational/technocratic processes. Running through all three themes are questions in respect of the purpose of sport; an issue, to date, debated most explicitly in Canada. Taken together, these themes afford an analysis of the wider social and political processes highlighted in this chapter – namely, the relationships between structures, agents and values/belief systems – in the construction of an elite sport development system in the three countries. In relation to these observations, it is now possible to draw further (but at this stage, tentative) conclusions with regard to conceptualising elite sport development models/systems.

First, it is argued that the model of systematic and asystematic talent selection and development (Fisher and Borms 1990) set out in Chapter 2 affords only a partial view of the complex processes that contribute to elite success. The model reveals little with regard to the wider social, political, economic and cultural environment within which sport policy discourses are constructed. Specifically, it has little to say regarding (i) the funding tensions permeating mass participation/ elite sport debates; (ii) the multi-organisational, multi-agent complexity that characterises frameworks within which policy direction at the elite level operates in the early twenty-first century (cf. Abbott *et al.* 2002; Digel 2002); and (iii) the technical/rational discursive context within which sport policy-making is increasingly framed. The second conclusion relates to the earlier discussion about the extent to which the nature of the objective – the achievement of elite success – determines/constrains the possible policy responses in different countries. The evidence presented in this chapter clearly identifies both Australia and Canada as 'early Western adopters', and the UK as a 'late adopter' of many of the principles of organisation and administration developed by former Eastern bloc countries.

However, the identification of broad similarities in policy responses to the issue of elite achievement still leaves unanswered questions regarding the existence, significance, composition and dynamics of any elite sport advocacy coalition. In addition, investigation of (any identified) advocacy coalitions would need to focus on the values and belief systems of both governmental and non-governmental members and the relative importance of coalition members, especially government departments/agencies. As Mintrom and Vergari (1996: 421) note, 'The "glue" that holds an advocacy coalition together is its members' shared beliefs over core policy matters'. A key question then for Chapters 4, 5 and 6 is whether there is evidence for shared beliefs (and value consensus) regarding elite sport development. In addition, in utilising insights into the 'context-shaping' asymmetries of (structural) relations of power (cf. Hay 1997, 2002) questions are also raised as to how the increasingly scientific/technical/rational approaches associated with elite sport development might serve to 'subdue' the concerns of those whose interests are not served by the objectives of elite sport.

Conclusion

4 Australia

This chapter draws on empirical data gained from interviews with key actors involved in the sport policy process and supplemented with documentary material, such as NSO annual reports, action/operations plans, financial statements and policy reviews, as well as policy-related documents from the federal government and the Australian Sports Commission. The three NSO case studies, Australian Swimming Incorporated, Australian Athletics Incorporated and the Australian Yachting Federation Incorporated, are organised in three sections. First, the organisational and administrative structure of each sport is outlined and the nature of the NSOs' relationships with other significant organisations is traced. Second, a number of sources have highlighted the most important areas involved in the development of elite athletes (cf. Digel 2002; Sports Council 1991; Sport Industry Research Centre 2002). Accordingly, four key areas of high performance sport policy are identified in relation to: (i) the development of elite level facilities; (ii) the emergence of 'full-time' swimmers, athletes and sailors; (iii) developments in coaching, sports science and sports medicine; and (iv) competition opportunities at the elite level. Finally, the chapter identifies briefly implications raised for the analysis of NSO decision-making with regard to high performance sport and also for the analysis of the wider policy-making process within which the NSO operates. A similar structure is used for the discussion of Canadian NSOs and UK NGBs in Chapters 5 and 6 respectively.

Australian Swimming Incorporated

Organisation, administration and relationships

In 1985, the Amateur Swimming Union of Australia, which was formed in 1909, was renamed Australian Swimming Incorporated (ASI); the removal of the term 'amateur' from the organisation's nomenclature was perhaps indicative of the gradual erosion of amateurism in Olympic sports in Australia (cf. Paddick 1997). Not only is ASI one of the oldest NSOs in Australia, it is also one of the most successful in terms of membership (98,945 in 2002–3) and elite level success – see Table 4.1 – (cf. ASI 2003; Commonwealth of Australia 1999; Howell *et al.*

1997). ASI has responsibility for the disciplines of swimming and open water swimming and is in the process of integrating disability swimming into its organisational remit. As the country's NSO, it also acts as the sport's parent body for Member Associations (State/Territory swimming associations), the Australian Swimming Coaches and Teachers Association Inc (ASCTA) and the Swimmers' Commission (ASI 2003). Other aquatic sports, which are independent organisations, but affiliated to ASI are: the Australian Diving Association, Australian Water Polo Inc, Australian Synchronised Swimming Inc and AUSSIE Masters Swimming. As a senior ASC official explained, it is interesting that some of these other aquatic sports have 'broken away' (Interviewee A, 6 June 2003) from direct control by ASI, providing some indication of tensions between disciplines, despite the sport enjoying increasing success in competitive swimming at the elite level (see Table 4.1).

An example of the tensions within ASI is provided by the debate following the 2000 Open Water World Swimming Championships where the Australian team failed, for the first time, to win a medal. A number of open water swimmers held ASI responsible. For example, a former secretary of ASI's Open Water Swimming Committee argued that 'This was the most under-prepared and under-developed group of swimmers ever to assemble in Australia and Australian Swimming stands responsible' (Guesdon 2001). Guesdon went on to suggest that, despite drawing up a five-year plan for the sport, ASI ignored the key elements of the plan and that 'The reason is always, no money in the budget left for open water to implement their plan'. There is also a tension between national ASI elite level objectives and the objectives of State/Territory swimming associations. In the late 1980s, for example, while ASI's President noted that 'Australian Swimming has enjoyed a harmonious relationship with these [State/Territory] organisations' (quoted in ASI 1988: 5), ASI's Executive Director argued that, 'Unfortunately, one of the four aims for 1987–8 was not achieved in totality. This being the development of greater co-operation between State Associations and Australian Swimming' (quoted in ASI 1988: 8). At this time, it appeared that 'co-operation', for the Executive Director, centred on:

> devis[ing] programmes and systems whereby all members ... can share in the success of our Olympic Teams and other elite teams .... Australian Swimming must ensure that its elite competitors are given every possible opportunity to succeed at world level.
>
> (quoted in ASI 1988: 9)

Tensions between the priorities of ASI and its State/Territory associations persisted into the 1990s (see, for example, ASI 1991, 1992, 1996), together with increasing evidence that the majority of the organisation's funding, received through the Australian Sports Commission (ASC), was being targeted at the elite level. Indeed, in a response to the Standing Committee On Recreation and Sport's Working Party on Management Improvement in Australian Sport, the following comments from ASI's Executive Director are illustrative of these enduring concerns:

Table 4.1 Australian swimming medals: Olympic Games/World Aquatic Championships, 1988–2001

| | Olympic Games | | | | | World Aquatic Championships | | | |
	Gold	Silver	Bronze	Total		Gold	Silver	Bronze	Total
1988	1	1	1	3	1991	2	5	1	8
1992	1	3	5	9	1994	4	2	3	9
1996	2	4	6	12	1998	7	6	7	20
2000	5	9	4	18	2001	13	3	3	19

> The challenge … is not to dismantle the State structure, but to make it work for the benefit of the whole sport. From personal experience, the conflict most often arises over the 'ownership' of the elite members of the sport. This can also be traced back to government funding – when the State Government also wants recognition for assisting elite rather than the grass roots level.
>
> (Murray 1997: 23)

More recently, tensions within ASI surfaced in a major review of the organisation's governance structures (ASI 2000). Many of those interviewed as part of this review, including ASI Board members, commented that the Board did not serve ASI as a whole. The review was unequivocal in its critique of the organisation, noting that comments from those interviewed expressed deep concern that ASI's priorities were focused on the elite few, with the interests of the wider swimming population and ASI's membership at large left to the State/Territory associations, districts and clubs to address. Of particular interest is that these conclusions were mirrored in the report of the Sport 2000 Task Force, which was charged by the Minister for Sport and Tourism to investigate 'appropriate strategies, arrangements and delivery systems for sport beyond 2000' (Commonwealth of Australia 1999: 9). The report concluded 'that the emphasis on elite sport has overshadowed the importance of delivering increased participation' (1999: 89).

Four areas of elite sport policy

Development of elite level facilities

It is important to note that, as in Canada and the UK, the largest providers of sports facilities in Australia are at sub-national levels of government. It is also worth recalling that a report commissioned in the early 1970s to investigate the establishment of an Australian Sports Institute found that 'Australia is desperately short of sports facilities of international standard' (Coles 1975: 33). Indeed, with regard to swimming, Coles found, *inter alia*, that 'There is no … heated swimming pool of international standard in Australia' (1975: 33). Reflecting these findings, in 1980, the federal government provided $AUS25 million over a three-year period for an International Standard Sports Facilities programme, with the aim of enabling 'Australian athletes to train and compete on a similar basis to their overseas counterparts' (Parliament of the Commonwealth of Australia 1983: 52). Yet, 10 years later, the ASC found that 'many other countries now have year-round facilities [indoor swimming pools] which Australia does not have nation-wide' (1993a: 42). However, as discussed in Chapter 3, the establishment of the Australian Institute of Sport (AIS) in 1981 provided the impetus for a more concerted approach to facility development for elite level training in many sports. The creation of Intensive Training Centre programmes (now known as National Training Centre programmes) during the mid-1990s in many States/Territories as part of the support for the Sydney 2000 Olympic Games further strengthened Australia's sports facility base (cf. Pyke and Norris 2001). The facilities and programmes provided by the AIS and State/Territory institutes/academies of sport have, however, been crucial for swimming. As the Director of the Australian Coaching Council (ACC) noted, 'The Canberra-based [swimming] programme is strong. However, State institute support and club programmes also contribute significantly to Australia's strong standing in world swimming' (Schembri 2000: 7).

Despite the growth in sports facilities in general and elite sport facilities, in particular, over the past 30 years, the Sport 2000 Task Force found that 'The issue of facilities was commonly raised in submissions to the Task Force' (Common-wealth of Australia 1999: 101), a key aspect of which appears to be the lack of a national facilities plan that identifies national sport requirements and operational objectives. As the NSO for the sport, ASI is therefore faced with a number of facilities-related issues. First, provision in the States/Territories is variable (cf. ASC 1993a) and out of the national body's control. Although provision is relatively healthy in Queensland, elsewhere the picture is one of decline. The South Australian Office of Sport and Recreation, for example, 'indicated that funding in the order of $AUS50 million is needed to refurbish local swimming pools and this is beyond the State or local communities to fund' (Commonwealth of Australia 1999: 101). A second issue concerns the control of 'water space' at local community level (ASI 1996: 2). For one senior ASI official, these concerns are:

> critical, absolutely critical ... we don't have control over the water. Most of the pools in Australia, traditionally, have belonged to local government authorities [and] they have devolved that responsibility to local management groups, and the bottom line is the most important thing.
>
> (Interviewee B, 5 June 2003)

Third, the issue becomes even more clouded if the school system is also factored into the equation. As one of ASI's senior high performance officials related:

> Most of our good facilities in Australia are in private schools ... [and] coaches who operate in private schools are not allowed to take kids from outside the school ... So the private school system sits outside the State school system

and they both sit outside the national and State [swimming] bodies and, unfortunately, they don't talk to each other.

(Interviewee C, 3 June 2003)

These observations point to a high degree of organisational complexity that has perhaps been masked by the success of Australian elite swimmers. The lack of dialogue is not helped by the noted over-emphasis, by the federal government, on elite sport objectives and the 2000 Olympic Games. Indeed, a senior official at one of the country's elite institutes/academies of sport stated that 'any investment the federal government makes into facilities is pretty much a knee-jerk reaction … it's more event-driven … There's no national co-ordination' (Interviewee D, 5 June 2003). The upshot is policy fragmentation, and for ASI, a concern over the future sustainability of the sport. As one of the sport's senior high performance officials explained, in the past, a large percentage of the most successful swimmers worked with professional coaches in clubs that had built their own pools and:

> that's really where all of our athletes have come from. They don't come from the amateur clubs. They come from professional coaches but now that's turned the other way because it's so expensive to build your own facility [and] most of our coaches are [now] in facilities that are owned by Councils and leased by clubs.

(Interviewee C, 3 June 2003)

A senior ASC official suggested that one recent initiative which might help to alleviate some of these problems is the signing of Memorandums of Understanding (MoUs), which usually involve the State/Territory swimming association and the State/Territory institute/academy of sport, and driven in large part by the ASC's requirement for NSOs to undertake the type of governance review described above (Interviewee A, 6 June 2003). According to this observer, the ongoing implementation of MoUs reveals evidence of an increasingly harmonious relationship between ASI and State/Territory swimming/sporting bodies. However, whether this initiative will have the desired long-term effect regarding access to facilities remains to be seen.

Emergence of 'full-time' swimmers

It is undoubtedly the case that in the early twenty-first century there are a small group of elite swimmers in Australia who can command endorsements fees, sponsorships and are in a position to compete for prize money on the Fédération Internationale de Natation Amateur (FINA) swimming circuit; in short, swimmers who train and compete on a full-time basis. It is also the case, however, as in Canada and the UK, that there are many others (at sub-elite levels) who can not. This group of swimmers would encompass many of those in receipt of Direct Athlete Support (DAS) grants allocated by ASI. In 2002–3, ASI allocated a total of $AUS379,500 to 93 swimmers, with grants ranging from $AUS1,000 to $AUS12,000 per annum (ASI 2003) and a further $AUS191,125, through a sponsorship arrangement with *Telstra*, to 50 swimmers (many of whom are included in DAS allocations). In addition, the Australian Olympic Committee (AOC) administers a medal incentive scheme, which, as one of ASI's senior officials observed, 'has been very, very, lucrative for some Australian swimmers because they [AOC] provide the funding every year, not just the Olympic year' (Interviewee B, 5 June 2003). The above scenario was summarised by one of the sport's high performance officials:

> With the exception of our major athletes like Ian Thorpe and Grant Hackett, and one or two others, we would have about six athletes earning about £35,000 [sterling] a year ... but the rest of our athletes rely on funding from ASI or part-time work ... a number of them are studying ... but basically most of them rely on money that we supply for them.
>
> (Interviewee C, 3 June 2003)

Yet, as for those that rely on ASI grants, 'It's not a lot of money' (Interviewee B, 5 June 2003). As was the case in Canada and the UK, the acceptance of professionalism in Australia has been slow and contested which, as Armstrong notes, 'is perplexing in view of the rather narrow-minded obsession with winning' (1997: 12). Indeed, while the creation of the AIS in 1981 clearly signalled a more professional approach to supporting elite sport, it was still the case that AIS scholarships were not to be characterised as a passport to outright professionalism. As Toohey observes, 'In order to maintain their amateur status, they [athletes] were expected to be gainfully occupied by undertaking studies or regular employment in addition to their training regimes' (1990: 130).

The slow embrace of professionalism was given added momentum by the award, in 1993, of the 2000 Olympic Games to Sydney. Through the ASC, the federal government introduced the Olympic Athlete Programme (OAP) in 1994; a clear (state-sponsored) acknowledgement that athletes now required extra funding support if the country was to achieve its stated goal of 60 medals at the Games: swimming was seen as a major contributor to this national goal of Olympic success (ASC 1994; Department of the Environment, Sport and Territories [DEST] 1994). The OAP provided an extra $AUS135 million over the period leading up to the Games and, while these funds were not just focused on payments to athletes, direct financial support to athletes increased significantly, with over $AUS1 million allocated for 1994–5 (ASC 1994). As stated in an OAP publication, 'Some major sports [swimming, athletics, rowing, cycling and gymnastics were the largest benefactors] will have National Training Centres which will support athletes on a full time, or almost full time, basis' (DEST 1994: 12). It is also clear that ASI's decision to continue with direct payments to its swimmers, post-2000 is a clear indication that sustaining the elite success achieved in 2000 (see Table 4.1) remains of paramount importance.

Developments in coaching, sports science and sports medicine

With regard to coaching, a significant factor in the success of swimming during Australia's so-called 'golden age' of sport – broadly acknowledged as the period covering the 1950s and early 1960s (cf. Phillips 2000; Woodman 1989) – was an apparent 'acceptance' of cutting-edge, scientific coaching regimes associated most notably with Forbes Carlile and Harry Gallagher (it should be noted that athletics was also a sport that embraced such techniques). Indeed, these coaches 'were paid by the Australian Swimming Union to attend special training camps to prepare swimmers for ensuing Olympic and Commonwealth games performances' (Phillips 2000: 158). However, as Phillips also argues, 'The success experienced at the top echelon was not representative of coaching in the majority of sports throughout the country' (2000: 83) and, from the London Olympics of 1948 to Montreal in 1976, 'athletics and swimming have provided the backbone of Australia's Olympic success' (2000: 84).

Before turning to some of the contemporary issues facing ASI, it is important to note briefly that the majority of developments in coaching education and training in general in Australia have emerged from federal government-inspired initiatives and reports (cf. Woodman 1989). Of note, are the reports in the 1970s by Bloomfield (1973) and Coles (1975) with the latter arguing the case for an Australian Sports Institute. In 1978, a National Coaching Council was established, which became the Australian Coaching Council (ACC) from 1979, and later that year a National Coaching Accreditation Scheme was set up (cf. Phillips 2000; Schembri 2000; Woodman 1989, 1997). The overriding theme running through these developments was a 'sport-government nexus [which was] so central to … the story of coaching development [in Australia]' (Phillips 2000: 91); a theme embodied by the relocation, in 1986, of the ACC's Director 'into Commission [ASC] offices at the AIS' (Woodman 1989: 216).

The first, and perhaps most significant, issue requiring closer examination then is that of the sport-government nexus. It is clear that, from the late 1980s, federal sport strategy documents such as *Going for Gold* (Parliament of the Commonwealth of Australia 1989), *The Australian Sports Kit (The Next Step)* (Department for the Arts, Sport, the Environment, Tourism and Territories [DASETT] 1989), *Can Sport be Bought?* (Parliament of the Commonwealth of Australia 1990), *Maintain the Momentum* (Department for the Arts, Sport, the Environment and Territories [DASET] 1992) and the *Olympic Athlete Programme* (ASC 1994; DEST 1994), signalled increasing federal government interest in supporting elite level sport. Interlocked with this increased interest was the prioritisation of eight sports for extra funding that were deemed most likely to achieve Olympic success – of which swimming was one (cf. Baumann 2002).

The second point is the evidence of considerable tension between coaches and the administrators of ASI, and between coaches and technical staff (ASI 2000). It appears that these tensions hinge, in part, on a perception from some within the swimming community that the coaches are 'running' the organisation. One contributor to the 2000 governance review argued that volunteers originally ran ASI but that paid coaches currently ran it (ASI 2000). Moreover, Schembri's (2000) argument that all levels of the Australian sports system need to function well is brought into sharp relief by another argument within the review. Although the elite end of the system in swimming was clearly considered to have functioned effectively, there was a strongly expressed view that the coaches' association (ASCTA) contributed to the development of elite swimmers but not to the overall development of swimming.

The third point concerns the role of the coach at the developmental/mass participation levels. This is a complex issue that has to take account of the following developments: (i) the ASCTA now has full stakeholder status within ASI and a vote on the Board following the recent governance review; (ii) the recent MoU, which allows for a more transparent set of agreements between ASI, State/Territory swimming associations and institutes/academies of sport; (iii) concerns regarding a lack of ASI involvement and influence in Learn-to-Swim school programmes; and (iv) the introduction, in 2001, of a federal government programme for a number of sports to increase participation levels – the Targeted Sports Participation Growth Programme (TSPGP).[1] Taken together, the upshot of these developments is that there is now a much more concerted effort by ASI to ensure that coaches operating at the sport's grass roots levels encourage children to become involved in competitive swimming. As a senior high performance official explained, the sport has now introduced a licensing scheme for coaches, which requires them 'to join a swimming club as a coach' and where one of their responsibilities will be to get 'kids from [the] playground to join the club' and 'encourage kids to get involved in the competitive side of the sport' (Interviewee C, 3 June 2003). In sum, it appears that, over many years, Australian swimming has relied on the expertise of a relatively small number of professional coaches who have had an overt focus on producing elite swimmers but with little thought given (until recently) to the overall strategic development of the sport.

In respect of developments in sports science and sports medicine, Australia remains in the vanguard of such developments (cf. Baumann 2002; Phillips 2000; Pyke and Norris 2001). The Australian Sports Medicine Federation was formed as early as 1963 (Vamplew 1997) although, as Coles observed in the mid-1970s, the level of provision at this time remained 'variable' (1975: 41). Although the creation of the Australian Sports Medicine Federation (now known as Sports Medicine Australia) was undoubtedly significant, it was the establishment of the AIS that provided the organisational focal point, and adequate funding, for cutting-edge sports science and medicine research in general. Swimming, however, was at the forefront in the use of sports science from as early as the 1950s (cf. Phillips 2000). As Howell *et al.* observe:

> The Helsinki [1952 Olympic] Games were far from successful for Australian swimmers, and after their mediocre efforts national coaches began to apply the scientific methods of training and conditioning suggested by the research of Professor Frank Cotton ... Cotton, assisted by Forbes Carlile, developed methods of training ... to prepare the Australian swimmers for the Melbourne

Olympics in 1956. The results were the most outstanding in Australia's swimming history.

(Howell *et al.* 1997: 418)

Across Australian sport in general, these developments did not emerge without some initial resistance. Wilma Shakespear – currently Head of the English Institute of Sport and former Australian national netball coach and Director of Queensland Academy of Sport – acknowledged that 'It took me a long time to ever accept that science was ever going to play a part, and it was not until I actually lost a world tournament that I thought the arrogance had better disappear' (quoted in Phillips 2000: 133). However, there was little evidence that such resistance has affected swimming in any significant manner. Indeed, Don Talbot, Head Coach at ASI from 1989 to 2001, and credited in many quarters as the key figure behind the elite level success enjoyed by Australian swimmers throughout the 1990s, extolled the virtues of leading sports science and medicine research (Phillips 2000; see also Baumann 2002). According to one senior high performance official, 'Australia is the leader in the application of sports science in the swimming world … And we now have an active national network with a co-ordinator [each] for physiology, bio-mechanics, nutrition, physio-massage and sports psychology' (Interviewee C, 3 June 2003). However, the need for even greater integration and coherence is clear as this observer went on to add that:

Before last year, the network didn't exist. If you weren't in the AIS, you weren't involved, and I could see that from when I was at [a State] Institute of Sport. Our guys just weren't involved in the national programme at all.

(Interviewee C, 3 June 2003)

Competition opportunities for elite level swimmers

The overriding factors shaping competition opportunities are distance from the quality of international competition available in Europe and North America and what a senior official at one of the country's elite institutes/academies of sport termed the 'tyranny of distance', i.e. the difficulty swimming teams face in travelling vast distances within Australia for competitive national meets (Interviewee E, 30 May 2003; see also Adair and Vamplew 1997). It is clear that concerns regarding the financial implications of sending Australian teams abroad for major swimming events remain as difficult as ever to overcome. Such concerns are, therefore, not new. In 1988, for example, the ASC/AIS listed some 16 funding grants to different sports for 'international programmes' and, although swimming received one of the largest allocations ($AUS100,000), it was made clear that 'one of the most significant problems facing sports today is the preparation and financing of Australian teams' overseas travel' (ASC/AIS 1988: 15).

Although the sport failed to establish the 'National Circuit Competition' structure in the early 1990s, a Grand Prix Circuit was successfully established in 1990–1 with the aim not only to provide 'much needed domestic competition', but also to generate significant revenues and prize money in order to encourage senior swimmers to maintain 'their participation at a National level' (Executive Director, ASI, quoted in ASI 1991: 6): elite swimmers were thus a clear priority for the sport's NSO. Competition opportunities for elite athletes in general in Australia, were also a priority at this time, with the federal government acknowledging that 'international competition and coaching are the keys to success. "Next Step" substantially increased the focus on international competition, recognising our physical isolation and the fact that we invariably compete out of season' (DASET 1992: 8).

The award of the Sydney 2000 Olympic Games provided a substantial impetus to improve the quality of international competition available to the country's elite performers. Crucially, additional federal funding was made available to allow increased participation of elite swimmers in international competition. Yet, while one of the OAP policy statements stated that 'Funding for international competition will be expanded' (DEST 1994: 15), it does not appear that there has been an equal emphasis on, and funding for, national domestic competition in swimming. As one senior high performance official acknowledged, 'We had a domestic league; we had a national league. We were given seed funding by the Sports Commission [ASC] but once that seed funding ran out ... [the] league fell over, we then haven't replaced it with anything' (Interviewee C, 3 June 2003).

The above discussion not only confirms the picture of a clear emphasis on the elite level over the past decade at least, but also points to the importance of putting in place domestic competition opportunities for the whole sport. As the high performance official explained, 'we're now in the process of changing, I guess, our philosophical direction in putting in place a domestic league' (Interviewee C, 3 June 2003). This observer also highlighted concerns over a 'crammed international calendar'. Although FINA's lack of planning and ASI's inability to influence the sport's international federation are part of the problem for Australian swimming, of equal significance is the geographical location of the majority of top-level competition opportunities. In other words, the major international swimming meets tend to be staged in the northern hemisphere; a situation exacerbated by the hiatus regarding funding from the ASC, post-2000, which constrained the number of swimmers sent to these events. The significance of a domestic national competition for the sport thus assumed far greater importance following the Sydney Olympic Games.

Summary

It is clear that Australian swimmers have enjoyed considerable success, both historically and more recently, in major international sporting events. As one of the targeted sports under the OAP during the 1990s the sport benefited from increased funding allocations provided by the federal government and the extensive array of support services at the AIS. The rhetoric underlying swimming's success, and indeed the success of many other sports at the elite level in Australia, is that of an integrated, coherent and systematic sport system. That the goals of integration and coherence have been at the heart of Australia's drive for elite sporting success is easily illustrated by an examination of various sport strategy statements over the past 10 to 15 years. In 1992, for example, in *Maintain the Momentum*, it was stated that 'In consultation with State institutes and academies, the ASC will co-ordinate a national approach to the delivery of sport sciences to Australia's elite athletes' (DASET 1992: 12). Two years later, it was claimed that 'To be successful, the *Olympic Athlete Programme* requires the co-ordinated input of many players ... High quality services must be delivered across the country through an integrated programme delivery system' (DEST 1994: 6).

For some commentators, it appears that the goals of integration and coherence have been achieved. For example, in 2000, in a pre-Olympic seminar, the Director of the ACC argued that 'A major strength of Australian sport is the nationally integrated system developed in recent years ... reflected at all levels of sport from physical education in schools through to management of large national sporting organisations' (Schembri 2000: 1). This investigation of ASI and Australian swimming, however, reveals a picture of a sport system where there might be integration among elite sport support services but where integration between different levels of the sport is conspicuous by its absence (cf. Commonwealth of Australia 1999). The picture that emerges of swimming in Australia is one where international success has been achieved through a clear emphasis on its elite swimmers but to the detriment of the development of the sport as a whole (ASI 2000).

The analysis of developments in four areas of high performance sport policy provides some corroboration of the view that, although the sport has enjoyed considerable elite success, it faces a number of concerns in the future. Perhaps the greatest concerns regarding facility development are the lack of control of water space and the need to develop further relationships with schools. Sufficient funding for swimmers to train and compete on a full-time basis remains a difficulty for the majority of the sport's athletes although, over the past 10 years or so, a small group of the very top Australian swimmers has benefited from the sport's high profile successes and has been able to train and compete on a full-time basis. The most telling divisions in the sport, somewhat paradoxically, have emerged in coaching where there has been a clear emphasis on the elite but with little strategic thought given to the development of sub-elite swimmers (ASI 2000). In a similar vein, the determination to provide the most conducive opportunities for the elite swimmer to achieve Olympic success has subsumed a similar level of determination to put in place a national domestic league that would provide a structure within which the sport's next generation of elite swimmers might emerge.

In summary, the two key interrelated issues facing ASI in the early twenty-first century are: (i) an urgent requirement to increase organisational relationships with those involved (primarily coaches) at the sport's grass roots levels in order to help close the gap between Learn-to-Swim programmes in schools and the onward progression of young swimmers to club levels; and (ii) the related issue of responding to the federal government's concern to increase participation levels in Australian sport through the TSPGP (cf. ASC 2004). In short, there appears to be evidence emerging of a qualitatively different emphasis within ASI, in large part reflecting a noticeable shift (in policy rhetoric at least) at federal government (ASC) level. This shift in emphasis away from the elite level is due less to the emergence of effective Sport for All advocacy coalitions and more to the 'loss' of the legitimising platform provided by the Sydney 2000 Olympic Games; providing powerful evidence of the impact that factors outside the policy subsystem have on influencing policy change.

Athletics Australia Incorporated

Organisation, administration and relationships

In 1897, the Amateur Athletics Association of Australasia was formed, comprising New Zealand and the Australian States of New South Wales, Queensland and Victoria. When New Zealand withdrew from this body in 1928, its name was changed to the Amateur Athletics Union of Australia and, more recently, to Athletics Australia Incorporated (AAI) (AAI 2003a; see also Jewes and Jobling 1997). AAI is part of the recently formed Australian Athletics Federation, an umbrella group that brings together the seven key athletics authorities in the country, including the Australian Track and Field Coaches Association (AT&FCA) (AAI 2003b). Aside from track and field athletics, our key concern here, AAI is the national body for the athletic disciplines of cross-country, road running and race walking (mountain running is administered by an affiliated association), and all States/ Territories are linked to the national body as Member Associations.

One of the defining characteristics of athletics in Australia is its organisational complexity, which has led to concerns regarding AAI's capacity to govern the sport. Indeed, in March 2004, it was announced that the sport and its NSO was to be subject to a wide-ranging investigation by the ASC, as 'the present criticism being levelled at the sport indicated the need for a more comprehensive review as the best way to take the sport forward' (Department of Communications, Information Technology and the Arts [DCITA] 2004). Concerns for the organisation and administration of the sport are not new however. As revealed in an in-depth study of the sport in the early 1990s (known as the *Landy Report*) (Daly 1994) and, more recently, in a review of athletics competition in Australia (Roe 2002), the sport appears to have suffered a spiral of decline from its heyday in the 1950s and 1960s (cf. Phillips 2000). Although it is beyond the scope of this study to provide a detailed analysis of the issues raised above, it is possible to identify three themes that have a bearing on the contemporary condition of athletics in Australia: (i) jurisdictional divisions, especially between federal/NSO and State/Territory organisations; (ii) a strong emphasis on the elite levels of the sport; and (iii) the organisational capacity of AAI to manage the many and various sectoral interests involved in the sport, most notably, Little Athletics, the body responsible for younger people up to 16 or 17 years of age.

The first two themes are inextricably related and will be explored as such. For the time-period under investigation, AAI's concern to promote itself as the body responsible primarily for the elite athlete can be traced back to the early 1990s. In 1991, for example, the President of AAI stated that 'We have deliberately set about changing the image of athletics at the elite level, strategically placing emphasis on our strengths, "the nation's best athletes"' (quoted in AAI 1991: 4). Whether policy direction within the sport can be characterised as 'strategic', and whether 'strengths' aptly embodies AAI's achievements over a number of years are moot points, as will become apparent below. As discussed above in respect of swimming, the overt elite emphasis at NSO level in Australia has clearly reflected the growing interest of, and (funding) interventions by, the ASC. In relation to this, the dilemma for NSOs was summarised neatly by AAI's President in the early 1990s: 'While our emphasis has targeted the elite segment of our sport, Athletics Australia is concerned that so many problems exist at the club level. The participation numbers in this segment have stagnated generally' (quoted in AAI 1991: 5).

Perhaps the key question here is whether AAI has had the capacity, the will or indeed the financial autonomy, to bring about significant policy change. The evidence suggests that the answer to such a question is emphatically negative. Throughout the early 1990s, as the build-up to, and emphasis on, bidding for the 2000 Olympic Games gathered momentum, AAI reported repeatedly on the difficulties involved in bringing together the sport's various interests (cf. AAI 1990, 1991, 1992, 1993), yet its organisational goals were clearly aimed at the sport's elite athletes. In 1993, for example, AAI's President lamented that:

> Participation levels in all sports continue to be the subject of expressed concern by politicians, administrators, and the media. It has been our dilemma that actual registration numbers have been declining and despite the strategy adopted of focussing on the elite end of the athletic model, we have not attracted new members to the club structure.
>
> (quoted in AAI 1993: 1)

Such observations might be construed in some quarters as rather naïve if the assumption underlying such a statement is that one outcome of a strategy that promoted the elite end of the sport would necessarily result in an increase in participation numbers at the grass roots levels. As Hogan and Norton observe, the participation structure in athletics has:

> been described as an inverted 'thumb tack'. This illustrates a relatively large junior participation base (for example, little athletics) which quickly narrows as drop-outs accelerate, often in concert with talent identification programmes … The fact that the focus of attention and money has been at the top level, often in the thirst for 'immediate' success, has left relatively little for junior development.
>
> (Hogan and Norton 2000: 215)

Hogan and Norton's reference to 'little athletics' is significant as it brings into sharp relief the third theme identified earlier, namely the capacity of AAI to bring together the sport's various peak bodies. As noted, Little Athletics is the organisation in Australia that caters for young people up to 16 or 17 years of age and, according to a senior ASC official, it is also an organisation whose 'President is very much anti Athletics Australia and very protective of the turf that they have ... essentially little kids up to about 16' (Interviewee F, 5 June 2003). This observer also stated that Little Athletics has over 90,000 members across Australia; yet AAI's membership was just short of 15,000 registered athletes in 2001–2 (AAI 2002: 29). Therefore, as the ASC official went on to add, 'they [Little Athletics] speak with a very strong voice in terms of the number of kids on the park'. Yet, in the opinion of this observer, Little Athletics 'doesn't do anything for the sport ... very little coaching, very traditional sort of structures ... but because no one else offered even that opportunity, they've become very strong' (Interviewee F, 5 June 2003).

The award of the 2000 Olympic Games to Sydney did little to unify the sport's various interests and in fact reinforced AAI's relative lack of concern with grass roots athletics and preoccupation with elite interests. In 1995, for example, in response to the new OAP, AAI's National Executive Director stated that 'it must be understood that this funding is very specifically allocated to the elite ... We must unite as a team to help our athletes perform' (quoted in AAI 1995: 8). Unfortunately, since 1988, Australia's elite athletes consistently under-performed on the international stage – see Table 4.2. Gullan (2004) expressed the frustrations of many in suggesting that, 'Instead of athletics feeding on the momentum a home Olympics brought, the sport is struggling on and off the track'.

There is evidence of an awareness of the damage that the perceived preoccupation with elite achievement has created. As a senior AAI official commented, 'There's no question [that] Athletics Australia has been criticised for a long, long time, going back 10, 20, 30 years for just having a high performance fixation ... we [the current Board] viewed that as a fundamental weakness in the organisation' (Interviewee F, 4 June 2003). However, the awareness of the problem by AAI officers has not prevented a groundswell of criticism aimed at the capacity of AAI to govern the sport in a manner which benefits the variety of interests in the organisation rather than just those of the elite. As Roe observes, 'some of the most committed people to athletics in Australia [have begun] to voice their fears that their beloved sport might die at its most fundamental level – its grass roots. There is no question that their fears are real' (2002: 42). In sum, the picture painted above is that of a sport which has struggled, for the past 10 to 15 years at least, to oversee what might be termed an inclusive set of policy initiatives.

Four areas of elite sport policy

Development of elite level facilities

In the previous discussion of swimming and ASI we detailed the significance of the creation of the AIS, State/Territory institutes/academies of sport and the National Training Centre programmes as part of the overall picture of facility

Table 4.2 Australian athletics medals: Olympic Games/World Athletics Championships, 1988–2001

	Olympic Games					World Athletics Championships			
	Gold	Silver	Bronze	Total		Gold	Silver	Bronze	Total
1988	1	1	0	2	1995	0	1	1	2
1992	0	0	2	2	1997	1	1	2	4
1996	0	2	0	2	1999	1	1	2	4
2000	1	2	0	3	2001	1	0	1	2

developments in Australian sport over the past 25 years (cf. ASC 1993a). Athletics has similarly benefited from such developments and, not surprisingly, also faces some similar problems, most notably those arising from the country's jurisdictional divisions. In 1995, for example, AAI's President argued that 'Athletics facilities are of major concern in every state of Australia, and not enough "hard nosed" athletic lobbying exists to develop our sport's desperate need for more facilities' (quoted in AAI 1995: 6).

The lack of support/facilities at club or grass roots level was an issue that had been signalled some six years earlier. In *Going for Gold, an Inquiry into Sports Funding and Administration*, it was noted that the need for adequate facilities remained a key concern in the country, with one contributor to the Inquiry arguing that a key reason for the lack of progression for junior athletes was that 'they just cannot continue because of the lack of facilities' (quoted in Parliament of the Commonwealth of Australia 1989: 81). In line with this argument, in 1993, the ASC found that 'As a result of the scarcity of facilities, good coaches tend to all coach in the one place, so that there is not as much dissemination of knowledge *to local level coaches* as is considered desirable' (ASC 1993a: 82, emphasis added). In short, the source of these problems appears to be that, for too long, the elite athlete has been the chief beneficiary of support and resource systems, with too little attention being given to the grass roots and developmental levels of the sport.

The regionalisation of the elite-focused State/Territory institutes/academies of sport has decentralised resources and provided some opportunities for collaborative use of facilities. However, as Hogan and Norton (2000) argue, these facilities, and coaching and sports science expertise, have centred on the development of talented athletes. However, it appears that rivalry between State/Territory institutes/academies has bedevilled attempts to put in place a fully integrated and coherent sports system in Australia (cf. Commonwealth of Australia 1999; Pyke and Norris 2001). As one senior ASC official explained:

> Institutes have been very good at raising the pockets of excellence around the country, and healthy competition between them has helped raise the bar but they've never acted co-operatively as a group to say [for example] do we want five track and field programmes around Australia? Why don't we put

that there and sprints there and pole vault there? .... There's never been a preparedness to adopt a national perspective on that.

(Interviewee F, 5 June 2003)

Despite the recognition of the need for greater coherence and integration, developments in elite level facilities in athletics typify many aspects of the way that the Australian sports system has developed over the past 25 years. Thus, for the Sport 2000 Task Force, not only has 'the system grown up in an ad hoc manner, resulting in duplication and fragmentation' but also 'participation has been starved of resources while Commonwealth Government programmes have focused on elite sport, and ... this situation needs to be addressed' (Commonwealth of Australia 1999: 73). Interestingly, the new federal government policy initiative (the TSPGP) to increase participation and membership numbers at grass roots levels highlights AAI's reluctance to address the skewed distribution of facilities towards elite athletes. In responding to the government's initiative, AAI has 'taken a clear and deliberate strategy of attacking the out-of-stadium events' as the basis for increasing AAI membership figures (Interviewee F, 5 June 2003). Out-of-stadium events include participants involved in 'fun-runs', road races and jogging – activities and events that do not require resources from AAI for facility development and whose membership of AAI is least likely to result in the strengthening of internal lobbies for a redistribution of facility resources.

Not only can the AAI strategy be criticised for avoiding any challenge to existing resource/facility providers but the strategy may also fail to deliver any genuine increase in participation as they are simply incorporating existing participants into AAI membership. As a senior ASC official argued:

if they [AAI] can lay claim to having some ownership over the 'trillions' of people who go out on fun runs, then they can deliver big numbers. The cynics would say that's not increasing participation, that's just territory. That's claiming territory that was already there.

(Interviewee F, 5 June 2003)

More worryingly for the sport as a whole, the same official suggested that the current recruitment strategy would not benefit the local AAI clubs and went on to add that AAI are 'getting out of the traditional club structure. They've recognised that there's a lot of concern that traditional clubs are not very inspiring and are kind of dying on the vine'.

Emergence of 'full-time' athletes

As Adair and Vamplew note, while 'There is now a public acceptance of the professional in Australian sport ... it has been a grudging and reluctant process' (1997: 30). As discussed in Chapter 3, from the late 1970s, increased federal government involvement for supporting talented performers in Olympic sports helped to precipitate the gradual acceptance of paid athletes in these former amateur sports. The two federal sport policy statements – *The Next Step* and *Maintain the Momentum*, in 1989 and 1992 respectively – signified increasing federal government support for elite level sport and particularly for full-time commitment. In *Maintain the Momentum*, it was stated that 'International sport is no longer a part-time occupation. The community needs to appreciate the sacrifices made and give our athletes the support they deserve' (DASET 1992: 7). As discussed, the announcement that Sydney had won its bid to stage the 2000 Olympic Games was key to a much more focused attempt to increase financial support for Australian track and field athletes through the OAP's Direct Athlete Support scheme. As AAI's President noted in 1995, the OAP will focus on 'programmes that will win medals and ensure the home team competes more successfully than we have at previous Olympic Games' (quoted in AAI 1995: 5).

As one of the ASC's eight targeted sports under the OAP, track and field athletes benefited greatly under this scheme, yet whether the medal returns at Sydney (see Table 4.2) merited such large amounts of public money is just one aspect of debates on the condition of the sport in the early twenty-first century. Although some commentators (cf. Adair and Vamplew 1997; Armstrong 1997; Booth 1995; Nauright 1996) have problematised the overt emphasis on supporting elite level athletes throughout the 1990s, their critique was confronted by the clear determination of the federal government that Australia should perform well at the 2000 Games. Whether this focus on supporting the country's elite athletes has achieved the intended outcomes for track and field athletics remains open to debate (cf. Gullan 2004; McAsey 2004; Mathieson 2004). What is clearer, however, is that, despite this increased support for elite athletes over the past 10 to 15 years, it remains the case that many of the sport's elite and sub-elite performers do not have the resources to train and compete on a full-time basis. According to a senior AAI official, 'some of them don't have two brass farthings to rub together … the majority of them, would be living at home … parental support, that type of thing'. This observer went on to add that:

> I would say that we've probably got around 40 athletes that don't work, in any meaningful sense, but if you ask me how many of them are making a reasonable living out of it, then it's probably less than 20.
>
> (Interviewee G, 4 June 2003)

In AAI's 2002 Annual Report it was noted that, of the 300 athletes in the national squad programme, 'About 100 … received needs based Direct Athlete Support. This ranged from a $[AUS]1,000 grant to help isolated/underprivileged young athletes to up to $[AUS]200 per week to assist international level athletes reduce their working hours' (AAI 2002: 11). An equally interesting comment is that 'Performance based DAS will also be introduced towards the end of 2002' (2002: 11); providing further confirmation that support for athletes who reveal medal-winning potential remains a high priority for AAI. Yet, whether such an initiative sends the 'right' type of message to the sport's broader community in a climate of organisational unrest is clearly open to question. The lack of depth within the sport's development squad has been raised as one cause of concern arising from the current pattern of distribution of athlete support. A former international athlete and current head of the Athletes' Commission has stated only recently that:

> It is a combination of athletics being in disarray and how viable it is for an athlete to afford to compete and train … That is definitely a consideration in people staying in the sport and I have heard it from more than one person.
>
> (quoted in Gullan 2004)

The shadow of the Sydney 2000 Olympics Games hangs over this debate and appears to have had some telling consequences for the sport. As Gullan (2004) notes, 'The selection philosophy for Sydney was "the more the merrier". More importantly, the money to make this happen was supplied in bucket loads'. A former senior AAI official endorsed this assessment, adding that in the build-up to Sydney:

> We had heaps more athletes competing in the domestic series; you had state institutes who had a lot of money to send people around. You had other athletes who were prepared to fund their existence, to get around, put their lives on hold to chase the dream.
>
> (Culbert, quoted in Gullan 2004)

As a post-Games legacy, AAI is faced with meeting the high expectation for support held by the large elite squad and their entourage at a time when the organisation is under pressure from internal critics who point to the neglect of other development levels and also from those who point to the relative failure of AAI to deliver Olympic medals. The latter problem is illustrated by Culbert's comments that, following the Sydney Olympics, much has changed and that 'The message has been very clear: Athletics lift your game or you don't get any money. You can argue that's harsh and unfair but that is the reality post 2000' (quoted in Gullan 2004).

Developments in coaching, sports science and sports medicine

Similar to swimming, the success of Australian track and field athletes during the 1950s and 1960s, was due in large part to a small number of renowned coaches, most notably Herb Elliott, Percy Cerutty and Franz Stampfl, and the application of cutting-edge scientific training regimes (cf. Adair and Vamplew 1997; Phillips 2000). Although such regimes did not meet with the approval of all in the sport, any potential resistance was deflected by the success of athletes on the international stage. In a similar vein, criticism has been more muted of the trend towards the professionalised coaching system that was put in place at the AIS in the early 1980s and in the State/Territory institutes/academies of sport. As Adair and Vamplew note, 'The message was clear: specialist coaching and advanced training techniques were going to rectify Australia's slide in international sporting competition' (1997: 93). Broader concerns at levels below the elite end of the sporting spectrum were thus subsumed under the weight of federal pressure for international sporting success. Thus, for Adair and Vamplew, 'In their quest for performance-based returns for their money, Australian governments have tended to be more interested in funding the coaching of top-level junior athletes, such as the few hundred recruited to the AIS annually' (1997: 94).

Developments in coaching within the sport of track and field athletics broadly mirror Adair and Vamplew's observations. In 1991, while the work of the AT&FCA was acknowledged, AAI's President also noted that 'Although athletics has a group of world recognised coaches, we need to spread the coaching base far wider if the sport is to progress at all levels' (quoted in AAI 1991: 5). Just three years later, the President argued that the 'Recruiting of more officials, administrators and coaches, at club and State level who can help move athletics forward in a professional manner, needs top priority' (quoted in AAI 1994: 3). Little appears to have changed in the intervening years. Indeed, a senior AAI official acknowledged that the sport has been overly fixated on its elite athletes and coaches (Interviewee G, 4 June 2002); a scenario borne out by a recent wide-ranging report into the sport's competition structures (Roe 2002). The implications of ignoring calls by the AT&FCA and other contributors to this report are set out in stark detail by Roe, who states that 'Much club level coaching is now being delivered in training groups rather than through clubs ... Clubs are becoming irrelevant' (2002: 36). Roe's report also found that 'It is evident that the number of persons coaching at all levels, with the exception of paid elite positions, has undergone a dramatic decline' (2002: 41).

Implicit in these observations is an undercurrent of neglect of the sport's grass roots. These findings are therefore in stark contrast to findings by the Sport 2000 Task Force that the creation of the National Coaching Accreditation Scheme (NCAS) 'has increased both the number and quality of coaches *at all levels*' (Commonwealth of Australia 1999: 80, emphasis added). It is undeniable that numbers have increased – the NCAS database reveals that there were 105,000 registered coaches in 1999, compared to around 40,000 in 1986 (Schembri 2000: 11–12) – yet these aggregate data clearly mask differences in specific sports. It would appear to be the case that, while the number of coaches is increasing across all sports, athletics remains an exception.

One of the chief concerns for AAI must be that the troubles regarding coaching permeate the entire spectrum of the sport. Indeed, some contributors to the Roe report 'believed that the coaching shortages were not only restricted to club level, suggesting that the situation was equally desperate for many elite developing athletes' (Roe 2002: 41). Of equal concern, if not more significant, is the sport's apparent neglect of the next generation of elite performers. In relation to this, Roe argued that:

> Coaches, whether active, inactive or potential, must be encouraged to participate in the coaching of athletics at grassroots, school and club level ...

and where appropriate, be willing to pass athletes on to other coaches in the interests of those athletes' further development.

(Roe 2002: 41)

Roe's final comments in the above quotation draw attention to an issue that has been raised elsewhere (cf. ASC 1999; Commonwealth of Australia 1999; Pyke and Norris 2001) as one of the primary stumbling blocks to a fully integrated and coherent sports system in Australia. This is what a senior official at one of the country's elite institutes/academies of sport referred to as the 'badging' issue, where those involved in the institutes/academies 'claim' athletes as their own rather than adopting a more national perspective to the development of athletes (Interviewee E, 30 May 2003). In a pre-2000 Olympic Games seminar, Schembri argued that the creation of a National Elite Sports Council had 'helped to minimise state-based parochial "ownership" of athletes in favour of a national approach to preparations for Sydney' (2000: 17). Yet, if the findings from Roe's report identified above are correct, it appears that the divisiveness permeating track and field athletics belies moves elsewhere towards a more collaborative approach to athlete development, and thus further indication of a sport in some disarray.

The issues raised above regarding coaching have not surfaced to the same extent with regard to the provision of sports science and sports medicine services. This is not surprising given that much of the recognition for Australia's resurgence as a major sporting nation over the past 10 to 15 years has been credited to the work conducted at the AIS's Sports Science and Medicine Centre (cf. Baumann 2002; Bloomfield 2003; Phillips 2000). It has also been well documented that a key element of the successful application of these support services is the co-ordination between coaches and sports science/medicine specialists at the AIS Centre and State/Territory institutes/academies of sport. As Baumann notes, 'Coaches have built strong practical relationships with sport scientists to develop new ways to enhance performance' (2002: 12).

Questions have been raised, however, about the efficacy of sports science/ medicine services in athletics (cf. Gullan 2004; McAsey 2004; Mathieson 2004). As former Australian international track athlete, Rick Mitchell, argues:

All of you now receive full Institute of Sport [AIS] support, sophisticated sports science and sports medicine, and better access to international opportunities than any one before your time … With all of these things in your favour, why are you unable to better the performances of those who long preceded you?

(quoted in Thomas 2002)

Two factors have been suggested which might explain the apparently limited impact of sports science/medicine on medal success. First, despite the many well-trained sports scientists, both in university departments and State/Territory institutes/academies of sport, 'their basic research is often limited because they have to rely mostly on university funding, which is not adequate for this type of investigation' (Bloomfield 2003: 149). Bloomfield goes on to note that 'The state institutes or academies of sport are in a similar situation ... none of them can afford to conduct basic research in order to try to solve many of the more funda-mental problems which arise in sport'. The second factor concerns the introduction of a new 'one-line appropriation' funding mechanism through which NSOs are allocated ASC grants. Under previous funding arrangements, NSOs had far less autonomy as to how/where these grants were spent. As one senior ASC official stated, in the case of sports science/medicine support, 'In the past, they [NSOs] didn't get the money. They got a notional allocation ... So it was value-in-kind' (Interviewee F, 5 June 2003). The new arrangements enable NSOs to appraise, far more critically, the delivery of these services from the AIS and calculate the opportunity cost of investment in sports science support. However, as the ASC official explained, there is also a feeling that decisions regarding sports science/medicine investment by NSOs may now lack the requisite qualified input from the relevant scientific experts.

Competition opportunities for elite level athletes

As noted above, the 'state of domestic athletics competition in Australia' has been exposed to the scrutiny of a recently published report (Roe 2002). The report does not concentrate in detail on what is known as the domestic *Telstra* A Series (or the *Telstra* A Championships) – the two major domestic track and field events in Australia. Both these events are, in essence, a national series for elite track and field athletes. Rather, Roe's report centres on domestic competition opportunities and structures below the elite level, yet the concerns raised by Roe have ramifications for the future health of the sport as a whole. These concerns have historical precedents and it is important, therefore, to examine briefly past policy statements in order to understand better the policy context for the current picture of competition opportunities and structures.

The inauguration during 1989–90 of a Grand Prix Series sponsored by *Mobil* was designed to establish head-to-head competition for the sport's elite athletes (AAI 1990) – this series can thus be viewed as a forerunner to the current *Telstra* A competitive events. Therefore, in the same period as the federal government strengthened financial support for NSOs 'to increase opportunities for international competition' (DASETT 1989: 15) under the Next Step programme, AAI established a domestic competition series for its elite track and field athletes. Throughout the early to mid-1990s, the Grand Prix Series was consistently reported as a key element of the sport's competitive structure as a whole. In 1992, for example, AAI's General Manager stated that 'the Mobil Grand Prix Athletic Series in Australia is the golden thread which ties together our domestic competition programme' (quoted in AAI 1992: 4). The picture emerging at this time was one of an integrated and coherent system that incorporated all levels of the sport:

> Athletics Australia has one of the most structured competition programmes
> of any country in the world. From the emerging talented juniors, through to

the developing 'espoirs' and onto the world ranked athletes, there is a competition programme tailored to suit.

(Executive Director, AAI, quoted in AAI 1996: 8)

These are interesting observations when set alongside current concerns with the effectiveness of the competitive domestic structure for elite level sport and the structure of competitive opportunities for sub-elite levels. With regard to the first issue, the two current flagship track and field events at the elite level – the *Telstra* A Series and *Telstra* A Championships – have not been as successful as AAI might have expected. As Mathieson (2004) notes, 'Athletics' governing body has been dogged by internal spats, debts topping $[AUS]1 million and poor crowds at its showcase A-series events'. Perhaps even more damning is the criticism from a former senior AAI official in a leaked letter to Australia's *Daily Telegraph*. Hurst reports David Culbert's argument that 'The series is currently at the lowest point in its history – its rapid decline due to the strategies and policies implemented by the current administration' (quoted in Hurst 2004). According to the Victorian Sports Minister, the decline appears to be affecting the capability of Australian athletes to compete internationally: 'The level of competition whether that be national or international doesn't seem to be of the quality that athletes need in preparation for a big event like the Olympics' (quoted in ABC Online 2004).

Alongside the concerns expressed about elite level competition structures, is an even deeper concern regarding the structure of opportunities for the sport's grass roots levels and thus future generations of international performers. Roe found that 'the level of participation in all formal arms of the sport by adult recreational athletes has decreased to levels where it is almost non-existent' (2002: 24). It may be the case that the decline in sub-elite/club competitive opportunities is a consequence of AAI's decision to target out-of-stadium events as one aspect of its Targeted Sports Participation Growth Programme (TSPGP). As mentioned earlier, the large majority of participants involved in out-of-stadium events are likely to be fun-runners, joggers and/or taking part in a 'one-off' run for charity. Therefore, it must be open to question whether these 'casual' participants will take up membership of AAI and whether such events support its more formal competitive structures in track and field athletics. Roe's report concluded that:

> The current obsession with graded individual competition throughout the length and breadth of Australia is gradually strangling the sport. This might be fine for the elite, but they now have the option of concentrating only on grand prix and championships competition …. Whilst some elements of seeded/graded competition should continue to be provided this should not be the sole 'bread and butter' delivery of the sport.
>
> (Roe 2002: 26)

Roe also quotes one contributor who viewed the decline in sub-elite competitive opportunities as a consequence of the successful bid to host the 2000 Olympic Games. This contributor argued that, while the A Series format suited conditions 'in the run up to the Sydney Olympics … we should [now] move on to something that provides not only competition for the elite but something for the next level down to aspire to' (quoted in Roe 2002: 31). In sum, it appears that AAI can be criticised for the decline of its showcase events for elite track and field performers and also that it has ignored to a large degree the structure of competitive opportunities for sub-elite/grass roots participants. For Roe, nothing less than fundamental change is required 'to the decision-making mind set if Australia is to turn around the almost inevitable demise of domestic athletics' (2002: 16).

Summary

Despite being one of the largest beneficiaries of federal government/ASC support over the past 10 to 15 years, AAI has neither achieved sustained success at the elite level nor managed to construct an underlying developmental platform upon which to build for the future. Indeed, AAI's grant allocation for 2002–3 from the ASC is reported as $AUS3,868,219 – the fourth largest allocation after swimming, hockey and rowing (ASC 2003). It may well be that the central support services/ programmes provided by the AIS, and to a lesser extent at the State/Territory institutes/academies of sport, has undermined AAI's capacity to take greater responsibility for the overall development of the sport. The recent announcement that the ASC will undertake a major review of 'some of the structural and governance issues facing the sport' (DCITA 2004) following the Athens 2004 Olympic Games, is illustrative of the seriousness of the problems confronting athletics in Australia.

In respect of the four areas of elite sport development discussed above, the level/quality of facility provision for elite sport is undoubtedly high, albeit with some variations across the States and Territories. Regarding the opportunities for athletes to train and compete on a full-time basis, it is the case that many athletes remain in part-time employment, are studying and/or rely heavily on parental support. As a senior ASC official explained, following the 2000 Olympic Games, 'The athlete support payments disappeared in, probably, the majority of sports' (Interviewee H, 5 June 2003). Indeed, a key concern for a senior AAI official is that countries such as the UK now have far more resources, through National Lottery funding, to provide greater individual athlete support than is possible in Australia (Interviewee G, 4 June 2003). Arguably, however, the most serious questions raised in the above discussion centre on the evident depth of concern regarding coaching and the structure of competition opportunities (Roe 2002). In the main, these concerns were directed at the sports grass roots levels, although the nature of the *Telstra* A Series and Championships have also faced criticism, primarily around the argument that these events do little for the levels below the elite (cf. Hurst 2004, Mathieson 2004; Roe 2002). In sum, it is perhaps not surprising that there are deep-seated concerns at grass roots levels of the sport given the emphasis placed on delivering elite success at the Sydney Olympic Games. However, even at the elite level, Australian track and field athletes have not matched the degree of success achieved in other well supported sports in Australia such as swimming.

Australian Yachting Federation Incorporated

Organisation, administration and relationships

Australia's climate, 12,500 nautical miles of coastline, steady, predictable winds and many of the world's finest harbours provide ideal conditions for participation in water-borne activities of different kinds. Although it is difficult to state with any certainty the total number of people involved, over 20 years ago D'Alpuget (1980) suggested that more than 500,000 Australians participated in some form of boating activity. By 1993, the ASC reported that 'it is estimated that there are about 2 million boaters in Australia' (ASC 1993a: 224). Water sports are thus clearly a high priority for the Australian public, yet the body now known as the Australian Yachting Federation Incorporated (AYFI) was not established until 1950, some 40 to 50 years later than the NSOs for swimming and athletics. Indeed, it was not until 1967, that this body 'severed its administrative apron strings from Britain's Royal Yachting Association' (D'Alpuget 1980: 70) and affiliated directly with the then International Yacht Racing Union. Moreover, moves towards a more professional approach to the organisation of the sport as a whole did not occur until the mid-1970s when:

> the States had at last come to recognise that only by truly co-operative effort and forward planning could they hope to administer a sport that had more than half a million adherents, and that they must agree to find the money to discard part-time honorary muddling and pay a national executive officer.
>
> (D'Alpuget 1980: 70)

This picture of a somewhat disorganised, fragmented approach to the leadership and organisation of the sport in general is paralleled by Australia's participation in yachting regattas at the Olympic Games, at least until 1980. Australia's participation in the Games, from its first entry into the Olympic programme in 1948 up until the 1980 Moscow Games (when the AYFI declined to send a team), is characterised 'by the herculean efforts of small groups of dedicated individuals and [yacht] class officials, hammering on the doors of all they thought likely to help them' (D'Alpuget 1980: 71). Over 10 years later, the organisation's President indicated that there was still some way to go if the AYFI was 'to keep pace with the growing international professionalism in sport' (quoted in AYFI 1993: 1). What is perhaps most striking here is that, despite the sport enjoying a widespread participation base, the overwhelming majority of these participants view their activities as a 'pastime' and appear to have little interest in, or engagement with, the sport's NSO and its programmes relating to Olympic yachting. As noted in The Sweeney Sports Report 2001/2002 (2002) there are over 1.5 million participants in sailing/yachting activities but the AYFI's membership numbers for the year 2002–3 are recorded as 39,786 across 392 affiliated clubs (AYFI 2003a, 2003b). Furthermore, an ASC analysis of yachting in the early 1990s found that 'the vast majority of people affected by the AYF's programmes are either non-registered (over 90%) or non-competitive (over 99%)' (1993a: 224).

There is also evidence that the sport has not been regarded as significant by the ASC/AIS, at least until recently. As one senior ASC official stated:

> [Before 1997] the Australian Yachting Federation, as I understand it … was an industry body. It didn't actually send teams anywhere. Once every four years they had to have a selection policy and they have to have a sign-off or whatever but they haven't had the money, time or inclination to produce a high performance team.
>
> (Interviewee J, 6 June 2003)

There is some evidence of AOC support during the 1980s for elite level preparation for the 1984 Olympic Games, with a substantial increase in overall funding to the AYFI in 1983–4, yet total ASC grant aid 'declined progressively after that until 1988/89' (ASC 1993a: 220). Yachting did benefit to some extent under the Next Step programme in 1989–90, but it was the award of the 2000 Olympic Games to Sydney that led to a radical change of fortunes for the AYFI and elite level yacht racing. The ambivalence of the ASC and the AOC towards the sport prior to the 2000 Games is captured in the following comment by a senior AYFI high performance official:

> within the Australian community, sailing was not a mainstream sport. Therefore, it really only got funding when it got close to the [Olympic] Games each quadrennium, and then there was an injection of funds for the team that went to compete at the Games. So, for the other three years … it was basically, if you had the money, you went and did it.
>
> (Interviewee K, 28 May 2003)

It is clear how far attitudes have changed in respect of the sport's elite level performers if we consider that, for the 1952 Helsinki Games, participation was only possible 'by shaking begging bowls for funds' and that 'officials … still regarded yachtsmen as dressed-up fishermen' (D'Alpuget 1980: 71). By the mid-1970s, while acknowledging the increased support from federal and State/Territory governments, D'Alpuget characterised this funding as 'paltry handouts' (1980: 90) in comparison to some of Australia's international competitors. However, in the organisation's 2000–1 Annual Report, the CEO drew attention to the changed funding environment for the sport since 1997, noting that the ASC grant support was approximately $AUS750,000 for 1996–7, whereas by 2001–2, this 'will amount to $[AUS]2,700,000 including the AIS programme. This represents an increase of 360%. A complete turnaround!!!' (quoted in AYFI 2001a: 1). Following the impetus provided by the 2000 Olympics, where Australian sailors won four medals (including two Gold), the depth of change achieved by the sport's NSO is noted by the organisation's CEO:

> In June 1997, you had no High Performance Programme. No staff, no coaches, no plan. In four years you have built a Programme that is the envy of most countries in the world. You have one of the best coaching and support teams, led by someone [Victor Kovalenko] widely acknowledged to be the best coach in the world.
>
> (quoted in AYFI 2001a: 1)

In the space of just six to seven years the AYFI (re-branded as Yachting Australia Incorporated in 2003) brought the sport to a position where it was regarded as one of Australia's leading contenders for medals at the 2004 Athens Olympic Games. The recent history of the sport suggests two important observations, the first of which concerns the lack of awareness on the part of the ASC of developments in elite sailing and possibly also an ambivalence towards sailing generally. Although the ASC provided OAP funding, sailing was not identified as a sport likely to deliver medal success at the Sydney Games (Commonwealth of Australia 1999). The second observation concerns the positive and rapid impact of OAP funding on Olympic success – see Table 4.3.

There are two interrelated factors that provide the context for the analysis of four areas of elite sport policy development and policy change that follows: first, critiques suggesting that the AYFI has been overly focused on its [Olympic] elite yachtsmen and women and second, the struggle to generate support among the State/Territory yachting associations (known as Member Yachting Associations [MYAs]) for the national strategy.

Regarding the first factor, as in swimming and athletics, the *national* sporting organisation for sailing has faced criticism that it focused too heavily on elite sailing to the detriment of other levels and also that it neglected the non-Olympic disciplines under its control. In 1996, for example, as OAP funding streams were becoming available, similar concerns to those raised in the UK regarding the Royal Yachting Association and cruising were highlighted. The organisation's President noted that 'There is a perception that the Federation addresses much of its activities to elite sailing to the detriment of other interests within our sport. One of these other interests is offshore sailing' (quoted in AYFI 1996: 2). A further

Table 4.3 Australian sailing medals: Olympic Games, 1988–2000

Olympic Games	Gold	Silver	Bronze	Total
1988	0	0	0	0
1992	0	0	2	2
1996	0	1	1	2
2000	2	1	1	4

concern was that knowledge gained from elite sailing initiatives should be filtered down to help with grass roots development (AYFI 1996).

During 1996–7, with OAP funding in place and with the organisation's President noting that 'Our elite athletes now have access to some of the best support available' (quoted in AYFI 1997: 2), the criticism intensified. Indeed, the President also observed that 'The AYF are often criticised over the amount apparently spent on Olympic preparation' but emphasised that this funding from the ASC and AOC 'is specifically earmarked for expenditure in this area. The money could not be spent to support other areas of our sport' (quoted in AYFI 1997: 2). In many respects, the national body has not ignored these issues and, throughout the mid- to late 1990s, re-structured its constitution, embarked on a strategic review process and published a comprehensive strategic plan for the sport (cf. AYFI 1998, 1999, 2002b). Yet, in addressing all those involved in water sport activities in the 2000–1 Annual Report, the CEO argued that 'You will only be successful by working together to common goals. Continue to waste time on fruitless in-fighting will not take you one step nearer to the objectives you have agreed' (quoted in AYFI 2001a: 3).

Reflecting the second factor mentioned above, it appears that one of the central sources of the continuing dissent within the sport was the AYFI's decision to raise membership fees at club and MYA levels and the subsequent questioning, by the latter, as to how/where these funds were spent. According to a senior AYFI official, the organisation is endeavouring to put in place clearer lines of communication between different levels of the sport (Interviewee L, 28 May 2003), yet it remains a struggle to convince the sport's diverse community that it is not only the elite sailor who benefits from the AYFI's funding streams. A recent Briefing Paper issued by the organisation highlights the core of this issue. On the distribution of funding, the Briefing Paper emphasises that only 'very limited funding that the AYF receives is from within the sport', while also noting that a 'popular misconception [is] that the AYF expends all membership funds on a small group of elite athletes. The High Performance Programme actually supports the AYF, not the other way around' (AYFI 2002c: 2). Indeed, just 16 per cent of the AYFI's income is generated from within the sport, while 69 per cent is from conditional grants distributed by the ASC.

The organisation is keen, however, to identify how ASC grants contribute to its general overheads and thus does not just benefit the elite. The Briefing Paper, for example, states that 'The HP [high performance] programme includes the increased provision of coaches for state youth camps, support for the National Youth Development Programme and support for representative Australian teams' (AYFI 2002c: 12). Despite such statements, the AYFI is still regularly challenged 'about the inequality of services that we provide to the States' (Interviewee K, 28 May 2003). However, as this observer went on to note, none of the States/ Territories prioritise resources in the same way, 'They allocate resources according to their priorities that they've pinned to high performance. Some of them don't have any Olympic [yacht] classes and the national programme is built around Olympic participation'.

In sum, on these issues, although the AYFI has not suffered the degree of dissent that was evident in both swimming and athletics, some disquiet has emerged over the period when federal funding for elite preparation increased substantially. On the one hand, the unparalleled success at the 2000 Olympic Games has been explained as a direct result of increased funding. On the other hand, some of the difficulties faced by sports with a far longer history of federal funding for elite participation are now emerging for the AYFI. Yet, it should be remembered that, as one senior AYFI official explained, it is only recently that the national body has attempted to address, in any meaningful way, strategies for co-ordinating activities at State/Territory level (Interviewee L, 28 May 2003). A more equitable balance between elite sport and community sport for Australian NSOs will remain 'elusive' (Lundy 1999) as long as federal funding for supporting elite sport far outweighs allocations to its Targeted Sports Participation Growth Programme (TSPGP) for example. The AYFI's new TSPGP – 'On Board' – received initial funding of $AUS300,000 over three years (AYFI 2003c: 6), whereas its total ASC grant for 2002–3 amounted to $AUS3,016,952, of which almost 90 per cent was listed under AIS and High Performance Programmes (ASC 2003). It is clear where the priorities of both the federal government and the AYFI lie.

Four areas of elite sport policy

Development of elite level facilities

A senior AYFI official explained that there is no national plan for the development of facilities, either at elite level or sub-elite levels (Interviewee L, 28 May 2003). Elite and sub-elite sailors use facilities provided by their individual yacht clubs and/or where there is provision at a State/Territory institute/academy of sport. There are suitable facilities in New South Wales, primarily around Sydney, as well as in Western Australia and Victoria, however, in other States/Territories, facility provision for elite training/competition is more variable (Interviewee L, 28 May 2003). It appears that the majority of the sport's elite sailors are now based around Sydney due, mainly, to the 2000 Olympics and, as one of the AYFI's senior high performance officials explained, 'the sailors that are here, the elite, they're not sailing out of clubs generally, they're sailing out of our training centre, which is a temporary base at the moment' (Interviewee K, 28 May 2003).

There was some indication, in 1993, that the AYFI had plans for the creation of a national sailing centre (AYFI 1993). However, since the Sydney Olympics, for which a training base had been established in Sydney at HMAS Penguin and a marina created for the Olympic regatta at nearby Rushcutters Bay, the issue of permanent elite level training/competition facilities has remained unresolved. This may be due, in part, to the sport's relatively recent emergence as a serious contender for Olympic medals and thus sustained federal support. In 2001, there was an attempt by the Yachting Association of New South Wales to lobby the federal government and the Sydney Harbour Federation Trust for the creation of a national sailing centre at an unused military training base as a legacy for the sport following the 2000 Olympics. It appears that this lobbying has failed. As stated in a media release, 'While the YA [Yachting Association] of NSW [New South Wales] has used its best efforts to pursue a legacy, it appears that the type of legacy the sport was hoping to gain will not be achieved' (Yachting Association of New South Wales 2001).

Similar efforts to maintain the marina site at Rushcutters Bay have not met with success. Indeed, in the same year, the Boating Industry Association of New South Wales, reported that 'Boating organisations have severely criticised the New South Wales Government over its plans to demolish the Sydney Harbour marina built for the 2000 Olympic Games yachting regattas' (Boating Industry Association of New South Wales 2001). Moreover, in the same media release, the Executive Officer of the Yachting Association of New South Wales argued that, 'Prior to the Olympic Games, sporting bodies were promised numerous benefits arising from the Olympic Games, but sailing has received nothing' (quoted in Boating Industry Association of New South Wales 2001). The lack of a strong lobby group within the sport is clear from the admission in 2002 that the AYFI will 'be developing a lobbying plan' (AYFI 2002b: 27). That the issue of a permanent training base remains unresolved is evident from the organisation's most recent annual report where the CEO states that, despite funding from the AIS and consulting all MYAs, '*efforts were renewed* to secure a High Performance Training Base in Sydney involving extensive discussions with the Federal Government' (quoted in AYFI 2003a: 9, emphasis added).

Emergence of 'full-time' sailors

It is clear that, up until the early 1980s, prior to federal funding for elite sport, Australia's Olympic preparations suffered, with sailors struggling to maintain a serious challenge to better supported elite athletes in other countries. The Corinthian nature of Olympic sailing during the early 1960s is captured in D'Alpuget's record of the 1964 Tokyo Games, 'when Grandpa Bill Northam performed the impossible and brought home the gold. Northam was the Australian public's ideal of a sportsman hero ... He had style [and] He was rich' (1980: 76). It appeared that little had changed by the 1976 Montreal Olympic Games. Unless they were rich like Northam, 'crews paid out years of personal savings for the privilege because the official subsidies barely covered the cost of transport' (D'Alpuget 1980: 90–1). Even as recently as the late 1980s, Addy Bucek and Jenni Lidgett, who both competed at the 1992 Barcelona Olympic Games, emphasised the financial challenges they had to overcome in order to compete at the highest level. Bucek, for example, observed that:

> About the only barrier I've had to overcome to be an international sailor, is finance, because when you compete at this level you have to compete overseas. There's no way around that and it costs a lot of money.
>
> (quoted in Bryceson and Herbert 1992: 104)

Bucek's experience was confirmed by the findings of an ASC report which suggested that 'The lack of sufficient funding and time was seen as a major cause for dropping out of the sport, as well as the athlete's perception that there was little to be gained financially from continuing' (ASC 1993a: 226). Indeed, Bucek's crew member, Jenni Lidgett, outlined the type of sacrifices required to compete as an international sailor at this time. Lidgett maintained that:

> Working full-time as well is the hardest thing, because it means that in some cases I will go to the gym in the morning and then go to work. Then I'll have to leave a little bit early to get down to the yacht club in time to make it out on the water.
>
> (quoted in Bryceson and Herbert 1992: 110)

The problem of support for Australian sailors has been/is exacerbated by a relative lack of interest in the sport from television companies and, therefore, fewer opportunities for advertising sponsorship deals to supplement income. In 1992, for example, the AYFI's President noted that, although the Olympic team returned its best result since Montreal in 1976, 'there was almost no TV coverage of yachting in Australia' (quoted in AYFI 1992: 3). Indeed, as recently as 1997, the CEO noted that the organisation 'had no commercial sponsors' (quoted in AYFI 2001a: 2). Undoubtedly, OAP funding streams, which were 'deliberately concentrated on a limited number of committed athletes' (CEO, AYFI, quoted in AYFI 2000: 4) were integral to the Olympic team's success in Sydney 2000. The association between ASC funding and Olympic success is clear from the CEO's statement that:

> Australia's best performance ever at the 2000 Olympics and the implementation of a new Strategic Plan contributed to the decision by the ASC to increase the High Performance Grant to the AYF …. The increase in funding enabled an increase in the number of programmes that are administered and supported, which in turn provided increased support to more athletes.
>
> (quoted in AYFI 2002a: 3)

In 2002–3, 116 sailors across eight programmes benefited from a total of $AUS832,854 through what was termed 'athlete reimbursement' (CEO, quoted in AYFI 2003a: 2). Although this figure is far less than the amounts currently available to elite sailors in the UK, for example, it nevertheless represents a substantial shift in attitude towards, and recognition of, the country's elite level yachtsmen and women. However, despite Australian sailors now benefiting from increased support, there are few, if any, sailors training and competing on a full-time basis. According to one senior AYFI official, the majority are either in education, rely on the modest sponsorship support generated by the 2000 Olympic success and/or prize money gained from the 'professional circuit', such as Round-the-World yachting events (Interviewee L, 28 May 2003). This view is mirrored elsewhere within the AYFI. For example, on the question of whether the sport's elite sailors might be classified as full-time athletes, a senior high performance official stated that:

> No, not all, depending on the athlete and depending on what career .... most of our athletes either have a job or are studying. Some of them run their own businesses, [which] therefore gives them the flexibility to come and go as they please. A couple who have been to the [Olympic] Games before have got special arrangements with their employers.
>
> (Interviewee K, 28 May 2003)

In sum, while acknowledging the amount of direct athlete support now available, the above observations reveal little change to the experiences of Addy Bucek and Jenni Lidgett some 20 years earlier (Bryceson and Herbert 1992). According to a senior ASC official, there are therefore real concerns in Australia that UK sailors, in particular, are currently better supported, and thus more likely to maintain their competitive advantage over their Australian counterparts at the Athens Olympic Games in 2004 (Interviewee J, 6 June 2003).

Developments in coaching, sports science and sports medicine

It appears that, until the introduction of OAP funding in the mid- to late 1990s, the notion of employing full-time professional coaches was not given the same consideration within the sport as had been evident in swimming and athletics. Sailors had often relied on interest from parents and fellow club members in their pursuit of international recognition. A running theme through D'Alpuget's (1980) account of *Yachting in Australia* is that of dedicated individual sailors, or crews, operating out of the local yacht club and succeeding (if at all) despite the system, not because of it. Moreover, Addy Bucek's account of the support systems available to aspiring Australian Olympic sailors during the 1980s reveals the somewhat haphazard approach to coaching in the sport at the elite level at the time. Bucek recalls that 'My father was our "coach" until I was about 19 or so. He and mum used to go everywhere with us. He taught us tactics and strategies, and watched every race that we sailed in' (quoted in Bryceson and Herbert 1992: 104). Indeed, as recently as the 1988 Seoul Olympics, Bucek went on to remark 'we had no coach. We were out there on our own'.

The establishment of the NCAS in the late 1970s had a clear impact on the volume of coaches at the lower levels with the numbers increasing from one yachting coach in 1979 to '823 level 1 accredited coaches and instructors' by 1993 (ASC 1993a: 225). It was the build-up to the 2000 Games and, more specifically, the award of OAP funding, that appears to have been a key source of policy change in relation to coaching at the elite level. During 1997, for example, a High Performance Manager and Head Coach were appointed, as well as Victor Kovalenko, the former coach to two Olympic medal-winning Ukrainian teams (AYFI 1997: 2). Indeed, one senior AYFI official stated that Kovalenko was the inspiration behind the successful team in Sydney (Interviewee L, 28 May 2003).

The influence of Kovalenko cannot be over-stated, as a senior ASC official revealed that, previously:

> there was a lot of sailing coaches around who would teach people to sail but they didn't necessarily coach, and the influence of Victor Kovalenko as a professional coach who comes in and says this is what a professional coach does was significant.
>
> (Interviewee J, 6 June 2003)

By 1999, as part of sailing's Olympic preparation, 16 staff were employed in coaching, management and support roles, which included a sports science co-ordinator and specialist sports science and sports medicine personnel (AYFI 1999: 3–4). According to a senior AYFI high performance official, sports science and sports medicine were available from the AIS on a 'user-pays' basis but take-up was slow:

> because we didn't have the funding, and we weren't able to afford the sports science and medicine support, then you become creative and you find it in other ways and I think we found it to a certain extent in volunteers up to 1992 and to a certain extent up to 1996 as well.
>
> (Interviewee J, 28 May 2003)

From 2001 yachting became an established AIS programme and could therefore benefit from the range of sports science and medicine support available as part of this provision (AYFI 2003a). By 2001 the significance of these disciplines was such that the organisation's strategic plan for 2001–4 identified a requirement to work with each State/Territory institute/academy of sport where there was no State High Performance Sailing Programme 'to provide support including sports science and sports medicine services to identified sailors' (AYFI 2001b: 22). Accordingly, there are now agreements in place with State/Territory institutes/ academies of sport and, as the AYFI's CEO notes, in 2002–3, 13 elite level sailors were inducted into the AIS programme, one aspect of which was 'intensive training … supplemented by sports science and sports medicine servicing' and which 'saw every member of the AIS squad finish on top at their first Olympic nomination regatta' (quoted in AYFI 2003a: 2). Therefore, in a relatively short space of time, the sport has moved from a position where the notion of sports science support for international sailors was primarily concerned with the preparation of boats and equipment to one where sports science and medicine support is now a vital aspect of elite sailors' preparation.

Competition opportunities for elite level sailors

In the build-up to the 1968 Mexico Olympic Games, Australia's elite sailors 'lacked hard race-training … had no craft of quality to train against … [and] whereas northern hemisphere competitors were fresh from international championships

[Australian sailors] had not had the resources to compete' (D'Alpuget 1980: 82). Although there was extra support provided by federal and State/Territory governments for the 1976 Olympic Games, it was still the case that Australian sailors suffered in comparison to their international counterparts. For example, European nations funded crews to attend up to six international regattas each year for four years as part of their Olympic preparations, whereas 'Australians got to one or two regattas each year' (D'Alpuget 1980: 90).

Over 10 years later, in 1988, the continuing difficulty of financing international competition opportunities across a range of sports was highlighted in a report outlining Commonwealth Assistance to Australian Sport (ASC/AIS 1988). As regards the AYFI, the organisation's President set out, in 1993, 'some of the important principal matters to be debated' (AYFI 1993: 2) for the future development of the sport, one of which was international competition, where it was noted that there were problems surrounding travel difficulties, funding and the need to initiate a new Asia/Pacific regatta circuit. At this time, although the AYFI was not yet in receipt of large amounts of federal grants, this issue was of some concern to the ASC. For example, in a study of its impact on sports performances and participation, the ASC found that 'Australian yachtspeople do not have access to yachting similar to those overseas which puts them at a disadvantage where race specifications are tailored to those conditions' (1993b: 15). By 1996 the impact of the impending 2000 Olympic Games was beginning to be felt as the AYFI sought to establish a 'SailDownUnder' series of international standard regattas in order to attract competitors from the northern hemisphere (AYFI 1996). This series of regattas was aimed not only at establishing better quality competition, but also at alleviating cost concerns. The latter remained a constraining element of the organisation's capacity to build a structure of competition opportunities for its elite level sailors, given that OAP funding for the 2000 Olympiad had yet to come fully on stream. Indeed, in this regard, the AYFI's President noted that 'These events ... provide an excellent opportunity for our sailors to race against the best in the world without the expense of travelling overseas' (quoted in AYFI 1997: 2).

With increased OAP grants from 1997, and the subsequent success of the Australian Olympic team in 2000, a senior AYFI official maintained that an emerging issue for the organisation is the development of a youth programme of events as a base for future success (Interviewee L, 28 May 2003). This development is in part a response to an increasing awareness by AYFI that 'rival nations are spending significant funds in this area' (CEO, AYFI, quoted in AYFI 2000: 5). Key to achieving such a goal is the co-ordination of levels below the elite and, as a senior AYFI official acknowledged, the process of co-ordinating national goals with those of MYAs has only recently begun (Interviewee L, 28 May 2003). A structured approach to competitive opportunities for younger sailors is inextricably related to funding levels and coaching development:

> The YDP [Youth Development Programme] will be achieved by devolving activities and sharing the knowledge with coaches through a coach education

and mentoring system and with young sailors through state squad programmes and camps. Given the size and difficulty associated with travelling to national events, the YDP must be predominantly state based.

(CEO, AYFI, quoted in AYFI 2000: 5)

However, the challenge of achieving co-ordination with the States/Territories was highlighted by the 2003 decision of the Victorian Institute of Sport to reduce its contribution to the State High Performance Programme for sailing (AYFI 2003a). In addition, the creation of a youth programme will require co-ordination with other AYFI activities at local levels, such as 'Get Into Small Boat Sailing', a comprehensive training programme for dinghies and catamarans. The AYFI acknowledge that, in order to achieve this aim, 'the sport must target young people, specifically through the education system' (CEO, AYFI, quoted in AYFI 1999: 2). This may prove problematic as a senior high performance official admitted that, although access to sailing activities in fee-paying schools is reasonable, there is little provision in the non-fee paying schools sector in Australia, primarily due to the costs involved (Interviewee K, 28 May 2003). In conclusion, it is only very recently that the AYFI has been able to establish a reasonably comprehensive set of 'competition development' strategies (AYFI 2003a: 3–4). In producing the competitive strategy, the Federation has had to overcome, and will have to continue to manage, three issues: first, the maintenance of adequate finance; second, the need to balance interests within the sport; and third, the co-ordination of national-federal/State-Territory objectives.

Summary

Arguably, the most notable feature of this review of Australian yachting and the AYFI is the scale of change achieved in a relatively short space of time. The results at the Sydney 2000 Olympic Games are perhaps one of the most obvious outcomes of such change, yet it is important to remember that the sport had struggled for many years to be accepted as a mainstream Olympic programme despite enjoying widespread popularity with a large section of the Australian public. Although it is always problematic to attempt to identify cause and effect relationships in such cases, it is clear that the allocation of OAP funding, in particular from 1996–7 to 2000, provided crucial financial support at the elite level.

One aspect of sailing's recent history, which is distinctive and requires comment, concerns the apparent neglect of sailing by the ASC and the rapid change of policy by the Commission. As the AYFI's CEO noted, 'In 1997 … interaction with the Australian Sports Commission was limited' (quoted in AYFI 2001a: 2). Yet, from 1996–7 to 2000, ASC grants and AIS programme support increased by some 360 per cent (AYFI 2001a) and, for the year 2002–3, sailing was the seventh largest (out of a total of 66 sports) recipient of ASC/AIS grants (ASC 2003). For one of the sport's senior high performance officials, OAP funding in the mid-1990s was crucial (Interviewee K, 28 May 2003) and was released by the ASC, according to another senior AYFI official, because the Commission was 'just waiting' for the AYFI to present a programme, or plan, for its high performance sailors in a climate of federal munificence in the build-up to the 2000 Olympic Games (Interviewee L, 28 May 2003).

With regard to the four areas of elite sport development described above, the issue of a permanent training base has yet to be resolved and would appear to be a major facilities-related concern for the sport's NSO. As discussed, the failure to secure significant support on this issue is perhaps indicative of the relatively recent emergence of the sport as an ASC/AIS supported programme. In a presentation to the ASC, the essence of this argument is captured in the following observations from the organisation's President:

> We are grateful for the recognition received from the ASC in increasing grant support to sailing and for the establishment of an AIS programme. However, we remain disappointed that despite our best efforts, there was no legacy from the Olympic Games and our elite athletes still have no permanent training facility.
>
> (quoted in AYFI 2002b: 1)

On the issue of financial support for the AYFI's elite performers, as in the sports of swimming and athletics, it is still the case that many sailors have yet to reach the stage where they can train and compete on a full-time basis. Sponsorship and advertising revenues also remain difficult to secure in a sport that has yet to attract the levels of media interest that Olympic sports such as swimming, for example, enjoy. In respect of coaching development, it is only recently that coaches have been linked to State/Territory high performance sailing programmes, yet the ability to establish a coaching team, and to secure the services of a world-renowned 470 Class coach (Victor Kovalenko) was widely credited as crucial to the success of the Olympic sailing team in Sydney. Finally, despite the residual concerns regarding the country's relative isolation from world-class competitive events, the AYFI has established a series of strategies aligned to competition development, most notably its SailDownUnder series and Youth Development Programme (AYFI 2002a, 2003a).

To conclude, the remarkable rise in the status of Australian yachting since 1997, such that it was the country's 'second most successful sport at the 2000 Olympics' (AYFI 2001c), indicates a high level of organisational and administrative acumen. Yet, there is perhaps one issue of paramount importance for the AYFI in the future if this success is to be sustained; an issue best captured in the following observation in the organisation's strategic plan summary: 'In the years leading up to the Sydney Games, Australian sport had a strong high performance focus. There is now a need to develop yachting for more Australians, without compromising our international competitiveness' (AYFI 2001c).

5   Canada

The focus of this chapter is a review and analysis of elite sport policy change in three Canadian NSOs – Swimming/Natation Canada, Athletics Canada, and the Canadian Yachting Association. In tracing developments in the same four key areas of high performance sport policy identified in Chapter 4, two further issues warrant consideration in respect of the Canadian sporting context. The first issue centres on the role of the federal government and Sport Canada. Questions here relate to the issue of NSOs' autonomy with regard to federal government policies for sport. The second issue concerns the changing nature of the organisation and administration of the three NSOs and the potential for tension between the values/belief systems of the NSOs' volunteer-based members and staff, traditionally more concerned with grass roots development, and those of the paid professional staff more likely to be involved in the implementation of rational planning systems, such as the Quadrennial Planning Process (QPP) and the Sports Funding and Accountability Framework (SFAF).

These rational planning systems can be conceived of here as 'planning dictates' – 'dictate' is used here in the sense of an order or principle that must be obeyed – which are important reference points for the following discussion as they help to clarify the 'conditions of action' (Betts 1986; Sibeon 1997, 1999) within which the three NSOs developed policies for high performance sport. These dictates are set within a broader policy discourse which, in the early 1990s, appeared to indicate a shift in policy direction towards a lessened emphasis on the elite level – a shift that appears to have strengthened more recently with the publication of the new Canadian Sport Policy and Bill C-12, both of which reveal, in their rhetoric at least, that federal policy direction has moved towards a far broader conception of sporting objectives and away from its previous focus on support for high performance sport. Thus, an interesting aspect of the ensuing discussion is the degree to which federal government rhetoric has been translated into substantive change at the NSO level.

Swimming/Natation Canada

Organisation, administration and relationships

Swimming/Natation Canada (SNC) has responsibility for three disciplines – swimming, disability swimming and open water swimming, with the related aquatic disciplines of water polo, synchronised swimming and diving all the responsibility of autonomous sporting organisations. At an international level, SNC represents Canada in Fédération Internationale de Natation Amateur (FINA) and International Olympic Committee (IOC) forums. As an organisation of 10 provincial sections, SNC is Canada's national swimming body charged with co-ordinating a variety of programmes, in conjunction with the Canadian Swimming Coaches and Teachers Association, across the sport's 350 clubs and 70,000 members (SNC 2001).

As with all the major NSOs in Canada, SNC depends heavily on the provincial club structure to provide a coaching and competition pathway to high performance levels. Yet, the capacity of the club structure to fulfil this development role is the subject of some controversy. Although one senior SNC official maintained that 'We still feel we have one of the best club systems in the world' (Interviewee M, 13 June 2002), Nick Thierry, editor of *SwimNews*, argued that 'Our club system … is now moribund' (Personal communication: 3 July 2002; see also Tihanyi 2001b), and Mark St-Aubin, age-group swimming coach and clinical kinesiologist, maintained that attempts to introduce talent identification and development programmes at club level have received little support or funding (St-Aubin 1994: 7). Others have variously described Canadian swimming as 'in crisis' (Colwin 1996: 12; SNC 1998: 11), 'not having a system' (Lowry 2000: 44) and 'stuck in the past' (MacDonald 1998: 37). Such criticisms raise questions as to the role, purpose, policy direction and strategic aims of SNC and, crucially, the nature of the organisation's relationships with its provincial partners, and with Sport Canada and the Canadian Olympic Committee (COC).

Chapter 3 outlined the policy direction of Sport Canada from the 1970s to the late 1980s; in short, the rationalisation, centralisation and professionalisation of Canada's major NSOs, the corollary of which was a focus on high performance sport, with the ultimate aim of medal-winning success at Olympic and World Championship events. It has also been well documented (cf. Kidd 1988a, 1988b, 1995; Macintosh and Whitson 1990; Whitson and Macintosh 1989) that regional and/or provincial/territorial interests in sport and physical activities, as well as wider (but interrelated) social policy concerns (e.g. equity, gender and official languages), have been routinely subsumed within the embedded systemic goal of elite success. That this 'ideology' of excellence, as Kidd (1995: 9) termed it, has in large part failed to realise the politically-motivated high performance goals in swimming is clear from Table 5.1. The priority given to Olympic and World Championship medals is clear from Sport Canada's funding mechanism for NSOs – the SFAF. As Sport Canada's documentation states, 'SFAF funding eligibility will be based on factors relating to the *level* of performance rather than on the volume of performance' (Canadian Heritage 2000b: 3, emphasis added).

Table 5.1 Canadian swimming medals: Olympic Games/World Aquatic Championships, 1988–2001

| | Olympic Games | | | | | World Aquatic Championships | | | |
	Gold	Silver	Bronze	Total		Gold	Silver	Bronze	Total
1988	0	1	1	2	1991	0	1	0	1
1992	1	0	1	2	1994	0	0	0	0
1996	0	1	2	3	1998	0	1	3	4
2000	0	0	1	1	2001	0	0	0	0

The high performance element of the SFAF was weighted (as at January 2000) at around two-thirds of the total funds available to a Canadian NSO. On this basis the funding formula has clearly failed to deliver the sought-after success for Canadian swimming. Such failure sharpens the paradox of the apparent increased emphasis on issues of 'participation', 'building capacity' and 'interaction' in the new Canadian Sport Policy (Canadian Heritage 2002) and the continued 'over-funding' of an under-performing elite. The policy paradox is highlighted by the comments of a senior official at Sport Canada who noted that:

> probably 65 per cent of the funding was in high performance. The funding is still, by and large, in that area, in part, because if the federal government does not support that high performance programme, then there are not a lot of other groups in the Canadian sport scene that are going to, other than the Canadian Olympic Committee.
>
> (Interviewee N, 12 June 2002)

Olympic and World Championship medals thus remain a criterion in the funding of NSOs and SNC remains an elite-focused body. This 'performance first' philosophy (SNC 2001: 4) is reflected in the comments of SNC's Acting Executive Director in 2001, who argued that 'Our mandate to progress SNC's focus to the international podium has never been clearer' (quoted in SNC 2001: 9). This position was reinforced by SNC's CEO in 2002, who stated that 'Our organisational structure has been realigned to better service the peak performance and technical areas' (quoted in SNC 2002b), largely in recognition of and compensation for the federal government policy shift away from high performance.

Moreover, at the same time as the new federal sport policy was formulated, which apparently downgraded the priority of elite sport, the COC adopted an almost diametrically opposed policy position, and 'approved a major shift in its funding practice' (COC 2002). In short, a large part of the COC's new High Performance Support Programme for NSOs/athletes is now linked to results at the Olympic Games. As a leading Canadian sports analyst argued, the COC 'live and breathe the philosophy of excellence and they have no critical distance as far as that's concerned' (Interviewee O, 19 June 2002); making it a likely core member of a potential advocacy coalition centring on high performance sport. Interestingly, a Sport Canada official stated that SNC has been an important supporter of the high performance lobby in Canada as it is clear that the organisation is aware of the funding implications of the COC's shift in funding priorities (Interviewee N, 12 June 2002); a point reinforced by SNC's CEO, who noted that the new COC funding model 'squarely places an emphasis on funding for peak performance … [and that] SNC is well positioned to benefit from the focus on high performance' (quoted in SNC 2002b).

Four areas of elite sport policy

Development of elite level facilities

Facility planning and development is an element of the Canadian sport delivery system traditionally located within the remit of provincial/territorial sporting organisations (P/TSOs) and municipalities. Accordingly, elite level facility developments in swimming have been shaped substantially by long-standing juris dictional divisions and federal responses to calls for assistance in facility development. The 1969 *Task Force on Sports for Canadians*, for example, noted, *inter alia*, 'that there has been no general study of such [sports] facilities'; and 'that we are woefully weak in the kind of facilities required for international competition' (Canada 1969: 55–6). The lack of elite level *swimming* facilities was also noted by the 1969 Task Force, which commended the federal government for its part in the construction of the country's first Olympic-class pool in Winnipeg (built for the Pan-American Games) and for its assistance in helping to build a similar pool in Halifax in preparation for the 1969 Canada Games. As Macintosh *et al.* note, 'the federal government restricted its support of facilities to those constructed for the Canada Games [from 1968] and international sports events' (1987: 103). This early indication of an emphasis on high performance sport was clearly related to a hosting policy for staging major events. Indeed, a senior Sport Canada official made it clear that 'The only way we support facilities is through our Major Games … our hosting policy' (Interviewee P, 12 June 2002). However, a facility building programme based on a hosting policy did little to realise either federal policy aims with regard to the development of high performance athletes or to assist in increasing mass participation in Canada (Macintosh *et al.* 1987).

In 1979, the federal government published a White Paper on sport – *Partners in Pursuit of Excellence: A National Policy on Amateur Sport* – which provided scant support for the building of sport/recreation facilities for the general public, but did signal the first indication that high performance (single sport) national and regional training centres would be federally-funded (Campagnolo 1979). By 1986, 78 sport training centres had been established, 55 of which were located at Canadian universities. Yet, it appears that the necessary co-operation for the optimum use of these centres, between federal and provincial governments, host institution, NSOs and P/TSOs and regional/local sports clubs, was lacking (Macintosh *et al.* 1987). In 1988, the federal government published yet another Task Force Report on National Sport Policy – *Toward 2000: Building Canada's*

Sport System (Canada 1988). With regard to facility development, the Task Force recommended, *inter alia*, that: (i) further emphasis should be put on co-ordinating the various organisations and agencies at national/federal, provincial and local (municipal/universities) levels; (ii) there was a need for 'adequate competition and training facilities' to support high performance athletes; and, crucially (iii) there should be an investigation into 'the possibility of developing national multi-sport training centres' (Canada 1988: 33–4). Regarding the last recommendation, the first multi-sport centre was established in Calgary in 1994, with swimming as one of seven 'client sports' included at the outset.

Many in the Canadian sporting community, including SNC, viewed the concept of multi-sport training centres (now known as Canadian Sport Centres [CSCs]) as an important ingredient in Canada's quest for success at the elite level. For example, SNC's National Coach/High Performance Director argued that the centre programme would help to reinstate a 'competitive attitude' back into Canadian swimming (Johnson 1995: 22–3). Despite the opening of the Calgary centre in 1994 coinciding with a round of severe budget cuts by the Canadian government, seven national swimming centres were established across Canada over the following nine years and it is clear that SNC has devoted a considerable (and increasing) percentage of its own resources to these establishments. For example, in 1994–5, $CAN86,000 – approximately 6.6 per cent of total SNC annual expenditure – was allocated to the centres (SNC 1997). By 2001–2 the forecast allocation had risen to $CAN433,000, almost 21 per cent of SNC's total expected expenditure for the year (SNC 2001). Unfortunately, despite the existence of the centres and the increasing percentage of income devoted to them, Canadian swimmers have not noticeably improved their success in major competitions (see Table 5.1).

In sum, it is clear that SNC has embraced the high performance training centre concept with some enthusiasm (Interviewee N, 12 June 2002; Interviewee M, 13 June 2002). However, a series of issues remain unresolved with regard to strategic facility development for swimming: (i) variable commitment to the CSC network from different levels of the sport; (ii) some provinces (principally the larger, more prosperous provinces, such as British Columbia and Québec) have high performance sporting ambitions of their own; (iii) the other side of this equation is that the smaller or less prosperous provinces, such as Prince Edward Island and Manitoba, struggle to provide adequate swimming facilities for the general public, let alone the high performance end of the sport (SNC 1997, 2001); and (iv) central to these issues are questions of organisational purpose and resource allocation.

Emergence of 'full-time' swimmers

One of the first initiatives to provide direct funding to elite athletes was the result of the *Proposed Sports Policy for Canadians* (Canada 1970), which allocated grants-in-aid to athletes while they were students. A number of other funding initiatives followed (e.g. 'Intensive Care' in 1972 and 'Game Plan '76') which were finally consolidated in 1980 under the auspices of Sport Canada's Athlete Assistance Programme (AAP). By the late 1980s, funding for elite athletes was sufficiently well established for Macintosh *et al.* (1987: 172) to suggest that a federal government-sponsored 'cadre of "state" athletes' now existed. However, few of the recipients of federal funding could afford to train full-time. The relative lack of funding for Canada's elite swimmers has proved to be an enduring issue for those involved in shaping policy direction for the sport (Interviewee N, 12 June 2002). Indeed, in the late 1980s, in a damning assessment of funding arrangements for Canada's high performance athletes, Kidd argued that:

> As underpaid professionals, athletes are 'sweat-suited philanthropists', subsidising the careers of hundreds of fully paid coaches, sports scientists, and bureaucrats, not to mention the ambitions of the federal state and the products and ideology of the corporations which sponsor teams and competitions.
>
> (Kidd 1988a: 300)

In response to the chronic under-funding of elite swimmers through the AAP, SNC established the 'Team Elite' programme[1] that involved a reallocation of resources in order to provide additional funding for its elite swimmers. According to SNC's High Performance Director, this reallocation of existing funding was 'something we felt we had to do, with or without new corporate support, if we want to be competitive' (quoted in Christie 2001b). However, elite funding remains modest by comparison to the UK where government funding through UK Sport is roughly four times that provided by Sport Canada through the AAP.

It is clear, Kidd's critique notwithstanding, that there is currently a discrete group of Canadian elite swimmers who might be categorised as 'full-time' – in the sense that they train and compete on a full-time basis – who receive direct support through Sport Canada's 'carding' (AAP) system, some additional funding from SNC and benefit from prize money and sponsorships linked to the professional swimming circuit. Unfortunately, as senior officials at SNC and Sport Canada acknowledged, many other Canadian swimmers just below this elite level rely heavily on parental support and/or migrate to universities in the United States (see also McWha 1998). However, the emergence of a group of funded full-time swimmers has implications beyond those who are recipients and those who are not. There are also implications for club funding and youth development.

First, SNC has funded a long-standing 'club grant programme', the aim of which has been to support grass roots developmental swimming at provincial/municipal levels. Yet, in 1997, in an economic climate of federal cutbacks to NSOs, and variability of resources for P/TSOs, SNC's club grant criteria were revised to allow clubs with medallists at national championships to be designated as 'high performance clubs'. As SNC's Manager of Swimming Development Services stated, 'it allows for linkage between the club grant and recognition of high performance clubs under the Sport Canada carding programme' (quoted in SNC 1997: 35). However, the policy also created a sharper hierarchy of clubs and sent clear signals regarding the priority in club development between nurturing elite swimmers and supporting the interests of the general membership. Second, a number of leading Canadian swimming analysts have suggested that the contemporary professional swimming circuit has contributed significantly to the demise of the sport's youth and sub-elite base. Tihanyi, for example, argues that 'Today the Canadian youth programme is virtually non-existent' (2001a: 6), while Colwin maintains that 'The advent of the professional swimming circuit has already caused an increasing gap between the vastly differing needs of the globe-trotting athlete and the lower-level participant, who still pursues the traditional daily routine of the amateur swimmer' (1998: 11). The concern is that elite swimmers are putting money-winning opportunities ahead of Olympic success. As Tihanyi argues, 'Our World Cup performances are very good and our [Olympic] Games performances are very poor' (2001a: 6).

Despite concerns about the adequacies of funding, it is clear that there is currently a small, but increasingly legitimised, cadre of elite full-time swimmers. The above discussion has revealed SNC as an organisation prepared to support the notion of full-time elite swimmers in order to achieve the goal of success at major international swimming events even if this results in an increasing remoteness from the interests of the grass roots. However, in recent years, the 'holy grail' of Olympic and/or World Championship success has eluded Canada's high performance swimmers, raising questions about the organisational and strategic acumen of SNC. That SNC has put in place, and pursues, financial incentives which allow full-time, high performance swimmers to 'subsidise' their own interests by competing for prize money at the numerous World Cup swimming meets across the globe, as well as Olympic/World Championship events, are but two examples of an organisation prepared to marginalise the interests of the grass roots for the benefit of the elite.

Developments in coaching, sports science and sports medicine

The first attempts to construct a coaching 'profession' in Canada were signalled in the 1969 *Report of the Task Force on Sports for Canadians*. While this report gave just one page to coaching issues and just two pages to what was euphemistically termed the 'medical situation', it found, *inter alia*, that 'there is no coaching profession in Canada [and that] few well-paid coaching jobs are available and very few men and women consider it as a full-time career' (Canada 1969: 64, 70). Over 20 years later, the 1992 Task Force on Federal Sport Policy, *Sport: The Way Ahead* (Canada 1992), cited the 1969 Report as a catalyst for a number of initiatives that led to the progressive development of coaching up to the early 1990s. Three key structural developments were cited: (i) the creation of the National Coaches Association in late 1970 – renamed the Coaching Association of Canada (CAC) in 1971; (ii) the development of the National Coaching Certification Programme (NCCP) in 1972; and (iii) the establishment of the Canadian Association of National Coaches in 1986 (renamed Canadian Professional Coaches Association in 1993) (cf. Canada 1992; Macintosh *et al.* 1987). While the 1992 Task Force

Report clearly recognised achievements regarding the professionalisation of coaching, it also inferred that this remained an unfinished project. Thus, while attempts to construct a coaching profession began in Canada in the early 1970s, over 10 years ahead of similar developments in the UK, a number of problematic issues remain in relation to Canadian swimming.

First, it is clear that coaching development in Canada remains an incomplete project. As Tihanyi (2001a: 8) argues, 'coaching has never been looked upon in this country as a profession' and, at grass roots levels, little is being done to help the many volunteer coaches to improve through coaching education. Second, the development of multi-sport training centres in the mid-1990s has not been recognised as a success by all in the Canadian swimming community. Here, problems centre on the progression of talented swimmers from municipal club level, through to clubs focused more specifically on high performance and, finally, into one of SNC's seven regional swimming centres. As a senior Sport Canada official related, tensions are apparent here as coaches at the two 'lower' levels are reluctant to release talented swimmers, who have spent many years with an individual coach, to a high performance centre (Interviewee N, 12 June 2002). Tihanyi is less equivocal on this issue, arguing that the principle behind the centres is 'that you bring in the swimmer to train in the centre for a while and the swimmer will still participate in and be part of the club. No such thing exists anymore – at least not 100%' (2001a: 6). Third, on the issue of coach education and development, doubts have been raised regarding the NCCP's effectiveness in building a coaching 'profession'. For example, an evaluation of the NCCP by the CAC raised the following questions: (i) 'Is the programme meeting the needs of both volunteers and professional coaches?' (ii) 'Why are so few coaches moving through the programme?' and (iii) 'How effective is a course-based approach?' (CAC 1996: 1).

A key output of the NCCP evaluation has been the transition to what is termed a competency-based education and training (CBET) approach to coaching in Canada (CAC 2002). This transition is ongoing, as each participating sport revises its coach training and certification. However, change has been slow. Indeed, Tihanyi (2001a: 7) argues that 'an old boys network has established itself in Canadian swimming at the upper level, which is making it very difficult for new ideas to emerge', while a Sport Canada official suggested that it has 'been quite a challenge', specifically for older coaches at club and provincial levels, to embrace fully the type of coaching innovations more readily adopted by national (high performance) coaches at SNC's regional network of swimming centres (Interviewee N, 12 June 2002; see also Colwin 1997).

With regard to developments in sports science/medicine disciplines, it is worth noting that, in the course of its inquiry, the 1969 Task Force Report found that many contributors were highly critical of 'the medical care and supervision provided [to] our athletes and national teams competing at the international level' (Canada 1969: 69). Following the 1969 Task Force findings, the Canadian Academy of Sport Medicine was established in 1970. This proved to be a catalyst for the creation of a number of related organisations, such as the Sport Medicine

Council of Canada and the Sport Physiotherapy Division of the Canadian Physiotherapy Association. Interestingly, despite this organisational evolution, the 1992 Task Force on Federal Sport Policy not only suggested that 'Sport medicine and sport science in Canada are still relatively young and evolving' but also that 'Coaches and sport scientists have not yet developed a strong partnership to use their assets to mutual benefit' (Canada 1992: 83). Moreover, this 1992 report also criticised the Sport Medicine Council of Canada for concentrating almost exclusively on national level, high performance sport.

SNC embraced sports science/medicine primarily through involvement in the multi-sport training centres. In its 1993–8 Strategic Plan, sports science/medicine programmes were highlighted as a 'high priority' (SNC 1993: 63), but only in the context of programmes to be delivered by the now established multi-sport training centres. More recently, SNC received funding through Sport Canada's Sport Science Support Programme, but the sums are small – $CAN1,000 per annum for two swimmers to receive support in areas such as strength training, sport psychology and physiology monitoring. However, elite swimmers have also benefited indirectly from the sports science/medicine support available for carded swimmers as one aspect of SNC's involvement in the multi-sport training centres since the mid-1990s. The training centres thus appear to be SNC's primary medium for delivering sports science and sports medicine services to its elite level swimmers.

To sum up, it is clear that Canadian swimmers now benefit from a relatively sophisticated framework of coaching and sports science/medicine support. However, this has been achieved at some cost, both financial and organisational. Financially, the elite coaching and sports science programmes absorb an increasing proportion of SNC income, while organisationally there are clear grounds for arguing that the benefits accruing to the elite are to the detriment of the club structure and the generality of club swimmers. Moreover, it is arguable that the current distribution of resources neglects the medium and long-term development of future talent. As Tihanyi argues, 'It is much too late to develop Olympians at the level of the training centres. [This] process must be incubated, nurtured, and brought to fruition at the club level' (2001b: 29).

Competition opportunities for elite level swimmers

The report of the 1976 Post-Olympic Games Symposium (CAC 1977) considered the issue of 'competition programmes' and argued, *inter alia*, that: (i) the size of the country was 'a logistical nightmare'; (ii) regular competition with other countries could not be guaranteed; (iii) competition programmes should be developed with the United States to offset the cost of travelling further abroad; (iv) at the same time, exchanges with countries that have achieved 'superior international performances' should be encouraged; and (v) the 'level of competition in Canada generally is low' (CAC 1977: 13, 17). The issue of competition structures/ opportunities appears to be enduringly problematic and inextricably related to the vexed question of jurisdictional responsibilities. For example, over 10 years after the 1976 Symposium, the 1988 Task Force on National Sport Policy argued for 'a national framework, which provides an increased range and quality of competitive opportunities for all levels of participants' (Canada 1988: 10–11). These concerns were echoed in the new Canadian Sport Policy, which acknowledged that, not only is federal-provincial/territorial co-operation essential to the successful implementation of the new policy, but also that there should be increased accessibility to 'development opportunities such as competition and training required to successfully compete at the highest levels of international competition' (Canadian Heritage 2002).

Although these general concerns help shape the broad conditions of action for elite sport, there are three more specific concerns central to our understanding of the particular issues facing swimming. First, Helmstaedt (1995: 19) argues that the international swimming calendar is now far too 'cluttered'; a problem which is exacerbated by the number of Canadian high performance swimmers opting to swim abroad in competitive events that offer financial reward rather than opting to 'swim fast domestically before heading overseas' (Johnson, quoted in Helmstaedt 1995: 19). Second, in recent years many Canadian swimmers have opted to move to the United States. As McWha argues, 'The level of competition in the NCAA [National Collegiate Athletic Association] is the best in the world bar none, as every year more and more non-American swimmers seek athletic scholarships at American schools' (1998: 32). The key concern here (for SNC) is that the NCAA competition schedule is not necessarily compatible with SNC's competitive calendar, and especially with the selection meets for major competitions, such as the Olympic Games and World Championships.

The final point questions the organisational and administrative acumen of SNC, especially in relation to the scheduling and number of meets that aspiring elite swimmers are expected to attend. Indeed, Tihanyi notes that, 'to add insult to injury and to continue the string of poor decisions, after the scandalous results [in Sydney], the high-performance leadership decides to designate *nine* meets for athletes in which to qualify' (2001b: 29, emphasis added). As Tihanyi concludes, this type of programme design 'will only help to destroy the preparatory training cycle of athletes and perpetuate the concept of just making the team rather than developing to the highest level' (2001b: 29).

Summary

From the evidence presented above, SNC is struggling to establish its prioritisation of high performance objectives at a time of a federal policy shift away from high performance sport. SNC's re-emphasis on high performance is perhaps indicative not only of the peculiar characteristics of the Canadian sport delivery system (geography and federal-provincial/territorial jurisdictions) but also illustrative of the lack of extra funding from Sport Canada with which SNC might implement federal government social policy objectives. Indeed, a leading Canadian sports analyst explained that there was 'clear tension in the room' at the National Summit on Sport in Ottawa in April 2001 as it became apparent that the government expected NSOs to realise federal goals on 'participation and co-ordinating the system and not to put all [their] money into high performance sport' (Interviewee Q, 11 June 2002).

It is clear that the past 10 to 15 years can be characterised as a period of policy confusion for Canada's major NSOs, including SNC. However, the evidence suggests that elite swimming has been able to insulate itself from the full impact of federal policy change. For example, as a senior Sport Canada official explained, the development of elite level facilities in Canada still benefits from Sport Canada's hosting policy for staging major international sporting events (Interviewee P, 12 June 2002). That Montreal has been awarded the 2005 World Aquatic Championships might, therefore, serve to stimulate an improvement in the number and quality of swimming pools suitable for high performance training/competition in the city. Despite the absence of a national facility strategy for swimming, and the variable enthusiasm for pool investment at the provincial/municipal level, elite swimming benefits from Canada's enthusiasm to host major events and the increasing number of CSCs that can offer world-class training opportunities for swimming.

With regard to the emergence of full-time swimmers, although AAP funding supported, in 2001, some 25 high performance swimmers who also benefit from SNC's in-house Team Elite and High Performance Swimmer Incentive programmes, the level of funding is clearly insufficient for elite level swimmers to train and compete on a full-time basis. However, this is not to suggest that there are no full-time Canadian swimmers as there is clearly a small group of swimmers who benefit substantially from sponsorships (e.g. Speedo Bonus programmes) and prize money (e.g. FINA World Cup series) that allows them to train and compete on a full-time basis and consequently puts them at the heart of an emerging coalition of actors/organisations centred on elite sport. While the size of the high-earning commercially sponsored elite is very small, and the state sponsored elite is only modestly funded, both groups fare better than the grass roots levels which are increasingly neglected through a lack of core funding and support.

In respect of developments in coaching, sports science and sports medicine, a somewhat confused picture emerges. Coaching is currently undergoing major structural change, with adaptations to the NCCP initiative promising increased professionalism. Yet, the greater professionalism is also leading to increased tensions between provincial clubs and elite centres as there is a perception among club/provincial coaches that they are developing talented swimmers only to 'lose' them to coaches within the CSC network. The quality of sports science/medicine available to elite swimmers through SNC's network of centres is a marked improvement on previous years, but the extent of support available is limited. For example, a leading Canadian sports analyst explained that 'research is going on in the universities but very few [studies]… directly contribute to the development of athletes … it is not a good structure' (Interviewee O, 19 June 2002), while a senior Sport Canada official suggested that 'there are only a handful of full-time sports scientists working in Canada.' (Interviewee P, 12 June 2002).

The final element of high performance swimming considered was the sport's structure of competition opportunities. Here, concerns centred on a 'cluttered calendar' (Helmstaedt 1995); the migration of talented swimmers to the United States (McWha 1998); the difficulties involved in integrating United States universities' programmes, and even those of Canadian universities, with SNC's competitive calendar; and a growing trend for high performance swimmers to prioritise short-term financial gain at competitions such as the FINA World Cup series to the detriment of a more long-term developmental strategy.

Athletics Canada

Organisation, administration and relationships

Athletics Canada (AC) was established in 1991 (previously known as the Canadian Track and Field Association [CTFA]) and is responsible for track and field athletics, cross country, race walking and road running. There are three themes which provide a useful context to the ensuing review: (i) AC's relationship with its provincial/territorial branches; (ii) concerns over the relative emphasis put on high performance sport in relation to grass roots developmental levels; and (iii) AC's struggle with the changing priorities of its primary funding partners, Sport Canada and the COC. The first two themes overlap and, like swimming, AC has relied upon its provincial/territorial branches to provide a framework for developments in coaching, athlete development and competition opportunities. However, as a senior AC official revealed, the issue of integration/co-ordination between the sport's various levels is one that has been debated at length (Interviewee R, 13 June 2002).

In 1983, the aims of the then CTFA were: 'to promote, encourage, and develop the widest participation and highest proficiency amongst its members' (Irons 1983: 23). Particular emphasis was given to 'The nurturing of young talent and the maintenance of enthusiasm at the grass roots level' (1983: 23). These laudable aims were easy to state but, as CTFA/AC has found, they were more difficult to fulfil in practice. A particularly persistent problem is the maintenance of a grass roots club structure as a foundation for CTFA/AC high performance objectives. In 1980, the CTFA National Performance Director, maintained that 'The development of a strong high level Club System is the main problem that the CTFA is confronted with at the present stage' (Mach 1980: 3). A few years later, in 1983, Wilf Paish, a former UK national athletics coach, voiced concerns regarding the profile of, and support for, Canadian track and field athletics. Paish concluded that, 'you appear to be trying to build a successful track and field structure without having a solid foundation ... Performance in depth is required' (1983: 15).

As regards the third contextual theme, changing federal funding priorities, the senior AC official, referring to federal funding cutbacks during the 1990s, argued that 'we let the grass roots die, but without your grass roots you can't compete at the elite level' (Interviewee R, 13 June 2002). This observer went on to suggest that, in relation to the promotion of participation and talent identification and development, 'I think they've [Sport Canada] pushed it down to the provincial level, hoping it's going to happen at that level [but] without that leadership from the national level it's not a consistent development programme'. The reluctance of the federal government to allocate sufficient resources that might allow NSOs to accomplish the many and varied elite/mass sport initiatives required of them was cited as a key structural deficiency in the Canadian sport system; a situation that is exacerbated by the variability of funding for sport and recreation programmes at provincial/territorial levels. As one of the larger provincial track and field bodies noted, 'The [provincial] government continues to reduce its funding of our sport, and future declines should be anticipated' (Ontario Track and Field Association 2002).

A further problem faced by CTFA/AC in fulfilling its range of objectives is the competition for resources between the four athletic disciplines within CTFA/AC's remit. The potential for disparity appears, on the surface at least, to be more apparent in track and field athletics than was the case for SNC. In the late 1980s, for example, Whitson and Macintosh found that, despite a significant increase in mass participation road running events at sub-elite level, the CTFA had 'not provided any support for road racing (and very little for cross-country events)' (1989: 441). It appears that the balancing of different priorities among the disciplines within AC's remit remains problematic. Indeed, a senior AC official acknowledged that the organisation has struggled to balance claims for resources between the four disciplines. As this official put it, 'if we've never been truly successful in race walking, should we continue to try and do it mediocre or should we try and focus on what we're better at?' (Interviewee R, 13 June 2002). AC's 2001 Annual General Meeting report endorsed these sentiments, with the High Performance Director for Endurance events stating that 'I believe it is still premature to … launch new programmes for the race walk' (quoted in AC 2001a: 13), with the parlous state of AC's finances given as one of the main justifications.

AC is clearly struggling to balance the variety of internal and external demands on its resources. As a senior Sport Canada official related, in respect of the new Canadian Sport Policy, 'Participation is the new pillar we're going to get involved in now [but] we're still not sure what to do with it [and] … there has been no announcement of new money' (Interviewee S, 20 June 2002). In marked contrast to the direction of Sport Canada, the COC has stated unequivocally that future funding for NSOs/athletes will be targeted at those sports that have achieved medal-winning performances at the Olympic Games and/or are able to demonstrate the potential to do so (COC 2002).

Four areas of elite sport policy

Development of elite level facilities

As with SNC, AC's remit does not include the production of a facility development plan: sports facility development remains the responsibility of provincial/territorial sporting organisations and/or governments and municipalities. As one senior AC official admitted, there is 'no national strategic plan' for facility development in athletics (Interviewee R, 13 June 2002). The scope of facility development at NSO level centres on the CSC network and Sport Canada's strategy for hosting major sporting events. On this issue, a senior Sport Canada official was unequivocal in stating that 'The only way we support facilities is through our Major Games' (Interviewee P, 12 June 2002). In this respect, track and field operates in a similar context to swimming, albeit with a number of significant distinctive elements.

The first distinctive element concerns the perception of track and field athletics by Canadians. Wilf Paish, while working at the University of Calgary in the early 1980s, observed that 'Track and field athletics is a very low-priority for your nation' (1983: 14). In other words, professional sports in Canada, such as ice hockey, baseball and basketball are more popular among Canadians than track and field in terms of participation and spectating. Comments made following the 2001 Edmonton World Athletics Championships suggest that little has changed in the perception of the sport held by Canadians. Buffery (2001), for example, reported in the *Toronto Sun* that 'Canada failed to win a medal at the world track and field championships ... But the good news is, by lunchtime today, it will all be forgotten ... [T]his is track and field and to North American audiences the only thing more boring than track is ... forget it, we're not going there'.

The second distinctive element is the volatility of commercial sponsorship. As a senior AC official explained, in 1990, the organisation recorded a $CAN600,000 deficit and, although this deficit had been turned into an accumulated surplus of $CAN178,000 by 1998, AC again recorded a deficit of $CAN500,000 in 2001 (Interviewee R, 13 June 2002). As this observer admitted, over the past decade, 'the majority of our sponsors left or didn't renew relationships because during this period there wasn't the ongoing communication and servicing of [our] sponsors'. Moreover, at the 2001 Annual General Meeting, AC's Treasurer reported that, 'corporate sponsorships are weaker than expected [and that] there is no further sponsorship revenue to be received by Athletics Canada at this time' (quoted in AC 2001a: 3). In short, in an economic climate of federal reductions in NSO funding and variability of funding support at provincial/territorial and municipal levels, AC is in a vulnerable position from which to elicit sponsorship from the private/corporate sector. The argument being developed here is that the political and/or corporate will to support any form of funding for facility development has been seriously undermined by the generally negative public perception of the sport over the past 10 to 15 years.

Yet, it is debatable whether AC possesses the organisational and administrative capacity to alter significantly the perception of the sport. Indeed, questions remain as to the organisational acumen of AC to implement its stated goal of strengthening partnerships with its provincial/territorial branches (AC 2002c) in order to leverage the degree of support capable of fostering facility improvements that might benefit all in the sport. It is recognised that AC's ability to provide policy direction for facility development is compounded by difficulties arising from federal-provincial/territorial jurisdictions. As a senior Sport Canada official related, while there is indirect help available for sport/ recreation facilities through a federally-sponsored general infrastructure programme, each province/territory and/or municipality has the discretion to spend these funds where they see fit, and it is by no means certain in today's economic climate, that sport/recreation facility development would be high on the agenda (Interviewee P, 12 June 2002).

A further distinctive element in AC's context, and an important difference between SNC and AC, concerns the emerging CSC network. Unlike SNC, which developed, through the 1990s, a network of swimming centres aligned to a number of the CSCs to support its high performance objectives, AC has been more ambiguous in its attitude towards the CSCs. Only in 2001 did AC establish its policy towards the centres. As the High Performance Director (Endurance events) reported, 'The National Sport Centre concept *has been clarified* and identified priorities established for the Endurance Group centres' in four locations (quoted in AC 2001a: 12, emphasis added). The Endurance Director goes on to state that these centres 'can not and should not try to be everything to everybody. That would be a recipe for confusion, inefficiency and poor results'. The slow pace of decision-making and the tentative involvement with the CSCs suggests an organisation unwilling to make the commitment to the pursuit of elite success that has been made by other sports such as swimming.

Emergence of 'full-time' athletes

In 1982 the Managing Editor of the *Track and Field Journal* discussed the IAAF's decision to permit athletes to set up trust funds 'to receive support for their efforts to achieve excellence' (MacWilliam 1982: 2). At the heart of MacWilliam's concerns was the refusal of elite athletes to agree to a CTFA policy to transfer 15 per cent of the money earned by individual athletes to an Athlete Heritage Fund aimed at supporting emerging athletes. MacWilliam concluded that 'it seems that self-interest among current national team members has reduced the opportunity for future team members to receive help along the way' (1982: 2). As in swimming, the tension between the interests (and self-interest) of elite athletes and broader talent identification and development objectives is the central theme of this section.

Since the 1980s, Canadian elite athletes have sought full-time status either by moving to the United States on sports scholarships or by relying on AAP carding support: both strategies pose problems for AC. As regards the migration of athletes to colleges in the United States and their competitions in the NCAA programme, a senior AC official admitted that, in the past, AC lost contact with these talented athletes. However, even if contact had been maintained, these athletes would not have been eligible for Sport Canada's AAP support as it was premised on Canadian residency (Interviewee R, 12 June 2002; see also Canadian Heritage 1999a: 2-2). A revision of this policy is now in place, such that AAP carding support is permissible for 'top ranked athletes' that return to live in Canada for the summer period (AC 2002a).

Although AC published a draft list of some 53 athletes for carding support at Sport Canada's 'Senior' levels for the period 2002–3 (AC 2002b), it is far from clear how many Canadian track and field athletes might be categorised as full-time. Indeed, a senior AC official stated that 'Some are ... at the very, very high end' (Interviewee R, 12 June 2002) and a leading Canadian sports analyst was equally uncertain, estimating 'that about half of them in Canada think of themselves as full-time' (Interviewee O, 19 June 2002). Moreover, although a senior Sport Canada official argued that 'we certainly have our fair share of what you would call full-time athletes', this observer also highlighted the important role that parents play, stating that 'You could not live off AAP money as an athlete. Parents carry a huge, huge, load in many sports in Canada' (Interviewee P, 12 June 2002). If we also consider recent pronouncements from the Canadian Association of National Team Athletes – known as Athletes Canada – on this issue, it is clear that any notion of 'full-time' track and field athletes in a Canadian sporting context should be treated with some caution. In 2002, Athletes Canada stated that 'To expect high performance athletes to represent Canada and win, without ... having the proper financial support to accomplish the task, is to invite confusion, frustration and ultimately, disappointment' (Athletes Canada 2002: 4).

AC has clearly struggled to cope with the ramifications of relatively low federal funding levels. In late 2000, for example, the organisation lost its Chief Executive Officer, John Thresher. On resigning, Thresher argued in the *Toronto Sun* that 'We're still seeing (national) junior and youth teams funding their own way to competitions in order to compete for Canada ... I would have liked to have changed that' (quoted in Buffery 2000). As mentioned above, AC has had to contend with financial difficulties over the past decade, and thus also the organisational uncertainty that arises from such difficulties. Indeed, the consultant who, in 2001, led a wide-ranging audit of AC maintained that 'AC lost its way through the 1990s' (quoted in Christie 2001a). Given such internal organisational uncertainty, variability of federal funding and the recent federal policy focus on levels below high performance sport, it is perhaps unsurprising that AC has not been able to lever extra monies to support its elite level athletes. In sum, unlike SNC, which has concentrated resources to support elite swimmers, AC has been more equivocal and restricted funding to the modest Elite Athlete Assistance programme (AC 2002c).

Developments in coaching, sports science and sports medicine

In the early 1980s Paish suggested that while Canada had 'a very sophisticated coaching scheme', many of the sport's 'senior records were set in 1976 or earlier' (1983: 14). The implication of this assessment was that, despite the sophistication of the coaching scheme, there had been a failure to deliver continued excellence at the elite level. Here, Paish argued 'It could be that for a while you [Canadian track and field] might have to take your better and highly motivated coaches away from the elite structure to process a grass roots programme. Such an investment ... would be worthwhile' (1983: 15). However, as a Sport Canada official revealed, 'in the mid-1970s the CTFA had [just] four full-time coaches as part of the lead-up to the [Olympic] Games in Montreal'. This official went on to add that since then there have been relatively few full-time coaches employed by Athletics Canada (Personal communication: 4 July 2002). Moreover, those coaches who are currently employed on a full-time basis are part of a cost-sharing agreement, primarily with CSCs and universities (Interviewee O, 19 June 2002). It appears, then, that despite the increasing professionalisation of much of the Canadian amateur sport infrastructure throughout the 1970s and 1980s, the issue of employing full-time, professional coaches in track and field athletics has yet to be fully addressed. As AC's recently appointed Head Coach stated, 'I feel we have undervalued and under-utilised this most important resource [coaches and coaching] … We need to change the regard for coaching' (quoted in AC 2002c: 8). In the light of these comments, Paish's assessment appears to be a serious overstatement.

Despite current criticism of the coaching system, it is not without merit and has benefited from the development of the National Coaching Certification Programme (NCCP) in the 1970s and the recent emergence of a competency-based education and training (CBET) programme for Canadian coaches. Yet, questions remain regarding coaching structures for track and field athletics. Indeed, AC's 2002 Semi-Annual General Meeting report revealed that a questionnaire circulated to provincial branches in 2001 elicited somewhat equivocal responses to the question, 'Do you think there is a clearly defined structure to develop coaches in Canada?' Typical responses included one respondent, who argued that, 'Yes there is, but it has lost its focus. Too fragmented. Too cumbersome' and another, who suggested that the 'Structure of coaching development is not clear. It may be on paper but not in practice' (quoted in AC 2002c: 44).

The depth of criticism was confirmed by the content of a recent internal audit of AC.[2] Christie reported in *The Globe and Mail* that 'The critique and blueprint for the future contains some stinging passages about the under-performing body [AC]' (2001a). Crucially, Christie goes on to report that AC was heavily criticised for '"failing to deliver coaching education programmes, failing to compensate coaches adequately and failing to develop coaches through appointment to national teams"' (quoted in Christie 2001a). A senior AC official acknowledged this damning assessment of the organisation's approach to coaching but pointed to the appointment of Alex Gardiner as Head Coach/Chief Technical Officer in early 2002 as indicating a significant shift in AC's underlying organisational values. The appointment of Alex Gardiner as Head Coach in 2002 is significant because he is Canadian track and field's first full-time professional coach not destined to be rotated for every major track and field games. It is also significant, as the nature of change appears to centre on a belief that a more professional, rather than a volunteer, ethos should now prevail. As the senior AC official explained, in the past, the position of coach (for major games) 'was almost like a reward for someone who's put in his (sic) time. It was a volunteer position and there'd be no stability or consistency between team to team because it would be a different coach every time' (Interviewee R, 13 June 2002). This official acknowledged how extensive the organisational ethos of voluntarism had been, as it was volunteer members who attended major events such as the Olympic Games and World

Championships, 'to the point where, if [professional] staff attended a major Games, that was almost taboo'. The AC official also pointed out that the recent internal audit had been a key catalyst for bringing about significant policy change in this respect, while also stating that 'we've changed all that around to say that the organisation will be driven by the professional, full-time, paid staff. But the volunteers are still very important' (Interviewee R, 13 June 2002).

Developments in the allied disciplines of sports science/medicine in track and field took place within the same broad context as swimming. Of especial note is the role of the federal government in the early 1970s in legitimising sports science/ medicine research that centred directly on elite athlete performance (cf. Macintosh and Whitson 1990). As discussed, this research was conducted as part of a wider reconstruction of the physical education system in Canada, which focused on the systematic and scientific production of athletic performance, and was legitimated by a conjuncture of interests between the federal government, NSOs and university physical education departments in the 1980s. That this was a federally-inspired policy direction premised on producing medal-winning outcomes at major sporting events is clear from the 1988 *Task Force on National Sport Policy*. One of the Task Force's recommendations was the urgent need 'To enhance the legitimacy and funding of the essential professions (coaching, sport science, sport administration, sport medicine, etc.) required to develop and sustain an effective high performance system' (Canada 1988: 36). Confidence in, and commitment to, sports science investment was, however, badly dented by the Ben Johnson scandal in 1988. The motives of Johnson's CTFA coach, Charlie Francis, were clearly revealed at the subsequent Inquiry. Francis stated that 'If you want to win ... then you must take anabolic steroids' (quoted in Boudreau and Konzak 1991: 90). In sum, it is clear that developments in sports science/medicine have been problematic for Canadian track and field leaders. Today, AC utilises the CSC network of support services for these disciplines, has developed its own internal sports science programme (AC 2001a) and has established an '"Ad hoc" medical committee' as part of its national team development programme (AC 2002c: 12). Overall, however, the investment is modest and the commitment by coaches and administrators equivocal.

Competition opportunities for elite level athletes

As illustrated in the sport of swimming, competition opportunities are an element of elite sport development in Canada that require discussion of levels below the high performance end of sport. The first point of note is that competition structures in Canadian track and field are many and varied and crosscut many different levels (cf. AC 2001a, 2002c). This observation highlights the jurisdictional problems faced by all sports in Canada as they struggle to provide a coherent and co-ordinated framework for competition and training which has to transcend not only the municipal/provincial/territorial/national divisions and responsibilities, but also the related divisions between developmental and elite level performers. A senior Sport Canada official summarised the complexity involved in providing an integrated framework for competition in stating that 'the dichotomy is not only between the provincial associations as a whole and the national federations [NSOs] but also between each individual provincial association and their national federation and each other' (Interviewee S, 20 June 2002).

The second point recalls the low levels of domestic competition in Canada. As the Director of Sport Canada argued in the report of the 1976 Post-Olympic Games Symposium, 'In most sports it is not up to international standards and that is a definite liability in our sport system' (quoted in CAC 1977: 13). Suitable competition levels remains an issue for those involved in Canadian high performance sport. As the editor of Cansport – a web-based service providing information and commentary on Canada's elite amateur athletes – argues, 'Is it any wonder many Canadian athletes struggle at the Olympics … because there's no money to send them abroad to compete regularly against the best in the world?' (Scammell 2000b).

The third point is that of Canadian athletes migrating to the United States, encouraged by offers of financially attractive sporting scholarships, where they are then expected to give priority to NCAA competitions. The tension in competition obligations is worsened by the fact that, apart from a small number of mandatory events, such as the Canadian national championships, AC does not have a comprehensive (mandatory) competition calendar for its elite athletes. Indeed, the AC official maintained that the 'competitive schedule is driven by the athlete and their coach, who takes a look at the calendar and determines where they'll go' (Interviewee R, 13 June 2002). It appears, therefore, that AC has relatively little influence over where, when and how often an athlete competes. Certainly, at the elite level, athletes are increasingly drawn to the IAAF Golden League and Grand Prix Circuit events, where the large prize money on offer is an attractive incentive to opt out of the Canadian developmental competition circuit. A Canadian sports analyst reflected these concerns, in arguing that a competitive framework 'exists but it's not very good … people have to go outside the country to get really good competition on a regular basis' (Interviewee O, 19 June 2002). Concerns regarding an increasingly wealthy, but relatively small group of elite athletes assuming control of where, when, and how often they compete, are not unique to Canada, as the discussion of UK Athletics in Chapter 6 reveals.

A fourth point concerns those athletes just below the elite level, known as *espoirs* (hopefuls) in Canada. Many contributors to this research, across all three sports, highlighted the 'gap' between elite and sub-elite athletes as, arguably, *the* key issue in attempts to provide a coherent pathway from developmental to elite level in Canadian sport. Indeed, a senior AC official admitted that 'the national office … hasn't strategically planned how to provide competitive opportunities for athletes who haven't been invited to a Grand Prix event' (Interviewee R, 13 June 2002). This official went on to add that this issue formed part of the organisation's recent internal audit and that AC has acknowledged the requirement for 'greater initiative and leadership in providing a competitive circuit for our athletes who aren't at that very, very high level'.

Recent comments from those involved with AC suggest that competition structures and opportunities remain problematic. It is perhaps not surprising, given the recent organisational and administrative upheaval within the organisation, that the issue of a coherent and balanced competition structure has been pushed down the policy agenda. As mentioned above, a key catalyst for change was the 2001 audit of AC. Indeed, AC's 2002 Semi-Annual General Meeting (SAGM) discussed the audit's recommendations and in the SAGM report, AC's National Team Manager 'recommended that AC must regain some degree of control over its flagship, the National Senior Championship' (quoted in AC 2002c: 52). On the one hand, such policy pronouncements in 2002 might be viewed as evidence of strong leadership from AC as it emerges from a period where, at best, there has been a policy void, at least in the view of AC's harshest critics. On the other hand, such pronouncements highlight the lack of policy direction, over the past decade at least. In the late 1980s, Kidd argued that 'The state [federal government] has transformed the once autonomous, voluntary, and largely regulatory sports-governing bodies into professionally administered non-profit corporations which conduct ambitious national and provincial training and developmental programmes under strict governmental direction' (1988a: 295). The evidence provided here suggests that track and field's leadership has struggled to develop the type of policy coherence required to fully embrace federal efforts to construct such programmes.

Summary

With regard to elite level facility development, as with all Canadian NSOs, AC has little policy involvement or influence. Facility development falls within the jurisdiction of provincial/territorial governments and their respective P/TSOs, and/or local municipalities and is often shaped by successful bids to host major events. However, as discussed, financial resources, and thus the level of facility provision at these sub-national levels, remain variable. Even in Ontario, one of the larger and more prosperous provinces, provincial government grants are variable and the Ontario Track and Field Association (OTFA), stated that 'Facilities in this province need to be improved' (OTFA 2002). AC is involved, however, at least on a collaborative level, in facility development with provinces/territories and local communities that put together bids to host major international sporting events, such as the 2001 World Athletics Championships in Edmonton. In short, AC's primary policy interest/involvement in facilities for elite level track and field is in leveraging partnership agreements in areas such as coaching and sports science/medicine within the emerging network of CSCs (Interviewee R, 13 June 2002).

In respect of the emergence of full-time athletes, it is clear that opportunities for Canadian track and field athletes to compete and train on a full-time basis are limited. For example, the small group of elite athletes in receipt of Sport Canada's AAP monies receive just $CAN1,100 (under £500) per month. As a senior Sport Canada official admitted, athletes at the elite level remain, in large part, reliant on parental support in order to train and compete to the standards required for international events (Interviewee P, 12 June 2002). This is a weakness in elite athlete development compounded by AC's financial difficulties over a number of years. Thus, the ability to provide financial support programmes such as those provided by SNC for elite swimmers has been, and remains, severely constrained. A further difficulty here, for track and field athletes, is the relatively poor public and media perception of the sport in Canada, coupled with the lack of significant medal-winning performances at major events (see Table 5.2) which results in difficulties in attracting corporate sponsorship to supplement federal government funding.

With regard to developments in coaching, the wider policy/organisational framework within which AC operates reveals a gradual evolution of programmes in these disciplines from the 1970s onwards. From the evidence provided, however, it is clear that AC's organisational and administrative capacity has been found wanting, most notably in coaching development. In respect of developments in sports science/medicine, it was noted earlier that support structures are in place for these disciplines within Canadian universities and the network of CSCs and that AC has developed structures to support these disciplines, such as its sports science programme and the creation of a medical committee. Yet, questions remain as to the efficacy of these structures for developing high performance athletes. For example, Mark Lowry of the then Canadian Olympic Association (now COC) indicated that there was still much to do to embed sports science/medicine within elite development strategy. Lowry suggested that one of the COA's five core strategies would be to 'establish support programmes for athletes and coaches, which include opportunities for personal training needs, e.g. access to sport science and medicine services' (2001). Moreover, as part of a recommendation to create a Canadian High Performance Sport Council, Lowry stated that a key priority is to establish 'a strategy for the integration and utilisation of sport science research, and medical best practices to benefit Canadian athletes'.

The fourth and final area of high performance sport development considered was that of competition structures and opportunities, and a series of interlocking issues were identified as constraining AC's capacity to provide and control such opportunities. These issues included: (i) the complexity of national/provincial/ territorial jurisdictional divisions; (ii) the lack of funding for athletes to travel abroad for international competition; (iii) the lack of domestic competitive

Table 5.2 Canadian athletics medals: Olympic Games/World Athletics Championships, 1988–2001

	Olympic Games					World Athletics Championships			
	Gold	Silver	Bronze	Total		Gold	Silver	Bronze	Total
1988	0	0	1	1	1995	2	1	1	4
1992	1	1	1	3	1997	1	1	0	2
1996	2	0	0	2	1999	0	1	0	1
2000	0	0	0	0	2001	0	0	0	0

opportunities for sub-elite athletes; (iv) the migration of talented young athletes to the United States; and (v) the preference of elite athletes to compete abroad for prize money, thus weakening the domestic track and field competition calendar. Whether AC's recently stated objective of providing 'a coordinated national domestic competition strategy' (AC 2002c: 10) for 2002–3 is attainable given the range and complexity of issues outlined here remains to be seen.

This discussion has clearly revealed the Canadian NSO for track and field athletics as, at best, lacking strategic policy direction and, at worst, as an organisation in some disarray. As AC's chair, Jean-Guy Ouellette, admitted, 'Many of AC's difficulties in recent years stem directly from a void in leadership' (quoted in AC 2001b) – a curious statement from one of AC's leading officials who has been in post for over 14 years. Ouellette also commented that 'The attractive thing is that the whole athletics community [is] behind us' (quoted in AC 2001b) in the organisation's attempts to rebuild the sport's credibility following recommendations from the independent audit in 2001. Despite this optimistic tone, antagonism towards AC's leadership, prior to the 2001 audit, should not be underestimated. In a report in the *Toronto Sun*, for example, Earl Farrell, chair of the Ontario Track and Field Association, suggested that 'provincial organisations are unhappy with the work of the AC board over several issues [and that] The branch presidents are not happy with the way business is being conducted or the way the sport is being run' (quoted in Buffery 2000).

In summary, AC has clearly not articulated a clear set of objectives to the extent achieved by SNC for Canadian swimming. AC appears to be more reluctant to state overtly that its organisational objectives are, in large part, committed to high performance sport. As one senior AC official explained:

> Our mission statement was always [about] delivering the elite and the high performance, but [also] providing leadership for grass roots and [as we've discussed] it's confusing ... long term, our strategic plan is going to outline that. I still see us providing leadership in grass roots, which will be a package that is consistent throughout Canada with all our provincial bodies.
>
> (Interviewee R, 13 June 2002)

One reading of these comments is that the organisation is merely reflecting the somewhat conflicting policy directions of its primary funding partners, Sport Canada and the COC for, at the same time as the federal government was realigning policy direction for sport, the COC adopted a diametrically opposed policy position to support only those organisations that had achieved, or had the potential to achieve, medal-winning performance at major games. In line with this reading, then, it is reasonable to suggest that AC is undergoing a period of policy consolidation and that, organisationally and administratively, a longer time period is required before a coherent statement of its core objectives, can be articulated. However, the production of a national programme that satisfies the elite and grass roots, balances the priorities of Sport Canada and the COC, embraces all levels of the sport's jurisdictional divisions, and meets the demands of all four disciplines within AC's remit, is a daunting task.

As regards changes in values/beliefs, Cunningham *et al.* provided an analysis in the late 1980s, which revealed not only the extent of structural change that NSOs were experiencing, but also the extent of change in dominant values/belief systems. Referring to Canadian sport in general, they argued that:

> change in voluntary sport organisations has involved a shift from organisations characterised by a balanced recreational/high performance focus, informal operating principles, and values that emphasised voluntarism, self-management, and participation, to organisations that now exhibit high levels of structure and values that embrace professionalism, bureaucratic rationality, and elite performance.
>
> (Cunningham *et al.* 1987: 69–70)

The key point to note here, however, is that AC does not appear to have undergone the degree of change evident in other sports and highlighted by Cunningham *et al.* This is not to argue that AC has remained an archetypal 'kitchen-table' organisation (cf. Slack *et al.* 1994). Clearly, bureaucracy, professionalism and an elite focus has formed part of the organisation's evolution over the past 10 to 15 years. It remains far from clear, however, quite how AC might be categorised today, given the noted organisational and administrative critique contained within the 2001 audit and the organisation's somewhat ambiguous policy statements in recent Annual and Semi-Annual General Meeting reports. As regards priority development groups, these reports appear to suggest that, in the near future, AC will direct policy initiatives and support along the entire spectrum of mass/elite sport requirements. However, the uncertainty within the organisation is reflected by one senior AC official's statement that 'To be everything to everyone on a limited budget isn't possible' (Interviewee R, 13 June 2002). This statement was made at the same time as AC's Chief Operating Officer was declaring that athletics' future goal is 'to go from good to great' (quoted in AC 2002c: 2).

Canadian Yachting Association

Organisation, administration and relationships

The Canadian Yachting Association (CYA) has responsibility for the aquatic-based disciplines of sailing/yachting, cruising and windsurfing and has more limited involvement in powerboating. The focus here is on policy developments for elite level sailing/yachting and, more specifically, on four 'policy-related' areas of the CYA's development of its high performance sailors in the 11 Olympic yacht Classes (the term 'Class' denotes a specific type of yacht). The CYA is involved in a matrix of relationships with numerous other bodies including the Canadian Coast Guard concerning safety-at-sea issues, industry bodies regarding yacht design, sailing schools on educational/instructional matters and, on coaching developments, with the two main coaching bodies in Canada – the Coaching Association of Canada (CAC) and the Canadian Professional Coaches Association.

An independent national single-sport body for yachting was established in 1931 and, in 1957, the organisation adopted its present title – the Canadian Yachting Association. In respect of high performance sailing, Howell and Howell (1985: 407) noted that, on the one hand, the 'high standard of Canadian yachting' was demonstrated at the 1932 Olympic Games where the Canadian sailing team won one Silver and one Bronze medal. On the other hand, the same authors also noted that 'Despite these successes participation in yachting has been waning since that time, primarily because of its reputation as a recreation for the wealthy and expansion of opportunities in other countries'. The decline in participation continued despite attempts in the 1980s to broaden the base of the sport by the establishment of less expensive and more accessible clubs, and a general promotion of sailing across different levels of society.

In their analysis of sailing, Howell and Howell (1985) identified two key challenges facing the sport, the first of which was the perception of the sport as elitist – a perception that has proved difficult to change. In April 2001, for example, the CYA convened what was termed a Strategic Pursuits Planning Workshop, one aspect of which was a discussion regarding the nature/type of language used to portray the sport. The discussion centred on the advantages/disadvantages of using the terms, 'sailing', 'boating' and yachting': the last being perceived as both 'elitist' and 'snobby' (CYA 2001: 15). The second issue identified by Howell and Howell was the expansion and development of the sport in other countries. Almost 20 years after their research, the CYA identified a number of 'future forces' that might have an impact on the sport, one of which was the steady rise in the standard of international competitive sailing. At the 2001 Workshop, the CYA stated that, in today's 'competitive global scene, it's the natural progression of trying to be the best which has seen many countries move to develop highly structured systems around their athletes to give them the best chance to perform on a global scale' (CYA 2001: 13).

Interestingly, elsewhere the CYA cite the UK as one of the world's leading countries at the elite level and, following the UK sailing team's performance at the 2000 Olympic Games, the CYA acknowledged that the UK are currently 'the envy of every sailing nation' (CYA 2002c: 1). Particular mention was made of the UK's 'extensive talent identification and youth development programme' (2002c: 1), a point reiterated by a senior CYA official, who suggested that, 'In the UK, it's a question of having worked … to make it work and the people in charge have had the patience to let it develop' (Interviewee T, 17 June 2002). Here, we may be witnessing a form of policy learning/transfer as the CYA look abroad at different sailor development systems as a way of improving recent international performances – see Table 5.3.

The past four Olympiads have been selected, following a similar format to that used for swimming and track and field athletics, but World Championship medal counts in sailing have not been included in Table 5.3 given the large number of world events in the sport. However, in the different (approximately 60) Classes that stage World Championships, Canada has won just three Gold, three Silver

Table 5.3 Canadian sailing medals: Olympic Games, 1988–2000

Olympic Games	Gold	Silver	Bronze	Total
1988	0	0	1	1
1992	0	0	1	1
1996	0	0	0	0
2000	0	0	0	0

and eight Bronze medals since 1988 (Personal communication: CYA, 22 August 2002).

Today, the CYA has some 400 affiliated member clubs, comprising approximately 80,000 members. Moreover, there are an additional 70,000 non-members who regularly participate in some aspect of aquatic sport on an informal basis (Personal communication: CYA, 26 November 2002). One of the CYA's key organisational objectives for 2002 was to increase awareness of, and participation in, aquatic sports (CYA 2001), thus contributing to the 'Participation pillar' within the new Canadian Sport Policy (Canadian Heritage 2002). At a Planning Conference in November 2002 a series of organisational objectives were presented under the heading 'Planning for the Future'. One of these objectives was closely aligned to the Canadian Sport Policy goal to achieve, by 2012, 'A significantly higher proportion of Canadians from all segments of society … involved in quality sport activities at all levels and in all forms of participation' (Canadian Heritage 2002). The CYA's own objective regarding participation is expressed in similar terms: 'To have a significant portion of Canadians take part in sailing and boating activities (Enhanced Participation)' (Personal communication: CYA, 26 November 2002). Indeed, all four CYA revised objectives mirror the Canadian Sport Policy's four pillars of Enhanced Participation, Enhanced Excellence, Enhanced Capacity and Enhanced Interaction (Canadian Heritage 2002). Thus, on the issue of high performance sport, the CYA's revised objective for excellence is 'To win medals and have athletes consistently achieving top 10 results internationally' (Personal communication: CYA, 26 November 2002). On 'Enhanced Excellence', the Canadian Sport Policy's objective is that, by 2012, 'The pool of Canadian athletic talent has expanded and Canadian athletes and teams are systematically achieving world-class results at the highest levels of international competition through fair and ethical means' (Canadian Heritage 2002).

Two important points are raised here. First, it is clear that federal government rhetoric is currently concerned with enlarging 'the pool of Canadian athletic talent' i.e. expanding participation at levels below the elite as a strategy for identifying and developing athletes capable of achieving 'world-class results'. The second point centres on the complementarity between the CYA's current organisational objectives that have emerged over the past three to four years with those of the federal government (cf. CYA 2001). It is clear, therefore, that CYA objectives are not just premised upon high performance objectives. As one senior CYA official explained, 'We need more depth in order to have consistently good athletes coming out at the top' (Interviewee T, 17 June 2002). The requirement for a well-developed grass roots base as a prerequisite for high performance success in sailing can be distinguished from recent policy developments in swimming and athletics. SNC has recently re-emphasised an unequivocal, 'COMM1T TO W1N!' philosophy (SNC 2002a: 4), while AC has yet to present a coherent set of organisational objectives following a period of policy transition. This is not to argue that SNC and AC do not (or have not) realise(d) the importance of constructing a framework that reaches beyond support for high performance levels. Rather, it is to suggest that the CYA has embraced the political – that is, federal policy – realities in a way that is qualitatively different from that displayed by the NSOs responsible for swimming and track and field athletics. As a senior CYA official explained:

> because of the [recent federal] sports policy and the way, politically, things are swinging now it makes it easier to take that approach [develop grass roots levels] than it has been before. It may make a lot of sense to you and me, that that's a logical way of doing it but if it also fits with how we're going to be evaluated for money, then, unfortunately, that's just the way it is. Money is an important part of it.
>
> (Interviewee T, 17 June 2002)

Interestingly, this official also acknowledged that, to date, there had been no firm indication that extra federal funding would be allocated to NSOs in order to meet federal participation objectives. However, the CYA appears to have realised that it is currently prudent to embrace federal-Sport Canada policy priorities rather than to attempt to obtain funding from its other (potentially) significant financial supporter, the COC. As discussed, the COC has stated that its funding priorities have sharpened such that monies will now be allocated to those NSOs/sports that have consistently won medals at major international Games, or at least show potential to do so. As illustrated in Table 5.3, the Canadian sailing team does not currently fall within either of these categories.

In sum, as with SNC/swimming and AC/athletics, the CYA has recently experienced a period of policy (re)-evaluation but which, unlike SNC and AC, has led to policy direction that closely mirrors the 2002 Canadian Sport Policy objectives in all four of its key pillars. Thus, while the CYA's Strategic Pursuits Planning Workshop in 2001 identified five key 'pursuits' (objectives) for the future, of which 'Pursuit 1' was to 'win medals' and 'achieve consistent top 10 results internationally' (CYA 2001: 1), the Association also recognised the need to develop a broad base for the sport, through club and provincial levels, in order to provide a strong foundation for its national sailing team. Key to attaining this objective is effective partnerships with provincial sailing associations. In the past, however, as for many sports in Canada's complex sport delivery system, effective partnership agreements between NSOs and P/TSOs have often proved problematic. A senior Sport Canada official was adamant that such jurisdictional complexities have 'caused all kinds of problems ... [The] provinces have their own priorities and ... [sport] doesn't necessarily rank as a very high priority' (Interviewee U, 20 June 2002). However, despite past difficulties, senior officials at the CYA and Sport Canada remain optimistic that a more positive policy relationship is emerging, and the Sport Canada official in particular argued that 'all the provinces are signed on to the new [Canadian Sport Policy] objectives. That's a first big step' (Interviewee U, 20 June 2002). However, as the same official cautioned, the recent federal/CYA/provincial co-operation has not yet 'translated into any ... specific outcomes in terms of funding decisions. We haven't solved that problem. That's still ongoing'.

Four areas of elite sport policy

Development of elite level facilities

That facility development for sailing is a concern for provincial/territorial and/or municipal level authorities is clear from a review of recent CYA Action and Operations Plans. There is no reference in these (national) plans to sailing facilities at any level (cf. CYA 1997, 2002d). Thus, facility provision for competitive and recreational sailing in Canada remains largely within publicly-funded bodies at provincial/territorial/municipal levels and especially within privately owned yacht clubs. Two examples illustrate the particular dependence of the CYA on sailing facilities available at private club level. First, in May 2002, the Toronto Sailing and Canoe Club – affiliated to the Ontario Sailing Association (the provincial authority for sailing in Ontario) – staged the Canadian Olympic Classes Queensway Audi Icebreaker Regatta, a major sailing event for Olympic Class yachts (Ontario Sailing Association 2002). Second, the Humber Sailing and Powerboat Centre, situated on Lake Ontario, and a member sailing/training school of the CYA, has recently updated one of Canada's largest sailing and boating facilities for training and education purposes (Humber Sailing and Powerboat Centre 2002). Thus, while the CYA has no direct policy input into the development and use of such club/provincial facility provision, it does benefit indirectly through its management of the national sailing programme, which includes youth level sailors who sail at such venues across the country.

Where the CYA does have more of a direct relationship with facility-related issues is with the emerging network of facilities and support services provided by the publicly-funded Canadian Sport Centres (CSCs) – a significant resource in the development of elite sailors. As discussed, these centres operate on a cost-sharing basis that involves, in the case of the CYA and sailing, federal and provincial governments, the CYA, the CSC and the sailing clubs involved in a particular area. Currently, the CYA utilises support services at three CSCs close to water, in Halifax, Toronto and Vancouver. However, an important difference in the sport of sailing, in comparison to swimming and track and field athletics is the requirement for equipment over and above the need for facilities *per se*. Consequently, it is important that the CYA ensures that the CSCs it works with are able to provide equipment vital to the support of elite level sailing development.

Namely, 'a coach full time, equip[ped] with a car, with a radio, with a computer and with a boat' (Interviewee T, 17 June 2002). Thus, a package of facilities/ equipment underpins elite sailors' development which, overall, necessitates additional monies to those required for high performance programming in swimming and track and field.

This package of facilities/equipment afforded by the CSCs is not, however, only centred on sailors currently considered to be at the high performance level. As discussed, the CYA has set out its organisational strategy in line with the 2002 Canadian Sport Policy. As such, developmental levels below the elite remain an important concern, not least because, historically, such development has taken place within club and provincial level facilities. However, club/provincial develop-ment has been severely curtailed in recent years due to the lack of funding available from municipal/provincial authorities. As one senior CYA official explained, 'the provincial associations have not been able to take care of their level and it has, in a way, forced the national body, like us, to try to cover' (Interviewee T, 17 June 2002). It appears, therefore, that the CYA is in a similar position to all major Canadian NSOs with regard to facility development, where the NSO is subject to unstable policy priorities at the provincial level, and thus uncertain funding allocations, with the consequence that facility development is reliant on private yacht clubs plus the growing network of CSCs.

These observations raise some important issues from a theoretical standpoint. Drawing on insights from the advocacy coalition framework literature, the CYA's relationship with the network of CSCs is clearly at an early stage, at least when compared to the degree of commitment to the network from actors at the high performance levels of Canadian swimming, for example. However, the CYA rationale for linking with the CSCs differs from swimming. SNC clearly views the seven dedicated swimming centres aligned to the CSC network largely in terms of its elite development objectives. In contrast, CYA policy mirrors the broader objectives of the 2002 Canadian Sport Policy with the consequence that the CSC concept is conceived of as one element in the overall development of Canadian sailing and not purely as a mechanism for the development of its elite sailors. This argument suggests that, while SNC might be conceived of as part of an advocacy coalition with values and beliefs centring on high performance sport, the CYA is much more equivocal regarding *high performance* sailing.

Emergence of 'full-time' sailors

By way of commenting on the nature of financial support for Canada's elite amateur athletes, in general, Scammell (2000a) gives the example of sailor, Richard Clarke, a Gold medal winner at the 1999 Pan-American Games, a Bronze medallist at the Melbourne 1999 Finn Class World Championships and considered to be a serious medal prospect in the Finn Class for the Sydney 2000 Olympic Games. Scammell argued that, 'Except for the privileged few with major corporate sponsors, bringing home the Gold has nothing to do with money. It's all about pride, commitment and the dream of winning an Olympic medal' (2000a). Richard

Clarke finished seventeenth at the Sydney Olympics and, on announcing his retirement form the sport, estimated that it had personally cost $CAN500,000 to remain sailing at the elite level over the four years leading up to the 2000 Games (Cansport 2000).

Although many Canadian commentators have called for increased federal level financial support for Canada's high performance amateur athletes, Clarke argued that 'I'd like to see some of corporate Canada rally behind the Olympic team [rather] than the government pick up the tab' (quoted in Cansport 2000). While a senior Sport Canada official agreed with this view, this observer cautioned that it was still unclear as to the extent to which the various government levels will be 'successful … in getting corporate Canada more involved' (Interviewee U, 20 June 2002). However, the CYA appears to have been relatively successful in this area. For the year 1997–8, for example, the CYA had the objective of maintaining $CAN88,500 (approx. £37,000) in sponsorship funding, with the figure of $CAN67,500 (approx. £28,000) being the target for new corporate sponsorship during this period (CYA 1997). These objectives were achieved and, by 2000, the CYA had set a sponsorship goal of $CAN240,000 (approx. £150,000) (CYA 2000). Three points are worthy of note here: first, unlike may NSOs, such as AC, the CYA has demonstrated an ability to raise sponsorship money in difficult economic times; second, these sponsorship sums are relatively insignificant if we consider Richard Clarke's estimate of his costs; and third, the chronic lack of federal funding to support Canadian NSOs.

While the CYA had 45 sailors (for 2002–3) in receipt of AAP support, the previous discussions of swimming and track and field athletics revealed that AAP grants are an important but insufficient support mechanism for elite athletes to train and compete on a full-time basis. Thus, much of the responsibility for funding the support systems for elite sailing development in Canada rests on individual sailors and/or parents. Moreover, the inadequacy of financial support in sailing is compounded by the sport's requirement for expensive equipment. As a senior CYA official explained, 'the equipment we use, and the transportation of the equipment, has become very expensive … we are able to cover only a portion of the operating costs, we're not even touching the equipment costs … We don't have full-time sailors at the moment' (Interviewee T, 17 June 2002).

Developments in coaching, sports science and sports medicine

In the period following the enactment of Bill C-131, *An Act to Encourage Fitness and Amateur Sport* in 1961, Morrow *et al.* (1989: 330) note that 'Funding was used for conferences and seminars held for coaches and administrators, and for graduate studies undertaken by many physical-education scientists; [and] research laboratories were established at several universities to study both sport and fitness'. However, while coaching has been a feature of sailing for some time it has been neither systematic nor especially well funded. For example, at the 2001 Strategic Pursuits Planning Workshop, CYA members argued that, 'to keep our sport strong for the next 20 years [the CYA should] invest in coaches' (quoted in CYA

2001: 14). More significantly, it is only recently that the CYA has identified a requirement for full-time national coaches. As one senior Sport Canada official explained, with regard to changing attitudes to coaching development, 'I'd say it started a few years before Sydney and even then a lot of the leadership in sailing weren't really convinced' (Interviewee U, 20 June 2002). This official also high-lighted the makeshift approach to coaching before the 2000 Olympics, as well as signalling aspects of policy learning/transfer:

> In Sydney, it sort of hit them ... and made them say, look at all the successful countries; they all have full-time coaches ... the CYA didn't have a full-time coach. A few of the rich clubs across the country had full-time coaches but otherwise they said [to sailors] go develop your own campaign ... It was pretty ad hoc.
>
> (Interviewee U, 20 June 2002)

The CYA now employs five full-time coaches and a High Performance Director for sailing who is responsible for the overall national programme (Interviewee T, 17 June 2002). In addition, the ongoing development of the CBET programme for Canadian coaches has been embraced by the CYA. This programme has three core elements: 'Community Sport', 'Competition' and 'Instruction' (CYA 2002b: 1). However, as Sharon Seymour reported, the CAC 'will focus on the community and racing [elements] first [but has] encouraged [the] CYA to put a priority on developing the Racing Coach stream of the CBET' (quoted in CYA 2002b: 2). Importantly, Seymour also explained that the CYA is required to present an application for funding to the CAC. Such an arrangement illustrates the lack of policy autonomy enjoyed by the CYA and, while not stated explicitly, it is reasonable to assume that the CYA will follow CAC policy direction and focus resources on the Racing Coach stream of the CBET. Arguably, these observations suggest an emerging policy priority on coaching development at the high performance end of the sport that is somewhat at odds with the CYA's rhetoric of support for more broad-based policy initiatives.

As regards developments in sports science/medicine, it is clear that these disciplines have not been fully utilised by the CYA. Indeed, the organisation's Strategic Pursuits Planning Workshop in 2001 revealed that attitudes to sports science are mixed and indicated a deep scepticism towards the benefits of sports science. Two key questions were posed at the Workshop: (i) 'To keep our sport strong for the next 20 years, what should the CYA *start* doing?' and (ii) 'To keep our sport strong for the next 20 years, what should the CYA *stop* doing?' (CYA 2001: 14–15). One answer to the first question was that all those involved with the sport should 'start believing the sport science system applies to sailing' (quoted in CYA 2001: 14). The following comment is indicative of replies to the second question, 'stop thinking that somehow the sports science stuff doesn't really make a difference, and that it's just "fluff". It's real, it works, it's what the other sailing countries are applying that are beating us at the youth and Olympic level' (quoted in CYA 2001: 15).

A senior Sport Canada official used these comments to illustrate that the CYA had not developed 'the type of physical preparation that athletes require. Beyond the CYA hiring, for a couple of weeks, a world expert and have the sailors work with this person ... That would be it' (Interviewee U, 20 June 2002). However, CYA Action and Operations Plans since 1997 have demonstrated a much greater commitment to the use of sports science, with the 2002 Operations Plan containing objectives 'To develop and implement a sport science based training and competitive programme for all high performance programmes (Olympic, Paralympic, Youth) by September 2004 [and to] Utilise Sport Science projects to develop skills' (CYA 2002d: 2–3). In order to fulfil these objectives, the CYA proposed further strengthening of relationships with the CSCs and 'other partners to improve holistic services (such as fitness programmes/fitness testing/mental training ...) provided to athletes' (CYA 2002d: 2).

It is clear that the CYA now appreciates, and has set policy objectives related to sports science/medicine. Importantly, these policy objectives appear to encompass not only the high performance end of the sport but all levels of Canadian sailing. The most likely explanation for the recent embrace of sports science is a process of policy learning/transfer from abroad, already suggested by the Sport Canada official's (Interviewee U) earlier comments and endorsed in a paper entitled *Long Term Athlete Development* in which the CYA acknowledged the success of the RYA's elite sailors, and asked 'What do they [GB/NI sailing team] follow?' The reply is instructive, 'Very simply, a programme designed around a Sport Science based approach to preparation. This includes an extensive talent identification and youth development programme' (CYA 2002c: 1). The CYA recognised that it 'can not copy all aspects' of the UK programme but it can, however, 'devise and deliver the same Sport Science Based approach to training and competition' (2002c: 1).

In sum, today, the CYA is fully embracing ongoing changes to coach education and training and has discussed adopting a more positive approach to sports science/medicine. Yet, while the organisational commitment underlying such policy direction should not be discounted, implementation might prove rather more difficult to achieve. The key concern is how such policies might be funded. As the CYA acknowledged in its 2002 Operations Plan, 'For all CST [Canadian Sailing Team] *Espoir* and Youth programmes, there is a considerable financial burden on the individual athlete, as [the] CYA is only able to provide partial support for operating costs and no support towards equipment costs' (CYA 2002d: 11).

Competition opportunities for elite level sailors

The CYA has a remit to provide 'nationally designated competitions to optimise competitive opportunities for Canadian sailors' (CYA 1997: 3). The range of designated competitions is long and includes Canadian Youths, Eastern/Western Intermediates, 23 and under-West and the Canadian Games. Programme support for major international sailing regattas is also an important element of the CYA's remit. However, as discussed, until recently, the approach to training and competition for Canadian sailors has been, at best, ad hoc. As a senior Sport Canada official explained, in the past, 'it used to be, if you decide you want to go down to Brazil [for example], you go down to Brazil' (Interviewee U, 20 June, 2002). However, as this official also acknowledged, 'in the case of sailing, there has been a major shift in outlook in Canada, in terms of what it takes to prepare a national team athlete'.

It appears that the poor performance of the Canadian sailing team at the 2000 Olympic Games was a major contributory factor for change, but not the only factor. Indeed, senior officials at the CYA and Sport Canada explained that the new Canadian Sport Policy has also been a major source of change. The CYA has embraced the emerging priorities of federal sport policy in all areas of programming for the sport of sailing, stating that its organisational objectives 'are within the direction of the new Canadian Sport Policy (CSP). The Vision, Goals and Pursuits approved by the CYA fit well with the priorities defined as the four pillars embodied in the CSP' (CYA 2002e: 1). With regard to competition opportunities, one senior CYA official explained that a 'core North American-based programme' has been established that takes account of the current financial conditions within which the CYA operates (Interviewee T, 17 June 2002).

In relation to this, the 2001 Planning Workshop identified the following issues for consideration in the development of a more structured competition programme for sailing: (i) the 'Level of Government funding [has been] reduced both by direct reduction and inflation'; (ii) 'The level of funding for International Competition has dropped drastically'; and (iii) 'Many nations have increased funding to their team enormously' (CYA 2001: 12). The rationale for a more structured approach to the designation of sailing competitions, based primarily in North American waters is, therefore, in large part, premised on financial considerations. As one CYA official commented, 'we're saying we need to train our athletes and to stay within the cost ramifications' (Interviewee T, 17 June 2002).

Despite the CYA's positive outlook on the development of a more structured, cost efficient and locally-based competition and training programme, a cluster of enduring concerns have yet to be fully addressed, all of which are associated with Canada's jurisdictional complexities. First, P/TSOs have seen their budgets reduced in recent years; second, P/TSOs differ, not only with regard to the emphasis given to sailing, but also in respect of the emphasis given to high performance sailing; and thirdly, as education is a provincial jurisdiction, Sport Canada and the CYA have little influence on sailing development in Canadian schools. The lack of a structured talent identification and development system in Canada was also cited by a senior Sport Canada official as a major contributory factor underlying the difficulties faced by the CYA at national level (Interviewee U, 20 June 2002). In sum, although the CYA has created a new North American-based programme of training and competition opportunities, funding levels and jurisdictional divisions remain constant concerns.

Summary

The emerging network of CSCs is at the heart of the CYA's elite level facilities policy. Centres in Halifax, Toronto and Vancouver are now utilised through cost-sharing partnership agreements with sailing clubs in the area, provincial governments and sailing associations and, in some cases, the CAC. However, from a review of recent CYA Action and Operations Plans, it does not appear that the Association has any direct policy influence within the numerous public and private sailing clubs where many of its sailors train and compete. This element of high performance sport policy might benefit, then, from the CYA's paralleling of the Canadian Sport Policy objectives; most notably, in this case, the 'Interaction' pillar. In short, the CYA could benefit from increased policy involvement with such clubs regarding facility development and use. The second element of high performance sport policy considered was the emergence of full-time sailors. It is clear, however, that few, if any, Canadian sailors can be categorised as full-time, in the sense that they have the financial means to train and compete on a full-time basis. While 45 Canadian sailors were in receipt of AAP monies through Sport Canada's carding system for the period 2002–3, it is evident that self-funding remains the paramount method of financial assistance for Canadian high performance sailors and that AAP grants are a necessary but insufficient means of support.

With regard to developments in coaching and sports science/medicine, although the CYA has embraced the recent coaching initiative (CBET) (CYA 2002b), it is only recently that the need for full-time coaches at the elite level has been recognised by the CYA leadership. In addition, it is also evident that the CYA has only recently adopted what it terms, 'a Sport Science Based system' within which coaches are trained and prepared to develop sailors (CYA 2002c: 1). One senior Sport Canada official suggested that this change in policy direction was driven by the lack of medals at the 2000 Sydney Olympic Games and the CBET initiative, inspired and funded by Sport Canada/CAC (Interviewee U, 20 June 2002). A further source of change has also emerged, however: policy learning/transfer from abroad, and from the UK in particular. It is useful in this respect to recall Sabatier and Jenkins-Smith's (1999) argument that endogenous factors alone are not sufficient for major policy change; exogenous factors (outside the policy subsystem) are also necessary. Following the logic of the ACF, there are indications here of both exogenous and endogenous factors in explaining changes in CYA policy. For example, the ramifications of poor performances at the Sydney 2000 Olympic Games and the developments in coach training/education can be viewed as examples of the former, while policy learning, in respect of changing attitudes to sport science benefits for sailing, is an example of an important endogenous factor. However, two further (potential) exogenous factors can also be noted: (i) the financial cutbacks suffered by NSOs in recent years – an example of 'changes in socio-economic conditions'; and (ii) provincial/territorial jurisdictional control of education policy – an example of the significance of 'policy outputs from other subsystems' (Sabatier and Jenkins-Smith 1999: 149).

The fourth and final area of high performance sport policy discussed was the structure of competition opportunities. A recent development for the CYA has been the implementation of a more structured, cost-efficient and North American-based programme of competition opportunities. This is in contrast to the ad hoc approach to training and competition in the past, where individual sailors would make unilateral decisions regarding when and where to train and/or compete. Reflecting the potential salience of the two additional exogenous factors cited above, the ACF might also offer potentially fruitful insights here with regard to policy change. Clearly, the lack of federal government funding has led, at least in part, to a change in socio-economic conditions. In addition, a senior Sport Canada official referred to policy outputs from the educational policy domain at provincial level, i.e. policy outputs from other subsystems in relation to 'under-developed sailors' (Interviewee U, 20 June 2002). Here, the inference is that neither the CYA, nor Sport Canada is able to influence educational policy in schools such that sailing is given greater priority at developmental grass roots levels.

There are four issues worthy of further discussion in respect of similarities in policy responses from the three NSOs considered in this chapter. First, all three NSOs have recently experienced a period of policy re-evaluation and scrutiny, albeit to differing degrees and with different consequences. Second, all three NSOs suffer from severe under-funding resulting in a lack of policy autonomy. For the CYA, and for high performance sailing, this is clear from the Minutes of the Association's Executive Committee Meeting in January 2002, which recorded that, 'In order to be in a position for medal performances at the 2004 Olympic Games, the Canadian Sailing Team needs $CAN3.6 million in additional funding immediately' (CYA 2002a: 3). Thus, all three NSOs are vulnerable, to a greater or lesser extent, to shifts in policy direction and funding allocations from Sport Canada, the COC or both.

Third, all three NSOs operate within the fragmented and complex Canadian sport delivery system, most notably in arrangements with their counterparts at provincial/territorial level. Whether the CYA's paralleling of the 'Enhanced Interaction' objectives in the new Canadian Sport Policy will help to reduce such jurisdictional divisions, however, remains to be seen. Fourth, all three NSOs are part of the Canadian amateur sport system, as opposed to professional sports such as ice hockey, basketball and baseball and consequently experience problems in attracting spectators; in attracting young people into the sport at grass roots levels; and in their ability to obtain sponsorship funds from corporate Canada.

To sum up, while acknowledging such similarities amongst the three NSOs, it is also important to highlight two significant differences between the CYA compared to SNC and AC. First, the CYA, as an organisation, has been relatively free from the type of damning organisational critiques that have been levelled at the leadership of Canadian swimming and track and field athletics. From the available evidence in the form of policy-related documents and interviews with actors closely involved with the Association and Sport Canada, the CYA can be characterised as an organisation exhibiting a clarity of (policy) purpose not evident to the same extent in the sports of swimming or track and field athletics. Second, (unlike SNC and AC) the CYA has clearly defined a set of policy priorities closely linked to the four pillars of the 2002 Canadian Sport Policy.

6   United Kingdom

This chapter focuses on three UK national governing bodies (NGBs) of sport – the Amateur Swimming Association, UK Athletics and the Royal Yachting Association – and is organised around the same three principal themes as Chapters 4 and 5: the organisational and administrative structure within which swimming, athletics and sailing/yachting operate; a consideration of developments in four areas of elite sport policy; and finally a summary of the key implications for the broader analysis of policy change.

Amateur Swimming Association

Organisation, administration and relationships

The Amateur Swimming Association (ASA), formed in 1886, is the governing body for swimming disciplines in England, with Scottish and Welsh ASAs having responsibility for the sport in these two Home Countries. The enduringly problematic question of the role of the Amateur Swimming Federation of Great Britain (ASFGB) also requires consideration in any analysis of swimming in the UK. Historically, the ASFGB's primary function had been the selection of teams for international events where England, Scotland and Wales compete as Great Britain. From the founding of the ASA, the relationship between the ASFGB and the three Home Countries has been beset with organisational, administrative and financial ambiguity. In the early 1970s, a three-part internal review (Martin Report) of the workings of the ASA stated that 'We regard it as a weakness that a satisfactory solution to this question of Great Britain swimming administration has not been resolved long ago' (ASA 1970: 20).

Despite attempts to clarify the relationship in the 1970s the ASA/ASFGB relationship remained fraught, centring in large part on the dominance of the ASA, both financially and in respect of representative voting rights (cf. ASA 1977, 1989). The jurisdictional disputes in swimming not only highlight the enduringly parochial nature of British sport's organisation and administration (cf. Godfrey and Holtham 1999) but also the potential impact of such parochialism on swimming's relative lack of success at an international level. Indeed, in 1970, the Martin Report stated that:

> There still persists in this country the relic of an essentially recreational attitude towards swimming … it does not help in the field of competition especially at the higher level, where a much more 'professional' approach and attitude is required.
>
> (ASA 1970: 18)

The findings of this report do not appear to have been heeded, as recent comments from Great Britain's National Performance Director of Swimming suggest. Bill Sweetenham has argued that 'Nothing about swimming in this country should remain the same. Either it stays the same and we get worse, or we change it and move forwards' (quoted in Parrack 2001: 24). There are indications, however, that the degree of change argued for by Bill Sweetenham is beginning to emerge. In October 2000, following numerous reviews of the ASA/ASFGB relationship over the past 30 years, the ASFGB was reconstituted as a limited company and branded as British Swimming. The ASFGB is now constitutionally distinct from the ASA, with a wholly-owned subsidary company – High Performance Swimming Ltd – set up to administer National Lottery monies, primarily, the World Class Performance funding (ASFGB 2001).

The ASA organises competition throughout England, establishes the laws of the sport and supports the national teams for swimming (including masters, disability, open water and synchronised disciplines) diving and water polo. The ASA also offers education programmes and certification for teachers, coaches and officials and operates an awards scheme. Three separate bodies are also involved in this area: the Institute of Swimming Teachers and Coaches – a fully-owned subsidary of the ASA; the British Swimming Coaches and Teachers Association – a separate organisation but with close links to the ASA; and the Swimming Teachers Association – a rival organisation that trains a small number of teachers and lifeguards. The development work of the ASA with children results in it co-operating closely with a wide range of education organisations including, the Youth Sport Trust and the English Schools Swimming Association. The ASA also supports some 1,600 affiliated clubs through a National/District/County structure and has close links with local authorities, which currently provide approximately 1,400 swimming pools for local communities (House of Commons 2002).

Four areas of elite sport policy

Development of elite level facilities

The 1970 ASA Annual Report stated that 'we do not have a single pool complex in Britain capable of staging Olympic, World or European Championships' (ASA 1971: 5). In the same era, the enduring dilemma of access to pool time in local authority facilities for elite level swimmers was highlighted by the Martin Report, which argued that 'the public must know the "price" that must be paid by swimmers in training and by the public themselves in the possible loss to them of their own facilities for a few hours weekly' (ASA 1970: 44). At this time, the economic crisis affecting Britain resulted in expenditure cuts throughout the public sector and, although 'swimming stood up well to the challenge' (ASA 1977: 4), there were inevitable cutbacks in local authority services and provision. An additional concern for the ASA was that new facilities that were being constructed or redeveloped tended to be leisure-oriented, with little provision for teaching swimming or for competition. However, elite level swimming was catered for to some extent, with centres of excellence established under a GB Sports Council scheme at Crystal Palace and Leeds (ASA 1980).

Concerns regarding the proliferation of leisure pools remained throughout the 1980s, culminating, in 1987, in the formation of a National Swimming Pool Strategy Working Party in conjunction with the GB Sports Council (ASA 1988). Specific reference to the requirement for competition standard 50 metre pools was not addressed, however, until the mid-1990s (ASA 1995). Interestingly, in the early twenty-first century, the ASA is still bemoaning the lack of elite level facilities, in particular, the lack of water space for elite training in local authority pools and the lack of 50 metre pools for long-course training and for international standard competitions (House of Commons 2002). Implicit in these observations is the enduring weakness in the lobbying capacity of elite swimming as well as an acknowledgement of the high capital and revenue costs of pools.

The sport of swimming in the early twenty-first century is thus in a situation where its primary facilities, i.e. swimming pools, are owned either by private operators whose aim is profit maximisation; local authorities, which are reliant on public monies and have to fulfil a broad range of sports-related social policy objectives; and educational establishments, which have their own organisational objectives. The Chief Executive of the Institute of Sport and Recreation Management encapsulates the problems of local authority provision for swimming at all levels, in arguing that local authorities are 'in a Catch-22 situation, where they have ever-decreasing funds for services, must therefore maximise income opportunities while also trying to ensure social objectives and Best Value and finding time for elite swimming' (Riley 2002: 7). Indeed, Bill Sweetenham has argued that if the 'government and the people want results, we need more facilities that are accessible and affordable. The Australian Gold Coast alone has at least eight heated 50m pools. In the whole of Britain we have a total of around 14' (quoted in Parrack 2001: 24). In sum, the enduring concerns of the past 30 years regarding facility development for elite level swimming remain despite the recent opening of three high performance training centres with 50 metre pools located in English Institute of Sport regional centres (ASA 2002b: 9).

Emergence of 'full-time' swimmers

Amateurism, in relation to both the quality of management and the payment of swimmers, has been a recurring source of controversy in the ASA and has affected coaches, judges and competition officials as well as swimmers and ASA managers (cf. ASA 1970; Keil and Wix 1996). The 1970 Martin Report noted that

'Swimming fortunately still remains one of the truly amateur sports in terms of the actual competitor' (ASA 1970: 57) and it was not until the late 1980s that this issue was addressed seriously by the ASA. For example, the internal policy review, *Which Way Forward?* acknowledged that 'it is apparent that our swimmers are now competing at a disadvantage with swimmers in other countries' (ASA 1987: 21) and that 'The ASA needs to move away from the "amateur" concept in an organised manner' (1987: 6). This recommendation was heeded, in part, in 1988, when the ASA abandoned any formal expression of what constituted an 'amateur' competitor, guided in part by FINA-approved laws relating to expenses and advertising. However, the abandonment of amateurism did not result in the emergence of a squad of full-time swimmers. Swimming always had problems attracting substantial commercial sponsorship and, in the late 1980s, the Thatcher government was unwilling to increase its funding for sport. Indeed, swimmers travelling to compete in the 1988 Seoul Olympics, and who were dependent on welfare support, had their benefits stopped for the two weeks of the competition. The issues surrounding the funding of elite level swimmers in the late 1980s were encapsulated in *Which Way Forward?*, which asked 'Why is success so limited? Does it really depend on swimmers training abroad or being without jobs?' (ASA 1987: 21). While the relatively successful performance in 1988 was not sustained (see Table 6.1), it did mark a significant change in ASA policy.

In the early 1990s the ASA-funded pilot scheme, 'Elite Funding for Top Swimmers', was introduced for the top 10 ranked English swimmers – an indication that a change in attitude was emerging and that the ASA was now prepared to provide assistance to 'enable the best performers to devote their full attention to training without being distracted by financial worries' (ASA 1992: 6).

It was the introduction of the National Lottery in 1994, however, that had the most profound influence on the financing of elite level swimmers. Swimming has benefited greatly from Lottery monies through the World Class Performance programme, with 47 swimmers funded, as of September 2002, and £1,550,000 committed for the period April 2002–March 2003 (UK Sport 2002a). In one sense, these 47 swimmers can be classed as full-time athletes. Yet, the notion of 'full-time' here remains a relative term, as many elite level swimmers remain employed, either full- or part-time (or unemployed and receiving state benefits). Moreover, as a senior official at the ASA/ASFGB explained, increased funding

Table 6.1 GB/NI swimming medals: Olympic Games/World Aquatic Championships, 1988–2001

Olympic Games					World Aquatic Championships				
	Gold	*Silver*	*Bronze*	*Total*		*Gold*	*Silver*	*Bronze*	*Total*
1988	1	1	1	3	1991	0	1	1	2
1992	0	0	1	1	1994	0	0	0	0
1996	0	1	1	2	1998	0	0	2	2
2000	0	0	0	0	2001	1	2	4	7

does not come without certain obligations for NGBs, which operate in a climate of increasing accountability (Interviewee V, 18 March 2002). This climate of increasing accountability is indicative of a notable shift in sport policy (rhetoric, at least) at central government level.

The Department for Culture, Media and Sport (DCMS) – plays a key structural role here in shaping the conditions of action within which sport policy-making takes place, a key aspect of which is that NGBs are now required to produce plans that identify the likelihood of success. The DCMS stated (in *A Sporting Future for All*) that NGBs would be required to set much more explicit medal targets and that their performance against targets 'will be an important factor in deciding future levels of funding' (DCMS 2000: 16). As a recent House of Commons Select Committee report on swimming noted, direct funding for elite level swimmers was reduced following the 2000 Sydney Olympic Games because no swimming medals were won (House of Commons 2002). However, as a senior UK Sport official related, 'In terms of a net scenario, swimming is not receiving less in this [current] four-year cycle than in the previous [pre-Sydney] four-year cycle' (Interviewee W, 28 October 2002) because although the World Class Performance funding was reduced, swimming benefited in other areas. For example, UK Sport now covers the costs of the athlete medical scheme (prior to Sydney these costs came out of the World Class Performance award) and, in addition, 50 per cent of the training costs at various English Institute of Sport (EIS) sites (e.g. Loughborough and Bath) are now met by the EIS (Interviewee W, 28 October 2002).

Although the impact of World Class Performance funding cuts was cushioned after the failure in Sydney, the message to the ASA from the government was clear – future funding is conditional on elite success; a scenario endorsed by one senior official at the ASA/ASFGB, who stated, quite unequivocally, that:

> the government will only judge swimming by eight days in Athens [Olympic Games] ... It isn't five days in Manchester [Commonwealth Games] this year. It wasn't five days in Fukuoka [World Championships], when we came back with seven medals. [That's] all very interesting but if [we] come back with seven medals from the Olympics ... that'd get people sitting up and thinking.
>
> (Interviewee V, 18 March 2002)

Yet, within the wider swimming community, there appears to be a residual tension with regard to an increasing focus on the elite level. This is clear from insights provided by an ASFGB official who also has many years of experience at the sport's grass roots levels. This official suggested that the recent changes, which gave the ASFGB control of National Lottery funding for elite level athletes and programmes, resulted in an inevitable loss of power and control within the ASA (Interviewee X, 19 March 2002). The official also observed that 'until recently, those at [ASA headquarters], the committee, they [used to] set everything and all of a sudden the money is in the Lottery and they have no say in the matter of how we spend it'. Notwithstanding these latter observations, the World Class

Performance programme award of £4,920,000 for the period April 2001–March 2005 (UK Sport 2001) provides strong evidence of the funding available to enable elite level swimmers in the UK to train on a full-time basis.

Developments in coaching, sports science and sports medicine

With regard to coaching, the 1970 Martin Report highlighted the lack of a well-developed coaching structure for the sport and maintained that 'there is much that could be done for the coaches that we have to improve their knowledge, status and the environment in which they work' (ASA 1970: 66). There were also calls at this time for a National Co-ordinator of Coaching, Facilities and International Swimming who would 'be concerned with directing and co-ordinating a coaching policy, the provision of facilities and the setting up of the right environment in which such a policy could function successfully' (1970: 68). These recommendations were heeded to the extent that the ASA set up the Institute of Swimming Teachers and Coaches in 1975.

Progress in the area of coaching development was slow, however, partly due to the tensions between the need to develop coaches/teachers to support mass participation and coaches for elite development. The tension is reflected in *Which Way Forward?*, which suggested that 'The ability to produce coaches of quality' was one of the Association's strengths, while also questioning whether the sport's relative lack of success at major international events was, in part, a reflection of the lack of coaches of the highest quality (ASA 1987: 4, 21). Concern over the development of elite level coaches was not just an issue for swimming. The GB Sports Council identified the 'lack of a co-ordinated structure for employing coaches' (Sports Council 1988: 48) as a general concern in sport and noted that despite the creation of the National Coaching Foundation (NCF) in 1983 – with an associated network of National Coaching Centres – there was 'still far to go'.

The introduction of National Lottery funding in the mid-1990s was crucial in improving coaching at the elite level of swimming. In 1996, the first National Performance Director for Great Britain was appointed, heralding a complete overhaul of the coaching environment at the elite level. In 1999, the ASA implemented a format for coaching development at the elite level outside its traditional educational structure. As the ASA's Director of Education noted, 'a programme has been put together specific to the needs of the coaches of elite swimmers … which might change a Bronze medal to a Silver, and Silver into Gold' (quoted in ASA 1999: 20). Clearly, the issue of a co-ordinated programme for elite coaching is now of paramount importance in the sport's drive to achieve success at major international events. Bill Sweetenham, the sport's National Performance Director, is widely credited as the key actor driving this new approach. Sweetenham's approach not only involves linking aspects of coaching certification with the quality of the swimmers being produced (ASA 2002a), but also has led to a shift away from the 'mass mediocrity' which results from a system where club coaches simply have to 'keep the local authority happy' (Sweetenham, quoted in Hassall 2001: 27).

With regard to sports science and sports medicine, as long ago as 1970 the ASA reported on these issues via its Scientific Advisory Committee (ASA 1971). However, during the 1970s and early 1980s, although there were instances reported of research into how these disciplines might be applied to swimmers' physiology and performance (cf. ASA 1973), the reports were largely concerned with matters such as pool lighting, public address systems and starting blocks (cf. ASA 1974, 1979). However, by the late 1980s and into the early 1990s greater consideration was being given to the physiological aspects of competitive swimming, such as lactate testing and hyperventilation, medical profiling of national squad members and medical injury research (cf. ASA 1990, 1993, 1994). This changing focus reflects wider changes occurring in British sport at the time. For example, the GB Sports Council's strategy for sport, *Into the '90s*, recommended that 'The need has never been greater for British sportspeople, especially but not only top level performers, to have access to adequate medical and scientific support when and where they need it' (Sports Council 1988: 49).

The value that sports science/medicine might bring to competitive swimming was not seriously acknowledged until the mid-1990s. The 1996 ASA Annual Report, for example, stated that 'scientific disciplines [physiology and biomechanics] are being used by athletes world wide in the development of improved swimming performance' (ASA 1997: 24). In this regard, the introduction of National Lottery funding has been crucial. In 1997, World Class Performance funding allowed for the appointment of the first ever full-time manager for Sports Science and Sports Medicine (ASFGB 1998). Currently, an integrated, multi-disciplinary sports science and sports medicine programme is now emerging, as swimming at the elite level benefits from the associated programmes provided by the United Kingdom Sports Institute (UKSI). It is important to put these developments into perspective, however, as it was only in 2001 that the first British Swimming Joint Science Conference was held.

Competition opportunities for elite level swimmers

The issue of a planned and managed approach to competition opportunities for elite level swimmers, and the interrelated question of the amount of time swimmers spend competing compared to their training schedule, was not seriously addressed until the appointment of Bill Sweetenham in 2000 (Ballard 2002). However, the Martin Report had made recommendations on this issue in the early 1970s, suggesting that 'the National programme [in England] must be planned with the season's major competitions in mind [and that] It is essential for the District and County Championships to be integrated with the national plan' (ASA 1970: 7). These issues remained a concern, however, into the late 1980s. Central to such concerns was the perception of a fragmented and dysfunctional system of competition opportunities. Indeed, *Which Way Forward?* acknowledged as much in highlighting a lack of effective control of the country's various swimming leagues and the proliferation of open meets (ASA 1987).

More recently, a senior ASA/ASFGB official explained that the combination of National Lottery funding and fundamental attitudinal change were crucial elements of the ongoing efforts to improve international performance (Interviewee V, 18 March 2002). Indeed, the recently appointed World Class Potential Director for swimming, acknowledged the importance of supporting Bill Sweetenham's attempts to drive through such fundamental change in arguing that 'we have to limit the amount of competition and do the right type of competition at appropriate times of the year. We should be looking to compete once a month in 12 competitions per year' (quoted in Ballard 2002: 23). A comprehensive planning calendar has now been established that takes account of the proliferation of competition opportunities at regional, national and international levels. The complexity of the calendar is such that it incorporates the dates of all major World and European championships, the GB programme of championships and stage meets, ASA, District and County championships, British Grand Prix meets, English Schools Swimming Association championships and National Swimming League dates up to 2004 (ASA 2002a). The acknowledgement that such a radical programme of change will involve changing deeply entrenched values, both for the swimmers as well as administrators at all levels of the sport, is clear in the ASA's admission that the need to develop a truly integrated competition programme 'will be the subject of much debate and consultation over the winter' (2002a: 19).

This is an argument supported by the World Class Potential Director's admission that such change 'may well provide a headache for schedulers of club meets and regional competitions' (quoted in Ballard 2002: 23), as well as by Lodewyke's (2002) report into recent changes to youth and age group competitions. Lodewyke points out that, while 'things are looking great for our top swimmers … there is also a growing voice around the country that believes the ASA only cares about the cream of the crop and that there isn't enough emphasis on grass roots swimming' (2002: 25). These contentions are reinforced by an ASFGB official who suggested that those involved at the grass roots level of swimming 'are resenting what the Start and Potential [Lottery programmes] people are telling them [with regard to] how they've got to run their events' (Interviewee X, 19 March 2002). It appears, therefore, that, even at this early stage in the restructuring of the competition programme, concerns remain at the grass roots level of swimming with regard to the type and extent of value change required in relation to the competition opportunities and training regimes currently gaining credence at the sport's elite level.

Summary

It is clear that policy direction in swimming over the past decade has shifted and, in the introduction of National Lottery funding and changing values/belief systems, we have two key sources of policy change. Arguably, these two sources of change underlie the putative development of an advocacy coalition, centring on an increasingly closed membership and a set of shared values/belief systems. This shared value/belief system permeates the increasingly professional-corporate approaches of the recently constituted ASFGB and the Lottery distributor, UK Sport – the two key organisational actors involved in setting the conditions of action within which elite swimming currently operates. As Dalton *et al.* observe, the 'language of policy matters … How things are named defines the sense of the problem and often circumscribes the nature of the solutions' (1996: 112). Within the ASA and the ASFGB the language is of professionalism, focus and Olympic success. The reconstitution of the ASFGB as a limited company and the setting up of the wholly-owned subsidiary company, High Performance Swimming Ltd are, arguably, the most concrete manifestations of these policy shifts and embody the rejection of amateurism (cf. Allison 2001) and the 'acceptance' of a rational-bureaucratic mode of operation (cf. Slack *et al.* 1994). The Lottery has provided funding at an unprecedented level, thereby creating a framework within which key actors/organisations have been able to legitimise the rhetoric of change. In short, a degree of consensus is now developing over the legitimacy of policies directed towards elite performance at the highest level. Changes in four key areas of elite sport development are indicative of such change: (i) the ongoing development of 50 metre elite-focused swimming pools (rather then the tradition of building short-course 25 metre pools); (ii) the emergence of 'full-time', or at least quasi-full-time, swimmers; (iii) the emergence of a coach-focused approach, not only at the elite level, but also throughout the sport, and the appointment of full-time sports science and sports medicine staff; and (iv) the streamlining of the competition calendar in order for elite swimmers to produce optimum performances at World and Olympic events.

Moreover, the introduction of World Class Potential and Start funding in England (and similar programmes in the other three Home Countries) for programmes below the elite level are instructive in highlighting the dynamic processes at work here, one aspect of which is the emergence of a powerful coalition of actors/organisations involved in putting in place initiatives centring on the pursuit of elite objectives. For example, the Potential programme, formerly funded by Sport England, and thus for English swimmers only, has now moved to a GB format (ASFGB 2002) and forms part of 'a fully integrated development model for age group/youth swimmers' (ASA 2002a: 15), which enables graduation to the senior team and onto the World Class Performance level of funding. In addition, a number of Regional Talent Camps for talent identification and development purposes have been set up in liaison with the World Class Potential Director and are linked to the ASA's grass roots initiatives, such as Sport England's Active Sports programme (ASA 2002a).

In short, the evidence points to policy shifts throughout the sport with the clear aim of producing sustained medal-winning performances at the highest level. However, such a conclusion also raises questions about the continuity of provision for the recreational swimmer of which there are 11.9 million participating regularly in the UK (cf. ASA 2001). The issue of resistance to change is thus brought into sharp relief and we should be careful not to over-determine the extent of, and agreement with, policy shifts towards the elite level. Questions remain, for example, as to the potential for tension between these latter policy shifts and the goals and aspirations of the sport's club-based grass roots membership, such as the District/County Associations, the voluntary elected members serving on various ASA committees, and coaches, teachers and young swimmers involved at a local authority level. For example, on the issue of encouraging young swimmers to embrace changes in age group swimming, i.e. the Competitive Development Continuum, the ASA acknowledge that 'not all the ideas were welcomed by everyone' (ASA 2002a: 17).

There is also potential for conflict between the various aquatic disciplines to consider. For example, on the one hand, the Past Presidents' Commission (ASA 1998) reported that there was some concern regarding representation of a particular discipline's interests on the ASA Committee, while one ASFGB official suggested that 'swimming predominates, it makes more money' (Interviewee X, 19 March 2002). On the other hand, as another ASFGB official explained, as swimming is the largest sport it can provide benefits for the smaller disciplines, such as access to the ASA's legal service, child protection and financial management (Interviewee V, 18 March 2002). In other words, as this official went on to add, 'there are tensions but overall the benefits outweigh the disadvantages'. In short, the evidence (cf. ASA 2002a) suggests that any resistance to the type of change outlined earlier remains relatively insignificant.

UK Athletics

Organisation, administration and relationships

UK Athletics (UKA) is the governing body for the six disciplines of track and field, cross-country, fell and hill running, race walking, road running and tug-of-war. It is important to note, therefore, that while this study is concerned with the policy processes in track and field, the breadth of UKA's remit shapes the conditions of action within which the organisation and administration of athletics in the UK has developed. As Ward argues, 'There is no more diverse sport than athletics and the problems of diversity have been and are compounded by the Byzantine committee structures that have come about over the past century which have become sacred cows to so many' (2002c: 23). Much of the history of the administration of athletics in the UK has been an attempt to cope with and reconcile the tensions between disciplines and between Home Countries/English regions (cf. Foster 2004). For example, in 1932, the constitution of an International Board was drafted, representing England and Wales, Northern Ireland and Scotland, largely in response to the Scottish Amateur Athletic Association's application for independent membership of the then International Amateur Athletic Federation (IAAF), the struggle for control of the sport in Northern Ireland and the IAAF's stipulation that only one body would be accepted to represent the UK at international championships (Lovesey 1979). The International Board became known as the British Amateur Athletic Board (BAAB) in 1937 and, while it is not appropriate to record in detail the history of the BAAB, its demise in 1991 when faced with bankruptcy was, in large part, due to the failure to overcome the jurisdictional tensions within the sport.

The formation of the British Athletic Federation (BAF) in 1991 as successor to the BAAB was seen as a major step forward, the principal aim of which was to unite the various organisations charged with administering the sport of athletics in the UK. The formation of the BAF, however, did not proceed smoothly, which draws attention to important aspects of power relations. With the formation of the BAF agreed in principle, and practically established, the Amateur Athletic Association (AAA) fought to retain much of its power and authority, albeit under the new name of the AAA of England. As a former senior BAF official explained, much of this power and authority resides in the financial wealth of the AAA of England (Interviewee Y, 28 May 2002). As the sport's largest (by club membership) and most prosperous organisation, the AAA (as it was then known) had come to the aid of the beleaguered BAAB in the late 1980s when faced with insolvency and it was now being asked to provide funding and to indemnify the BAF for the first five years of its operation. With disagreements over the BAF's draft constitution and distributions of funds to the other Home Country associations, this scenario is indicative of the parochial nature of sport's governing bodies in the UK (cf. Godfrey and Holtham 1999).

The intention was that the BAF would provide a single autonomous body and also one which would give greater accountability to grass roots athletics, with clubs, of which there were 1,500, having a vote at the BAF's annual meeting and in so doing 'dodge the masonic order of the old constitution' (Ward, quoted in Gillingham 1991: 3). However, the BAF's short history (it was declared bankrupt in 1997) was plagued by a series of damaging events, including: power struggles between the various English regions and Home Country associations; financial squabbles regarding payments to elite athletes; media condemnation over the discredited promotions director, Andy Norman; and the drug abuse case against the athlete, Diane Modahl. In short, the BAF was an organisation struggling to come to terms with a sport that had attracted increasingly large amounts of television and sponsorship monies throughout the 1980s; a trend, moreover, which led inexorably towards professionalisation of management and an elite group of 'professional athletes'. Mackay encapsulates these 'struggles' in the *Observer*:

> As the Nineties progressed, sponsors lost interest. The sport became more professional and the value of an athlete kept going up; but the amateurs, many of whom had been in positions of power for more than 30 years, continued to resist the need for more professional input.
>
> (Mackay 1997: 9)

The upshot was insolvency for the BAF, which went into administration in 1997 with debts of over £1 million. The AAA of England was once again called upon to provide financial aid for a body called UK Athletics 98, which managed the sport until January 1999, when the organisation now known as UK Athletics Ltd (UKA) was formed. Given the history of organisational in-fighting described above it is not surprising that UKA outlined the following three principles underlying its purpose:

- 'It should *co-ordinate* and *support*, rather then intervene, govern or control.
- It should be designed to be *effective*, rather then be driven by political or representative concerns.
- It should have *defined and stronger links with clubs and athletes*' (UKA 2002a).

Four areas of elite sport policy

Development of elite level facilities

This section is concerned, primarily, with the development of track and field athletics in relation to the building or refurbishment of facilities and stadiums on a nationwide basis within which athletes can train and compete at the highest level. However, the construction of a national stadium capable of hosting athletics for major events such as the Olympic Games and World Athletics Championships is also worthy of consideration. The latter is of particular interest as the recent debates surrounding the policy processes underlying the refurbishment of Wembley Stadium as a venue for athletics, and the now defunct proposals for a dedicated athletics stadium and facilities at Picketts Lock in north London, raise questions as to the enduringly dysfunctional nature of athletics' organisation and administration.

Up until the 1930s, when cinder tracks began to proliferate, track and field athletics took place primarily on grass tracks, a situation that remained largely unchanged until the 1960s. The first synthetic track in the UK was provided at Crystal Palace in 1967 and the growing popularity of track and field athletics during the 1970s fuelled the growth in synthetic surfaces. By 1986 there were over 100 synthetic tracks and over 400 cinder tracks in the UK (Farrell, quoted in Sports Council 1987b). In 1987, the GB Sports Council hosted a National Seminar and Exhibition entitled 'Athletics: On the Right Track', out of which a number of policy documents were published (cf. Sports Council 1987a, 1987b) which highlighted the shortage of outdoor synthetic tracks and also of indoor facilities.

That the lack of indoor facilities has remained a recurring issue for the sport is clear from findings of a review in the late 1960s, which found that there were many 'expressions of regret that the facilities for the practice of indoor athletics are so few and far between' (Byers Report 1968: 28). By 1992, May reported that, although facilities improved dramatically in the 1980s due, in large part, to local authority investment, 'the UK still lags behind the rest of Europe' (1992: 36) and, as recently as 2001, the Olympic heptathlon champion, Denise Lewis, was reported as branding Britain's facilities 'third world' (quoted in Mackay 2001: 30). In the same report, Mackay also noted that, in Haringey where Lewis trains, 'she has no access to indoor facilities, the track is in a bad state, the weights room antiquated and the atmosphere generally not conducive to preparing for world-class performances'. Two key issues are signalled here: ownership and cost of facilities. The GB Sports Council's 1987 research, for example, found that 79 per cent of tracks named by clubs belonged to local authorities and 'that athletic facilities have placed a large burden on municipal finances' (Sports Council 1987a: 58, 71).

The sport's failure to rationalise its overly complex organisation and finances may, at least in part, be responsible for the deficiencies in facilities. A 1983 GB Sports Council report – *Financing of Athletics in the UK* – stated that a situation 'in which 20 bodies manage, develop and control athletics and receive grant aid for these purposes, [does] not provide the most cohesive pattern throughout the United Kingdom' (quoted in Sports Council 1987a: 22). That the BAF and its successor, UKA, have not managed to overcome difficulties regarding the financing of facilities is clear and led Mackay to report that 'UK Athletics simply does not have the financial resources to pay for the repair of tracks, which are normally owned by local authorities' (2001: 30). On the issue of the competing demands for finance, Gains sums up the problem as follows:

> For clubs it might mean assistance towards travelling costs, financial support for coaches to take courses, even help towards that ultimate of objectives – a 'clubhouse'. For UKA it probably means identifying talent, fast tracking likely medal hopes, creating development centres and prestige projects that grab immediate attention.
>
> (Gains 2002: 50)

At the heart of these observations are questions of purpose in relation to the role of NGBs in the early twenty-first century and, more importantly, their discretion to determine those purposes. As one senior official at UK Sport explained, with regard to UK Sport's 'modernisation' programmes for governing bodies, 'One of the key things I want to get out of the modernisation project is [for UKA and all NGBs] to go back to basics and identify what it is a governing body is here to do' (Interviewee Z, 28 October 2002). This official also explained that funding for NGBs is increasingly tied to meeting government-driven social policy and elite achievement objectives; thereby drawing attention to the financial constraints within which UKA operates. This is clear if we consider that some 81 per cent of UKA's combined income for 2001–2 was 'tied to the delivery of specific activities and programmes' (UKA 2003: 19); largely from Lottery monies, sponsorships and promotions (including television rights), and all linked tightly to the elite level: this financial situation leaves little income for the development of grass roots. In contrast, the elite level now benefits from the ongoing development of facilities linked to the UKSI network of high performance centres (UKA 2001). Indeed, on the issue of planning for athletics facilities for all levels of the sport, a former senior BAF official explained that 'There's never been a development plan. Well, they've written things down but no one has taken any notice of them … and they haven't really pushed for indoor facilities enough; there's been no drive' (Interviewee AA, 30 April 2002).

This perceived lack of drive within the sport's governing body with regard to the development of elite level facilities is also evident in the sport's inability to argue effectively for a major national athletics stadium capable of staging a World

Athletics Championship or an Olympic Games. According to Ward, a key source of the organisation's lack of effectiveness on facility development 'is that UK Athletics has little or no funding of its own' (2002c: 21). A membership scheme, which would provide the sport with greater self-sufficiency, was mooted as long ago as 1968 (Byers Report 1968). However, in the mid-1990s, a BAF strategic review and consultation document (*Athletics 21*) found that 'the willingness to pay a realistic price, through, for example, club subscriptions, is very low' (BAF 1995: 35). The power struggles between the sport's leading organisations are at the heart of resistance to such a scheme. As Ward notes, 'the opposition to a membership scheme ... stems from the suspicions of the AAA of England and the territories [English regions] to central authority' (2002c: 22).

On the one hand, the values embodied at a 'central authority' level (e.g. UKA and its High Performance Directorate) centre on professionalism, commercialism and corporate objective-setting in relation to the sport's elite athletes. On the other hand, grass roots values are still those of amateurism and voluntarism. Such a contention is borne out by findings in *Athletics 21*, which revealed that club officers, and other volunteers with close club connections, felt threatened by 'a sense of loss for the tradition of amateurism and the values associated with it' (BAF 1995: 20), and considered that 'The elite are eroding all the grass roots values of the sport because there is so much concentration on their money' (quoted in BAF 1995: 20).

Today, however, such values are increasingly subsumed as the investment in elite services and facilities through National Lottery funding further expands the UKSI's network of high performance centres (UKA 2001). Lottery funding is also providing UKA with £50 million towards the implementation of its 1998 £80 million National Facility Strategy. This strategy is, in part, addressing the paucity of indoor athletics facilities as one element of a development programme comprising some 27 new projects across the country (UKA 1998). Yet, concerns remain as to whether this investment will benefit the majority of the sport's club athletes (Interviewee AA, 30 April 2002) or merely create clearer pathways, opportunities and facilities for those with elite potential. A clear example of this changing structure is provided in UKA's 2001 Annual Review, which reported on the progress of its five-year development strategy, *Fun to Fulfilment* (launched in 2000), which claims to support the development of opportunities for all involved in the sport, but acknowledges that '*its primary* objective is to establish a clear pathway of development activity for young people' (UKA 2001: 10, emphasis added).

Emergence of 'full-time' athletes

The selection of Juan Samaranch as President of the International Olympic Committee (IOC) in 1980 was a significant moment for the emergence of full-time athletes. According to Allison, Samaranch 'had little interest in strict interpretations of the amateur principle' (2001: 169) and the President's equivocal approach to this issue is clear in the IOC's acceptance of a proposal from the IAAF during 1982–3 that athletes should be allowed to earn money from the sport. However, the outcome of the IAAF's proposal was characteristic of the sport's enduring ambiguity over the issue of amateurism. Athletes were now permitted to earn money but these earnings were to be placed in a trust fund controlled by their national association or federation. At this time in the UK, the BAAB administered this trust fund, and athletes could draw on these funds only for 'valid athletic expenses', which covered living costs such as food, transport and accommodation, as well as expenses for sports equipment and clothing, insurance, medical treatment and coaching services (BAAB 1986: 1–2). Moreover, as a former senior BAF official explained, this was a period characterised by what was known as 'shamateurism' – typified by payments to athletes not sanctioned by the governing bodies of sport and International Federations (Interviewee Y, 28 May 2002).

From the early 1980s, when the IAAF sanctioned trust funds for athletes, athletics authorities in the UK began the process of transforming, albeit in a somewhat piecemeal fashion, a traditionally amateur sport into one that is now openly professional and commercial in nature. However, this restructuring was a complicated and difficult process. Of particular concern was, and remains, the ability of a small number of elite athletes to command appearance fees, prize money and sponsorship deals. In short, athletics was now a commodity to be sold and the most valuable aspect of this complex commodity was the elite athlete. The commercial attractiveness of the sport peaked in the mid- to late 1980s, with ITV's commitment of £10.5 million for a five-year television contract in 1985 indicative of the large amounts of money coming into the sport at this time (Watman 2002).

The sport's attractiveness to commercial interests also led to the setting-up of a number of Grand Prix events across Europe, staged by private organisations that negotiated worldwide television contracts, and which gave these organisations the resources to meet the high fees demanded by the select group of athletes that the events hoped to attract. This aspect of structural change had dire consequences for the BAF in the 1990s. As Mackay reported in the *Observer* in 1995, the BAF struggled to compete with the amounts of money generated by the Grand Prix organisers with the consequence that British elite athletes failed to compete in home competitions and television and sponsorship money 'started to run dry after the 1993 season' (1995: 11). The BAF attempted to solve this problem by offering contracts to a number of elite athletes with the intention that they would support domestic competition, but also, and equally more importantly, compete less often. During the early 1990s there had been a growing concern that participation in Grand Prix events was harming the country's medal chances at major events. The performance of the GB team at the Atlanta Olympic Games, where only six medals were won (see Table 6.2), appeared to provide confirmation that participation on the Grand Prix circuit was damaging the chance of Olympic success. Although the Atlanta Olympics might represent a nadir for the sport, it was also, according to a former senior official at the English Sports Council, 'one of the catalysts for the [increased] emphasis on elite sport' since the mid-1990s (Interviewee BB, 26 February 2002).

Table 6.2 GB/NI athletics medals: Olympic Games/World Athletics Championships, 1988–2001

	Olympic Games					World Athletics Championships			
	Gold	Silver	Bronze	Total		Gold	Silver	Bronze	Total
1988	0	5	2	7	1995	2	1	1	4
1992	2	0	4	6	1997	1	1	0	2
1996	0	4	2	6	1999	1	4	2	7
2000	2	2	2	6	2001	1	0	1	2

An equally important catalyst for change, and one that predated the poor performance at Atlanta, was the publication of the Conservative Government's sport policy document *Sport: Raising the Game* (Department of National Heritage [DNH] 1995) which signalled a significant sea-change in British sport policy. Whereas the setting-up of the Sports Councils in the early 1970s heralded initiatives largely concerned with mass participation and Sport for All programmes, *Sport: Raising the Game* focused on two key areas: young people and sporting excellence. This emerging focus on the elite level was maintained by the Labour Government's policy statement on sport – A *Sporting Future for All* (DCMS 2000). A third stimulus for change was the introduction of the National Lottery in 1994, which was to prove crucial to developments at the elite level.

Despite the impending availability of Lottery funds in 1997, the BAF was declared insolvent due, in large part, to its failure to adjust to the new demands of a sport that was now openly professional and intensely commercial. Significantly, the BAF owed £600,000 to Britain's elite performers and £200,000 to 'overseas stars' (Frecknall *et al.* 1997: 12). The paradox of this situation was that the organisational and administrative restructuring that the sport undertook, largely at the behest of the government, merely reinforced the influence of elite athletes. Indeed, the BAF went into administration at the same time as it was being encouraged by Sport England to operate in a more professional manner. On this issue, one former high ranking BAF official explained that:

> Sport England saw the mess that the amateurs made of the BAF, and the terrible in-fighting which brought it down, and Sport England determined that, when the new organisation [UKA] came into being … funded via tax payers' money and by Lottery funding, they weren't going to have any nonsense. They were going to appoint professional staff; it would be a professional organisation from top to bottom.
>
> (Interviewee AA, 30 April 2002)

Perhaps the most important aspect of the BAF's demise was the setting-up of a company called Performance Athlete Services Ltd (PAS)[1] in 1997, which was charged with managing Lottery funding for elite athletes. As Mackay reported in 1998, '[PAS] received the £10m Lottery money and ensured that the funds were kept away from the BAF' (1998a: 24). Moreover, as Frecknall *et al.* noted in 1997, 'the 195 or more elite athletes plus the four coaching directors recently appointed under performance director Malcolm Arnold are the only people in the sport who are at all sure of what the future holds' (1997: 12). The subsequent distribution of World Class Performance Lottery funding confirmed the priority to be given to elite athletes. Athletics (excluding disability athletics) received £2,800,000 for the period April 2002–March 2003, which helped to support (as at September 2002) 82 athletes (UK Sport 2002a).

In sum, if results at major international events such as the Olympics Games are the benchmark of a 'healthy' sport, then the six medals won in Sydney 2000, two of which were Gold, was a marked improvement on the performance four years earlier – see Table 6.2. However, defining a successful sport primarily by the achievements of the elite is a deep-seated source of tension within athletics, especially as the elite benefit, not only from Lottery funding, but also from the various commercial opportunities open to them. A typical attitude from the grass roots is summed up by the following comment: 'How can it be right that some athletes are making obscene amounts of money while I stand out in the rain for three nights a week for nothing?' (quoted in BAF 1995: 20). Thus, although this was a view stated in the mid-1990s, UKA is still perceived by some as too willing to accept the drive for international success at the expense of the sport's grass roots levels.

Developments in coaching, sports science and sports medicine

Although the 'real breakthrough in British coaching was the BAAB report that set up the first AAA summer school at Loughborough in 1934' (Lovesey 1979: 120), coaching development was mainly defined as 'the teaching of teachers and the coaching of coaches' (Interviewee AA, 30 April 2002), with little attention given to coaches working explicitly with athletes or linking coaching and performance planning at the highest level (Sports Council 1991). The development of coaching was thus piecemeal and hardly strategic, and the increasing cost of administering coaching schemes almost resulted in bankruptcy for the AAA, which led to the BAAB taking responsibility for coaching in 1972 (Lovesey 1979).

Coaching development in athletics appears to have been bedevilled by disagreements between coaches and administrators, as well as disagreement over the methods used by coaches. As one former BAF official revealed, athletics coaching from 1948 – when Geoff Dyson was appointed Chief Coach – to 1961 – when Dyson resigned following clashes with the amateur officials running the sport – was very much 'theory based' (Interviewee AA, 30 April 2002; see also Radford *et al.* 1989). Consequently, the two senior coaches who succeeded Dyson were constrained by the sport's lack of enthusiasm for coaching innovators and their methods. In short, coaching development stagnated despite the formation of the British Association of National Coaches in 1965, which gave a clearer voice to coaching interests in UK sport. However, the appointment of Frank Dick as Director of Coaching in 1978 offered the prospect of a more innovative approach.

Yet, despite Dick's undoubted contribution to British athletics coaching throughout the 'Golden Decade' of the 1980s, reservations remained regarding his approach. Indeed, a former senior BAF official argued that 'to be truthful about it Frank didn't bring in all that much innovation either. So we get to the late 1980s and into the 1990s and the [coaching] scheme was almost as it was back in 1948' (Interviewee AA, 30 April 2002). Moreover, commenting on Dick's resignation in 1994, a leading athletics official stated that 'People have vastly over-estimated his [Dick's] worth to the sport in this country' (quoted in Hubbard *et al.* 1994: 11). However, Dick was credited with setting-up a National Coaching Strategy in the 1980s, of which the UK Coaching Scheme was arguably the most prominent manifestation (Sports Council 1987a), with the formation of the NCF in 1983 the first real indication that the development of coaching as a profession was now a priority for sport's administrators. Indeed, in 1988, the GB Sports Council stated that the setting up of the NCF and its associated network of National Coaching Centres throughout the UK was 'one of the major successes of the past five years' (Sports Council 1988: 49) but with the caveat that more work was still required.

It was also during the 1980s that athletes began to consider the specific requirements for elite coaching. In 1984, for example, Frank Dick published a review of the sport's National Coaching Strategy, within which proposals for a National Performance Strategy were outlined (BAAB 1984). This appears to be the first acknowledgement that a structured and co-ordinated approach to coaching development was imperative to achieving success at major international events. As Dick argued in the late 1980s, 'The precept central to a National Coaching and Performance Plan is that a *national* scheme to provide a *local* service for the cutting edge of performance development – quality coach/athlete contact – is in pursuit of achievement in the *international* arena' (quoted in Sport Council 1987b: 10). While Dick's comments can be viewed as an attempt to garner support for elite performance development at club level, this has proved to be an enduringly difficult objective to achieve.

That the direction and nature of coaching development in athletics remained unresolved is evident from contributions to the 1989 *Independent Review of Coaching* (Radford *et al.* 1989), which called for a complete restructuring of coaching. One contributor to the review claimed not only that there was 'too much emphasis on the academic development of coaches' (quoted in Radford *et al.* 1989: 67), but also criticised the lack of utilisation by athletics coaches of NCF resources. Many of the criticisms contained in the review were endorsed in the 1991 GB Sports Council publication, *Coaching Matters* (Sports Council 1991) to which both Peter Radford, then Chairman of the BAAB and Frank Dick were key contributors. The publication of *Coaching Matters* highlighted the stagnation in the organisation and administration of many sports in the UK and the need for the report to 'be a catalyst not only to bring about changes in coaching but to create closer relationships between coaches and performers on the one hand … and the administrators … on the other' (quoted in Sports Council 1991: 5). *Coaching Matters* also drew attention to the failure to address the overly complex structure of British sport, especially in the light of the change of emphasis towards the elite level by Sports Councils and the implications of this changing emphasis for coach education and development. Finally, the report argued that 'there has to be nation-wide access to sports science and sports medicine services' (1991: 6) as part of an integrated and co-ordinated approach to the development of athletes.

The GB Sports Council report, far from prompting an investigation of the contribution of sports science/medicine to athletics, was followed by a further period of neglect. For example, in 1994, Peter Coe, the father and coach of Sebastian Coe, commenting on his involvement with the South of England's elite coaching scheme, stated that 'The idea of actually sitting down and sharing experiences, training information and anything new in sports science – in short the very keys to success – was never mentioned' (Coe 1994: 9). Moreover, as a former senior BAF official explained, in 2000 the Genesis Report into the governance of UKA was not only critical of the sport's High Performance Director and the Performance Athlete Services [PAS] team but also of the neglect of sports science (Interviewee AA, 30 April 2002). As this official went on to add, 'until then, they'd pretty well ignored things like sports psychology, sports science and all the rest of it. Frank Dick certainly ignored it throughout his tenure'.

Concerns about the quality and organisation of coaching in athletics were echoed in the consultation document, *The Development of Coaching in the UK* (UK Sport 1999). After noting that the 1991 *Coaching Matters* review 'did not address some critical areas such as the development of coaches working with high performance athletes' (1999: 1), this document provided explicit acknowledgement of the importance of integrating sports science/medicine support into the coaching environment, with a specific emphasis on the needs of 'high performance athletes and their coaches' (1999: 43). However, the UK Sport report stimulated little immediate action within athletics. It was not until 2002, following the poor performance of the GB/NI team at the Edmonton World Athletics Championships in 2001, that UKA undertook a review of sports medicine support (cf. Powell 2001). It is clear, then, that concerns remain as to the development of, and provision for, coaching, sports science and sports medicine, despite the significant impetus provided by National Lottery funding.

Overall, the past decade has witnessed significant change in the national framework for the provision of coaching, sports science and sports medicine in the sport of athletics, with the introduction of Lottery funding being the most important development. However, the values, principles and belief systems, which underlie the sport's organisation and administration, have changed more slowly. Although there has been a broad acceptance of the prioritisation of elite achievement, this has been controversial and there must be doubts regarding the degree to which this value change has permeated all levels of the sport. The BAF's mid-1990s strategic review explicitly investigated the changing nature of the values underlying the sport, from those linked with notions of amateurism and voluntarism, to those associated with professionalism and commercialism (BAF 1995). The 1995 review exposed antagonisms between the sport's grass roots level club members – who were more closely linked to the traditional values of amateurism and voluntarism – and the growing cadre of elite athletes and professional staff – who embraced (and benefited from) the type of values linked to professionalism and commercialism. That concerns persist as to the adequacy of coaching, generally, in the UK is clear from the latest review of coaching published in 2002 by the DCMS. In the review's Foreword, Sports Minister, Richard Caborn, observes that 'Much good work on coach education has been done in the United Kingdom, but there is a need for a concerted effort to improve the quality and quantity of coaches in all sports' (quoted in DCMS 2002: 2).

Competition opportunities for elite level athletes

In 2000, UKA acknowledged that 'the existing [competition] structure is a confused organisation to those participating, with an overload of fixtures resulting in falling levels of participation and volunteer support' (UKA 2000: 1). Yet, this issue does not appear to have been a major concern for the sport over the years, at least as reflected in the key policy-related documents reviewed here. It was an issue addressed, albeit briefly, in a review of the sport in 1968, which argued that 'there is an urgent need for the introduction by the BAAB of a co-ordinated competition structure' (Byers Report 1968: 26). If the issue of competition structures failed to receive sustained analysis, there has been plenty of comment.

In 1987, for example, Frank Dick argued that club competition had limited value as preparation for the international arena, while suggesting that 'The door had to be opened to graduated competitive opportunity beyond national level for those athletes who were ready for the experience' (quoted in Sports Council 1987b: 7). In the same year, Alan Pascoe, former Olympic athlete, but commenting here in his capacity as head of the sponsorship company, Alan Pascoe Associates Ltd, argued that the success of the sport throughout the 1980s at the elite level was due to a 'well-developed competition structure' (quoted in Sports Council 1987b: 74) in referring to the types of events organised by promoters such as Andy Norman. However, as already noted, the BAF faced bankruptcy in the late 1990s, with much of the blame attributed to competition structures at the elite level based on large appearance fees and prize money being paid to a small number of elite athletes.

Part of the problem was due to too many similar international meetings staged for the elite, which resulted in a decline in public interest and thus less income for the BAF. Part of the problem also lay with the elite athletes' reluctance to compete in these (BAF-staged) home internationals, preferring instead to compete abroad for higher rewards (Mackay 1995). At the heart of this issue was the concern that competition structures were designed to provide opportunities for elite athletes to earn high fees rather than facilitate the development of potential elite talent. Indeed, Ward (2002a) suggests that the athletics calendar should start later than the traditional May meetings (when the weather is often inclement), which would then allow the season to extend into August and September. This does not happen, Ward argues, because 'our whole fixture calendar is geared to those few ... who carry the flag at major championships. About [0.] 001 per cent of the athletic population at a reasonable guess' (2002a: 50). In other words, the months of August and September are left free of competition for the benefit of elite athletes to compete at events such as the Olympic Games and World Athletics Championships. The paradox of this situation is that many of the elite athletes cited by Ward above do not compete in the various events held in the spring. For Ward, then, the structure of competition opportunities for the generality of athletes in the UK is increasingly determined by the needs of elite athletes. While such evidence might be interpreted as further confirmation of the organisational atrophy affecting athletics in the UK, a more plausible interpretation is that the existing competitive structure reflects the strength of the coalition of actors and organisations centring on the elite level and thus the relative weakness of the grass roots levels of the sport.

Summary

The past decade has witnessed quite radical changes in the organisation of and context for elite athletics, most of which have been substantially underpinned by Lottery funding. Lottery funding has enabled a programme of facility improvement and development particularly designed to improve indoor training opportunities. There is also the prospect of a further £40 million – the bulk of which will come from Sport England's Lottery fund – for facility development as a 'legacy' of the government's broken election manifesto promise to provide a suitable venue for the 2005 World Athletics Championships (UK Sport 2002b). Lottery funding has also enabled the emergence of 'full-time' athletes. In September 2002, 82 athletes were funded through the World Class Performance programme for the period April 2002–March 2003 (UK Sport 2002a). However, as was the case for swimming, the notion of 'full-time' remains a relative term here as a number of these athletes continue to work in other employment, either, full- or part-time (cf. Ward 2002b). The emergence of a more structured and integrated approach to coaching development and sports science/medicine provision is a third key indicator of change. However, one dimension of change where the sport has been less successful is in reforming its competitive structure.

Although the availability of National Lottery funding has been a key factor in strengthening the focus of UKA on elite achievement, there has been a strong residual tension within the organisation over the implications for the strategic direction of the governing body and particularly for clubs and the grass roots. Questions surrounding resistance to a shift from the once-dominant values of amateurism/voluntarism to those of professionalism/commercialism are at the heart of debates within UKA. More specifically, there is a deep-rooted reluctance by some to accept the notion that the sport of athletics should be structured in such a way that 'excellence' is the only outcome of participation and commitment. As discussed, questions surrounding values, principles and belief systems were a key aspect of the BAF's strategic review in the mid-1990s. Instructively, the review noted that 'British athletics today exists in an environment which is essentially a battlefield ... [wherein] The values that people hold determine their activities and help to define what they consider to be success' (BAF 1995: 10, 17).

The 1995 review raised fundamental questions regarding the values and principles underlying the sport and highlighted the tension between a commitment to elite achievement and 'Nostalgia and a sense of loss for the tradition of amateurism and the values associated with it' (BAF 1995: 20). As one volunteer commented, 'I am concerned that a more professional approach by everyone in the sport tends to put us all on a conveyor belt, trying to move on to the next stage. We risk losing the "fun" aspect of athletics' (quoted in BAF 1995: 20). This view contrasts sharply with that of UKA's Chief Executive:

> One thing I am worried about is that track and field is becoming more and more recreational ... People are saying ... 'I'm not bothered whether the sport prospers or not' ... there's nothing wrong with recreational athletes. I used to think that they only existed in running but now triple jumpers and discus throwers are appearing solely to compete at weekends in league competitions. The problem is that it's becoming the norm.
>
> (quoted in Ward 2002c: 23)

The Chief Executive's subsequent comment that 'any future funding will be directed towards those clubs and competitions ... that are all about raising standards', only serves to reinforce the impression that those charged with organising and administering the sport in the early twenty-first century are becoming increasingly hidebound to their paymasters, most notably, UK Sport. Not only has the strategic focus within UKA shifted clearly from support and development of clubs and grass roots participation to elite achievement but the focus has also narrowed to the exclusion of the other five disciplines, beyond track and field, that are the responsibility of UKA. This narrowing of focus is doubtless reinforced by the attractiveness of track and field to sponsors and television companies and the ready availability of Lottery funding.

The skewing of resource distribution within UKA towards elite track and field prompted some criticism, particularly during the 1990s, from road running and cross-country. Indeed, in 1994, Chris Brasher, founder of the London Marathon, lamented the BAF's lack of interest in road running, citing it as 'One of the reasons Britain has never had an Olympic marathon champion' (quoted in Mackay 1994b: 3). Moreover, in the same year, Mackay queried why cross-country has 'long been considered the poor relation of British athletics' (1994a: 7), while Rodda posed the following question, 'If British athletics can annually organise six major outdoor international meetings and another three indoors ... why do so many facets of cross-country look antiquated and gaffe-prone?' (1994: 17). Although there appears to be more evidence of confrontation between the different sub-disciplines within athletics than that found in the sport of swimming, the extent of such confrontation does not (yet) appear powerful enough to alter the conditions of action within which the sport currently operates. In sum, the evidence suggests that the structure of the sport is centred on professionalism and the meeting of corporate (funding-related) objectives, most notably, medal-winning performances at major international events: a shift from those values that traditionally underpinned the '"fun" aspect of athletics' (BAF 1995: 20) to those centring on achievement and excellence at the elite level.

Royal Yachting Association

Organisation, administration and relationships

The Royal Yachting Association (RYA) is the recognised governing body for sailing in the UK. The Association's remit has broadened considerably over the years and it now encompasses the interests of all water users under sail or power. In 2002, the RYA had 95,000 personal members within 1,580 affiliated clubs and across 181 Class Associations. It also administered training standards for over 200,000 students per year at 1,400 Recognised Teaching Establishments (RYA 2002a; RYA and Sport England 2001). However, these figures exclude recreational participants who are not official members of the Association, estimated at between 1.5 million and some 'four million or so boaters' (RYA 2001a: 18).

Given the significant safety aspects connected with the sport, an important element of the RYA's operations concerns the regulation and stakeholder consultation over instructional and safety issues. For example, the Association's important role in safety-at-sea issues involves working closely with the Royal National Lifeboat Institution and HM Coastguard amongst many others. In addition, the RYA headquarters currently houses the Secretariat for the European Boating Association, which is regarded by the European Commission as a key consultative body on all boating matters (RYA 2001b). Finally, a pressure group called the Boating Alliance was established in June 2002, which includes the RYA, the British Marine Industries Federation, the Inland Waterways Association, as well as other water sports, such as canoeing, rowing and surfing. The Alliance's aim is to provide a forum for these groups to 'take a co-ordinated and united approach to strategic issues of major importance to the boating industry and boat users' (Boating Alliance 2002). As a former Olympic Coach related, the RYA is renowned as a forceful lobbying organisation in its relationships with bodies responsible for shaping the context within which the Association operates (Interviewee CC, 11 September 2002).

The complex nature of the RYA's remit is clear in that it not only encompasses 181 affiliated Class Associations – which include dinghy, keelboat, motor cruising and powerboating – but it also has responsibility for the sports of windsurfing and personal watercraft (jet skis) (RYA and Sport England 2001). This wide-ranging set of responsibilities, at different levels and across many water-related activities, suggests considerable potential for conflict between groups of members. However, the jurisdictional power struggles so prominent in swimming and athletics do not appear to have blighted the RYA to the same degree. The relative lack of intra-organisational friction has a number of potential explanations.

First, as a senior official at UK Sport related, membership of the RYA is not compulsory for competitive or recreational participants (Interviewee DD, 28 October 2002; see also RYA 2001a). Second, 'by comparison with most sports, boating is unusual in having a very large number of participants who enjoy their sport as an outdoor recreation and leisure pursuit with no competitive element' (RYA 2001a: 35). Third, sailing is not recognised by the various Sports Councils as a priority school sport (2001a: 3). Finally, a senior RYA racing coach explained that sailing has not been part of the Commonwealth Games programme; therefore, the sport only ever competes as the UK (or Great Britain and Northern Ireland, depending on the nomenclature used) at major international events and thus avoids the Home Country jurisdictional problems faced by swimming and athletics (Interviewee EE, 25 March 2002).

The absence of many of the sources of conflict found in swimming and athletics is not to argue that the RYA is an organisation free from internal dispute. As the accounts of the NGBs in swimming and athletics have revealed, the notion of what constitutes an amateur or indeed amateurism, was an issue with which most, if not all, UK NGBs have had to contend: the RYA was no exception. For example, Fairley notes that 'The debate … about how to maintain amateur status was really of considerable interest' (1983: 42), but this was in 1910 and concerned the British Olympic Association's general guidelines on the issue of amateurs. In general, the internal debate on amateurism at this time lacked the bitterness found in swimming and athletics (and rowing). The more relaxed approach to the issue is clearly reflected in a letter found in the then Yacht Racing Association's (YRA) Minute Book from Lord Desborough who argued 'As for yachting – don't be in a hurry. You may have to formulate a rule for International competition for the purpose of each event' (quoted in Fairley 1983: 43). The inference being that the sport should only concern itself with this issue for major international events such as the Olympic Games. That this remained an enduring, but not overly-divisive, issue for the sport's national governing body is reflected in the next major debate on the issue in the late 1950s, where it was noted that 'the question of amateur status only rears its head in specific events which stipulate that only amateurs may compete for such-and-such a cup or, of course, in Olympic competition' (1983: 132). The RYA seemed content to deal with the issue of amateurism in a highly pragmatic fashion. Of greater concern to the membership, especially the recreational cruising arm in more recent years, has been the use and distribution of Lottery funding. In 2001, for example, the RYA Chairman felt compelled to reassure 'Cruising members … that the Olympic and Youth Training Programmes are almost entirely financed by Lottery Funding, and monies generated by membership and commercial trading are used to represent the rights of boaters and develop the grass roots of the sport' (quoted in RYA 2000: 4).

The only other issue that has been a source of tension in recent years concerned the decision to designate nine zones throughout the UK for organising youth race training activities and the appointment of salaried High Performance Managers. As a senior RYA racing coach explained, before the appointment of High Performance Managers, the RYA used volunteer, regional race-training co-ordinators who worked on the principle that the 'region was there to task them, which was not the reality. Now with High Performance Managers, there is no conflict. We've professionalised the race-training side of it and the committees have less involvement than they used to' (Interviewee EE, 25 March 2002). Thus, while there is some evidence of internal disputes within the YRA/RYA, such disputes have not been characterised by the bitter in-fighting evident in swimming and athletics over the years. Indeed, as one senior UK Sport official pointed out, 'I get the impression that there is more support for the necessity of a governing body in sailing [than in athletics] due to things like safety, training and education … and there is a common interest about legislative issues, anything that might restrict sailors' access to water' (Interviewee DD, 28 October 2002). Whether there is a common interest in the development of elite sailing is discussed in the sections that follow.

Four areas of elite sport policy

Development of elite level facilities

While the focus of this section is on the development of facilities for elite level training and competition it is nevertheless important to reiterate the diversity of the RYA's remit, which encompasses many different levels and types of water sport activity (cf. McKinsey and Company 2002). The significance of such a diverse remit is that it raises questions of emphasis; in short, how has the RYA managed to balance facility development for recreational sailing, and the various other disciplines within its remit, with the development of facilities for Olympic and World Championship level racing? This question can be addressed at governmental and at governing body level. First, at a governmental, or Sports Council level, the issue of sailing facilities for both recreational and elite sailors has not assumed the same importance as found in swimming and athletics. This is not to argue that the Sports Councils have ignored facility development for sailing activities. For example, in 1978, the GB Sports Council published the *First Report of the RYA Facilities Committee*, the main objective of which was to 'encourage the orderly and planned provision of facilities for cruising and racing under sail or power' (Sports Council 1978: 2). Of note, is the report's conclusion that 'there is still a deficiency in the facilities available for yachting', as well as its concern that 'it is important to give everyone the opportunity to enjoy the benefits of boating' (1978: 10). There was no reference at this time to expanding elite level facilities, although it was noted that the National Sailing Centre at Cowes (opened in 1965 under the jurisdiction of the Central Council of Physical Recreation) was now well established.

It could be argued that the relative lack of intervention (or interest) in the provision of sailing facilities at Sports Council level was due, at least in part, to the acknowledgement by the RYA that the sport is perceived as wealthy and elitist and that sailing is not recognised by the various Sports Councils as a priority school sport. Indeed, with regard to the first point, Coghlan and Webb suggest that the National Centre at Cowes was perceived as a 'bastion of privilege', and that yachting was not 'available to any considerable extent to the artisan or the working class' (1990: 75). Thus, intervention by the Sports Councils was limited to issues related to access to water and the countryside in general, and for disadvantaged groups in society in particular.

That the GB Sports Council's concerns in the late 1980s centred primarily on issues surrounding increasing provision for designated disadvantaged groups is clear from its strategy document – *Sport in the Community: Into the '90s*. With regard to water sports, a Countryside and Water Recreation Policy was established centring on issues of access to water and the countryside (Sports Council 1988), and provision for other areas/levels of the sport was not deemed a priority. This may also be due to an enduring perception that the sport requires expensive equipment, clothing and travel in order to participate and that it remains elitist, in the sense of economically exclusive (RYA 2001a; but see Proctor 1962). *Into the '90s* did, however, refer to the closure of the Cowes National Sailing Centre in 1987, stating that 'discussions [would] continue to find a replacement on the mainland for the National Sailing Centre' (Sports Council 1988: 73). That a National Sailing Centre had still not been established by late 2002 is perhaps a useful indicator of the relative importance given to this issue by the GB Sports Council and its successor bodies. Interestingly, in 2001, Sport England published a Planning Bulletin for water sports, prompted in large part by sailing's successes in recent years that 'have given the various water sport disciplines a high profile' (Sport England 2001: 1), and which reflected the change in Sports Council priorities over the past 20 years and its greater willingness to support sports that delivered Olympic success, but contributed little to social policy objectives.

The second level on which the question of facility development can be addressed is at the level of NGB organisational priorities. It could be argued that the relative lack of intervention by government and quasi-governmental organisations over the years on this issue is due, in part, to the RYA's determination to remain as independent as possible from such bodies. Indeed, the RYA argues that the 'very best reason' for joining the organisation is to contribute a voice to those who 'wish to have influence over the future of leisure boating in the UK, rather than some Government Department. The RYA has been very successful in "self governance" of boating. We want this to continue' (RYA 2002b). It should be recognised, however, that sailing and water sports generally have benefited in the past from the establishment and development of Sports Council-funded National Sports Centres, notably Cowes (in 1965), Holme Pierrepont (in 1973) and Plas-Y-Brenin, Wales (in 1955). As discussed, of these, Cowes was the principal Sailing Centre. Yet, as a former Olympic Coach explained, 'Cowes was never really used a great deal for elite level sailing and training as it was not an ideal location for that purpose' (Interviewee CC, 11 September 2002).

It appears that the RYA adopted an ad hoc approach to the development of facilities for the specific use of elite level sailors' training and competition from the 1960s to the early 1980s. As Fairley (1983: 171) notes, RYA Minutes in 1970 recorded that 'A base for Olympic training and major regattas was desirable'. Yet, by January 1971, the idea of an Olympic base 'had been dropped' (1983: 171–2) and a working party was created to investigate the possible establishment of a National Yacht Racing Centre. The concept of a National Yacht Racing Centre was subject to three separate reports by the RYA in the early 1970s (RYA 1972, 1973a, 1973b); the premise being that, 'If Britain is to remain at the top of the international "yachting league" in Olympic and other forms of racing, this centre must be built' (RYA 1973a: 2). However, the planned centre was never built and, in 1995, 'the RYA rejected the previously promoted concept of a single National Sailing Centre … [as] High level sailing competition has advanced considerably and a single national sailing venue no longer meets the needs of the sport' (RYA 1998c: 24).

By the late 1970s, however, there was a growing consensus within the RYA's various racing committees that the sport required training centres of some form, based around specific club sites where Olympic Class racing could be guaranteed. As Maynard argues in an internal RYA report, entitled *The 1977–1980 Olympic Effort*, 'these centres would also encourage the Olympic fleets to grow and do much to raise overall standards' (1976: 3). The growing consensus around a more organised and strategic approach to the development of elite level racing facilities gained support in 1992. Following the 1992 Olympic Games, where the Olympic sailing team won just one Bronze medal, the RYA's Race Training Committee proposed six potential options for change in the organisation of the sport's Olympic programme (RYA 1992b). Later in the same year, the Yacht Racing Divisional Committee accepted the option to improve Olympic preparation by a reallocation of existing resources (RYA 1992a). In order to achieve this objective it was resolved to establish a small Olympic panel (known as the Olympic Steering Group – OSG) the primary responsibility of which was to direct the overall organisation of the Olympic programme. Although the issue of facility development was not a primary concern of the OSG, the creation of this Group nevertheless signalled a significant change in the objectives of the RYA.

Today, the RYA is one of the largest recipients of National Lottery funding across the World Class Performance, Potential and Start programmes administered by UK Sport (UK Sport 2002a) and Sport England (and the respective Sports Councils in the other three Home Countries). Reflecting this shift towards a closer (resource) relationship with these quasi-governmental bodies, a joint policy statement from the RYA and Sport England was published in 2001, entitled *Facilities Strategy for Sailing*. The strategy notes that 'England still lacks high quality racing facilities' and confirmed seven sites for Sailing Academies in England 'originally identified in the RYA's [1998–2001] World Class Performance Plan as priority projects for development of competition and training facilities to an international standard' (RYA and Sport England 2001: 4). Collectively, these sites are capable of providing sailing conditions that emulate those found at major international sailing events – an important aspect of competition training at the elite level (cf. RYA 1998c).

In sum, it is clear that, although the RYA adopted a policy in the early 1990s to establish an OSG – a policy development that was somewhat ahead of the sports of swimming and athletics – it has taken over 10 years for this group to realise substantial policy change with regard to elite facility development in the form of Sailing Academies. This may be due, in part, to the particular character-istics of the sport and the relationships it has had to develop with numerous organisations involving the physical environment, harbour authorities and the marine industry (RYA and Sport England 2001). However, what is also clear, and particularly significant for this study, is that a coherent organisational and administrative framework is now in place, not only for the development of elite level sailing facilities but also for many of the other elements essential to the preparation of an elite sailing team. That a more coherent and strategic approach to this level of the sport was adopted earlier by the RYA than by the governing bodies for swimming and athletics is also significant. It is significant given that the advent of National Lottery funding appears to be as important in sailing as in the two other sports. While there remains a significant resistance in swimming and athletics to the emergence of a coalition of actors around the objective of elite level success, such resistance is not apparent to the same degree in sailing. As a senior UK Sport official explained:

> paid staff in the RYA have tended to take the attitude that, well, there are some structures and policies that we don't necessarily like, but let's just get on with it and stop whingeing and make things work for the best in our sport … that's not always the case in some of the other governing bodies.
>
> (Interviewee DD, 28 October 2002)

Emergence of 'full-time' sailors

Although there are parallels to swimming and athletics, there are also important differences in the ways that this issue has developed in the sport of sailing. Although there was extensive discussion of the issue of amateurism within sailing (cf. Fairley 1983), it has not proved to be as contentious as in many other sports. In the late 1950s, the International Yacht Racing Union's (IYRU) Rule 22 stated that an amateur 'yachtsman [is one] who engages in yachting activities afloat as a pastime as distinguished from a means of obtaining a livelihood. Acceptance of any profitable benefit … is inconsistent with amateur status' (quoted in Fairley 1983: 131). This ruling led to problems with those engaged in the sport but not as race sailors. For example, sailing instructors and those running sailing schools were deemed to have breached the amateur rule as outlined by the IYRU. Yet, the RYA appears to have taken a somewhat relaxed position on this issue.

In 1960, for example, RYA Council Minutes reveal that 'The Council supports the view that, except for Olympic regattas, the amateur status rule could be abandoned' (quoted in Fairley 1983: 132). By 1989, in line with changes in other sports (cf. Allison 2001), the IYRU had relaxed its rules over amateur status and now allowed sailors who were also working in the sport in areas such as yacht design, construction and similar professions to compete without loss of amateur status (Pera 1989). Moreover, following the 1988 Olympic Games, the IOC voted 'to declare all professionals eligible for the Olympics, subject to the approval of the international federations in charge of each sport' (Wallechinsky 1996: xxii). The IYRU did not dispute the IOC's ruling and as the sport entered the 1990s opportunities emerged for sailors to compete at major 'non-professional' events such as the Olympic Games and World Championships as well as in professional sailing events such as the America's Cup and various Round-the-World yacht races. At the same time, an emerging elite-oriented coalition within the RYA, centring on the OSG, enhanced its position as a powerful voice within the organisation with the sanctioning of a 'Top Sailor' grant award scheme in 1994 (RYA 1994: 2). Yet, even with the implementation of the 'Top Sailor' grant scheme and the introduction of National Lottery funding in 1997, the cost of training to compete at the highest level, remains a significant problem. In order to achieve success at the highest level 'The RYA considers personal ownership [of a boat] to be the only realistic way of producing top sailors' (RYA 1998a: 4). Given the cost of Olympic Class boats – the Three-Person Keelboat-Soling at £30,000, and the Multihull-Tornado at £17,000 being the most expensive (RYA 1998c) – it is clear that, in order to participate at this level, substantial financial support is paramount.

At the elite level of sailing in the UK, in September 2002, there were 42 sailors on the sport's World Class Performance programme, which received Lottery funding amounting to £1,750,000 for the period April 2002–March 2003 (UK Sport 2002a). The RYA was the first NGB to benefit from Start and Potential Lottery funding from Sport England in 1999–2000, support that, in large part, underpins yacht racing's developmental levels, including the Champion Club programme (sponsored by *Volvo*) and Junior, Youth and Olympic Development squads (RYA 2000). The inauguration of the OSG in the early 1990s can therefore be viewed as the first substantial indication of a shift in policy emphasis that was to continue throughout the 1990s and led to the creation of a framework of development programmes aimed at medal-winning success at the Olympic Games and World Championships (RYA 1998b).

In sum, a clear performance pathway for talented young sailors is now in place, the aim of which is to create a set of conditions that will eventually allow these sailors to train and compete on a full-time basis. The RYA acknowledged as much in its 1997–8 Annual Report, in stating that 'Many of our increasingly full-time sailors are now on a par with those with whom we compete on a world stage' (RYA 1998b: 9). Unlike swimming and athletics, many sailors benefiting from World Class Performance funding and training on a full-time basis also have the opportunity to benefit financially at a later date by transferring to professional events such as the America's Cup and Round-the-World yacht races.

Developments in coaching, sports science and sports medicine

Coaching development in the sport of sailing reflected the ad hoc approach found in most sports in the UK (cf. UK Sport 1999). For example, the RYA had no structured approach to coaching development until the early 1970s when a new

RYA Coaching Scheme was established (Fairley 1983). Moreover, it was only in 1970 that the RYA took the decision to appoint a paid Olympic Training Coach, a decision that was complicated by the prevailing IOC eligibility rules which debarred any person taking up the paid position of Olympic Training Coach from competing in future Olympic Games as a racing sailor (RYA 1970). This remained an issue for the sport throughout the 1970s, although an Olympic Coach was appointed for the 1972 Games, albeit on a short-term contract (Interviewee CC, 11 September 2002). The appointment was further complicated by the shortage of suitable candidates. As Maynard noted in a review of sailing's performance at the 1976 Olympic Games, 'Good class coaches (as opposed to good class *helpers*) were not available for most classes in '76' (1976: 2, emphasis added).

Securing the services of high quality coaches was not helped by the RYA's decision to boycott the 1980 Moscow Olympic Games. As a former Olympic Coach explained, the boycott resulted in a degree of disillusionment amongst coaches and sailors which contributed to the loss of the modest momentum established in the 1970s (Interviewee CC, 11 September 2002; see also Coghlan and Webb 1990). By the late 1980s, however, there was a move towards employing full-time coaches in sailing and the 1988 Olympic Games sailing team utilised five coaches in this capacity. It should be remembered that this was at the elite level and, as a senior RYA racing coach related, before the introduction of Lottery funding, coaching was not 'the normal part of how you learned to race competitively … at international level … most people taught themselves to sail and race and they continued to do that until, perhaps, they came into contact with the RYA coaches' (Interviewee EE, 25 March 2002).

At the RYA's post-1992 Olympic review conducted by the Race Training Committee the decision was taken to not only establish the OSG but also to revise the sport's coaching policy (RYA 1992b: Appendix). There was to be a move away from the notion of full-time RYA staff coaches employed for elite level training and towards the setting-up of 'a group of experienced and respected sailors … to act as "ad hoc" coaches to groups of competitors, Olympic Classes or individual sailors' (1992b: Appendix). This policy shift thus signalled the gradual decline of staff coaches, and a move towards a larger but more diverse pool of coaches for the elite level that could offer the wide range of expertise required by sailors (Interviewee CC, 11 September 2002). The revision was prompted by the many and varied disciplines associated with sailing. In short, not only did elite sailors gain access to a wider range of expertise but the RYA and partner organisations also benefited from the ability to develop coaching/educational/training courses for the many different aspects of the sport and to profit financially from such courses.

Despite recent innovations in coaching, the RYA still faced problems. As the RYA's 1998–2001 World Class Performance Plan states, 'The RYA's system for training, allocating and funding coaches has suffered from a severe lack of resources. There are, therefore, not enough coaches of sufficient quality available' (RYA 1998c: 11). The recommendation to appoint a full-time coach education officer in 1999 formed part of the RYA's strategy to improve coaching quality, and the application for Lottery funding for its 1998–2001 World Class Performance Plan helped to provide the necessary resources (RYA 1998c). Whereas other NGBs suffered from a lack of both strategic direction and resources, the RYA has had a much clearer (and less fiercely contested) elite strategy, but lacked the resources for operationalisation. The strength of the RYA strategy development regarding elite coaching is easily illustrated.

First, there was the decision to create a dedicated OSG in the early 1990s, which resulted in a more strategic and coherent approach to the support of elite level sailing. Second, the decision to use high quality part-time coaches in a sport incorporating numerous and complex technical requirements allowed the RYA to contract coaches to work with Olympic, Paralympic and recognised youth Classes. Thus, the RYA facilitated, rather than provided, coaching centrally from headquarters. In May 1998, for example, the RYA employed just four full-time staff racing coaches, two of which were for windsurfing and match racing disciplines (RYA 1998c). Third, as a senior RYA racing coach explained, there has been a restructuring of the race trainer/instructor/coach system such that every club now has a properly trained, qualified individual providing club level training rather than 'someone who was on the club committee' (Interviewee EE, 25 March 2002; see also RYA 2001a). Finally, as the Chairman of the OSG noted in a post-2000 Olympic review, the decision to employ overseas coaches and technical experts, which began in the lead up to the 1996 Olympics, is now a vital element of sailing's elite level preparation (McIntyre 2000).

In short, the picture painted above suggests that those involved in the organisation and administration of sailing have adapted to the changing conditions of action, not least with regard to changing resource conditions resulting from the introduction of Lottery funding, with greater clarity of purpose than that witnessed in the sports of swimming and athletics. The changing resource conditions cited above increasingly emphasised medal-winning success at Olympic and World Championship events. On this basis, there is strong evidence to suggest that policy changes implemented in this area have played an important part in the recent success of the sport. In the 1996 Olympic Games, for example, where performances of the GB/NI team in all sports were generally poor, the RYA notes that 'sailing won two of Britain's fifteen medals – both Silver … Scoring the [Olympic] regatta on a crude medal count Great Britain was [the] fourth country but scoring it unofficially on points we were the top team' (RYA 1998c: 3).

With regard to the development of sports science and sports medicine disciplines, in a sport as complex and physically demanding as yacht racing (cf. Pinaud 1971), the requirement for scientific/technical expertise in these disciplines is considerable. However, in common with most sports in the UK, the application of sports science and sports medicine knowledge is a relatively recent phenomenon in sailing. In 1976, for example, the Association's embrace of sports science was limited to an acknowledgement that 'it [physical training] is now an integral part of Olympic sailing' (Maynard 1976: 2), while the contribution of sports medicine depended upon the services of a voluntary team doctor (Interviewee CC, 11 September 2002). One of the first indications of a greater acceptance of the value of sports science/medicine can be found in the RYA's successful grant application to the GB Sports Council in 1985, albeit couched in the language of 'fitness programmes and medical services' (RYA 1985: 25). As revealed in the January 1986 Yacht Racing Divisional Committee Minutes, 'The additional "Olympic Preparation" grant had totally altered the situation for our [1988 Olympic] campaign' and extra support was allocated to a 'Sports psychology programme' and for 'Sports medicine' (RYA 1986: 3) – thus laying a foundation for a discussion of a 'Sports Science Support Programme' following the 1992 Barcelona Olympic Games (RYA 1992a: Appendix A).

By utilising funding from the GB Sports Council's Sports Science Support Programme, the Association established a project that would apply 'scientific principals to the analysis of sailing to deepen the understanding of elite performance' (RYA 1992a: Appendix A). The terminology of 'fitness' and 'physical activity' underlying this area of RYA policy in the 1970s and 1980s had been replaced with a discourse reminiscent of the former Eastern bloc programmes. In short, by the early 1990s, the RYA had begun to embrace contemporary developments in sports science/medicine, utilising the services of a part-time physiologist from 1993 (full-time from 1998, when a second (part-time) physiologist was also appointed) and winning approval from the GB Sports Council for the funding of physiological and psychological projects. Today, as acknowledged by a senior UK Sport official, the RYA is one of the country's leading governing bodies of sport with regard to elite level preparation for major sporting events (Interviewee DD, 28 October 2002). The effectiveness of elite preparation is also supported by the strength of sailing in the Olympic medal table since 1996 (see Table 6.3).

Competition opportunities for elite level sailors

The complexity of competition opportunities and structures in sailing is due to the large number of different Class Associations involved in the sport and the potential for up to 60 World Championships. In the UK, and for the RYA, there are primarily three levels (regional, national and international) to competitive opportunities and structures supporting the Junior (11–15 years) and Youth (16–19 years) Classes. At regional level, there is no official competitive structure and most competitions are located at clubs that have a strong following in a particular Class. In a number of Classes, regional competitions are based around a series of events leading up to what is termed, a 'travellers' trophy' (RYA 1999: 10). At UK

Table 6.3 GB/NI sailing medals: Olympic Games, 1988–2000

Olympic Games	Gold	Silver	Bronze	Total
1988	1	0	0	1
1992	0	0	1	1
1996	0	2	0	2
2000	3	2	0	5

level, the national Class Associations organise separate, single annual National Championships and often a national traveller's series for different Classes. At international level, as noted above, the various International Class Associations organise annual World Championships and Continental Championships. In addition to these competitions there are also other prestigious, stand alone multi-Class events, primarily in Europe and North America, forming part of a wide-ranging array of opportunities for elite level sailors in preparation for the pinnacle of this complex competition structure: the Olympic Games (cf. RYA 1999).

It is clear that sailing and individual sailors require a well-managed competitive calendar if success at the elite level is to be realised. As a senior UK sport official suggested, in contrast to athletics, where 'people tended to do their own thing, elite sailors have to be focused, organised individuals in order to manage all the logistics around the many different events across the world' (Interviewee DD, 28 October 2002). Moreover, much of the coach's work at the sport's elite level now centres on managing the logistics involved within available resources. The reference to 'available resources' is instructive. The RYA's 1999–2008 Start and Potential Plan, for example, acknowledges that 'The development of the current high performance programmes has always been constrained by the amount of resources available. This has significantly restricted the width, depth and quality of their implementation' (RYA 1999: 11). However, the concern with resources has not prevented the Association investing heavily to ensure optimal preparation conditions for the Olympic Games (McIntyre 2000). Before 1990, Olympic training and selection trials were held in UK waters. However, following the 1990 policy change, training and selection trials for the 1992 Barcelona Olympics were to be held, as far as possible 'in Mediterranean waters' (RYA 1990: Appendix 1) and for the 1996 Atlanta Olympics, a decision was taken to establish a residential and training facility close to the Savannah location for the Olympic regatta. Later, in 1997, a Sydney Training Base was established at the Woolahara Sailing Club in Australia for the 2000 Olympiad at a total cost of £193,400 (RYA 1998c). The rationale underpinning this policy change is also clear. As the RYA's 1998–2001 World Class Performance Plan states, 'It cannot be stressed too highly how important detailed knowledge of the local weather and tidal currents will be to *winning medals* in 2000' (RYA 1998c: 23, emphasis added).

In sum, the RYA has constructed a training and competition framework, encompassing Junior, Youth and Senior levels of yacht racing, to ensure that 'British Sailing achieves consistent success in future Olympic and World competitions' (RYA 1999: 49). Policy decisions taken in the late 1980s and early 1990s have been facilitated by National Lottery funding and legitimated by consistent Olympic success. As a former Olympic Coach explained, any disquiet within the RYA in relation to the increasing emphasis on preparations for the Olympic Games and the large amounts of Lottery monies on which such preparations were based, 'was silenced by the results in Atlanta and Sydney' (Interviewee CC, 11 September 2002). A clear manifestation of the development of these earlier changes is the now established policy of overseas training and preparation. Indeed, one of the lessons learnt from the 2000 Olympic campaign was that sailors required preparation time of 'at least five months … for the Olympic regatta following the final selection trials'; just one aspect of the quest 'to be the dominant force in Olympic sailing for the next two Olympiads' (McIntyre 2000: 4–5).

Summary

It is clear that, over the past 10 to 15 years, the RYA has embraced the corporate, and increasingly contractual obligations, that are now an integral element of the resource relationships it enjoys with UK Sport and Sport England. Although progress has not always been rapid, the RYA has steadily moved to a position where it has in place, across all four key areas of elite development, a strategically focused and integrated framework. With regard to developments in elite level facilities, the publication of a *Facilities Strategy for Sailing* in 2001 highlights the construction of seven regional Sailing Academies in England 'as priority projects for the development of competition and training facilities to an international standard' (RYA and Sport England 2001: 4). The emergence of full-time sailors was the second area of elite development considered and 42 sailors were (as of September 2002) funded through the World Class Performance programme for the period April 2002–March 2003 (UK Sport 2002a). However, as for the sports of swimming and athletics, 'full-time' remains a relative term as a number of these sailors continue to work in other employment, either, full- or part-time (Interviewee CC, 11 September 2002; see also RYA 1998b).

The developments in coaching, sports science/medicine provision broadly reflect those found in swimming and athletics, however, the RYA appears to have embraced change in these areas somewhat earlier. The structure of competition and training opportunities for sailors was the final area considered, where there has been sustained investment since the early 1990s to establish training bases, which reflect conditions similar to those expected in the forthcoming Olympic Games. Part of the explanation of the relatively uncontroversial development of a sophisticated and expensive elite sailor support system lies in the absence of the organisational, administrative and jurisdictional power struggles evident in swimming and athletics. The establishment of the OSG in the early 1990s signalled the embryonic development of a coalition of actors within the RYA with a clear focus on the elite level. The development of the OSG was driven by the RYA's review of the 1992 Olympic performance where the team won just one Bronze medal. The review also prompted the decision to improve the RYA's system and organisation of Olympic preparation by a reallocation of existing resources (RYA 1992a).

With regard to the two sources of policy change (i.e. Lottery funding and changing values/beliefs) identified in the sports of swimming and athletics, changing values/beliefs do not appear to have had the same significance in explaining change within the RYA and sailing. In relation to this, it was suggested earlier that the RYA is comprised of members who possess a substantial amount of social, economic and/or cultural capital. This is clearly related to the perception of the sport as socially exclusive; a contention reinforced by Aversa (1986), who investigated different 'entry routes' taken by newcomers to the sport, albeit in an American context. Aversa identified three such routes: (i) traditional: joining a yacht club; (ii) commercial: through commercial sailing schools; and (iii) most informal: learning the rudiments of sailing from boat dealers who offer sailing instruction as a by-product of purchasing a boat. Interestingly, Aversa concludes that it is through the first of these routes where sailors become most accomplished: 'the elite of the sport' (1986: 52). However, joining yacht clubs is not socially or economically straightforward, and the RYA has acknowledged that the sport tends to be perceived as elitist 'partly due to the cost of equipment, clothing and travel and partly because the older, more traditional sailing clubs are seen as being largely white, male, upper to middle-class organisations' (RYA 2001a: 15). That the Association has drawn up an action plan in order 'to increase opportunities for everyone who wishes to take part in the sport' (2001a: 15) is notable. Of greater significance for this study, however, is that this socio-demographic profile might, somewhat paradoxically, help to explain how policy towards elite sailors could change so smoothly. More specifically, there are a large number of people participating in water sports activities who: (i) are not involved with the RYA; (ii) are not concerned with competitive events; and (iii) can afford to participate in their chosen activity unaffected (and unconcerned) by RYA policy direction and/ or resource allocation that 'favours' elite level sailors. In other words, what the RYA does with its money (especially Lottery money) has little impact on the quality and quantity of opportunities for the vast majority of sailors.

To summarise, today the RYA has a Performance Directorate comprising some 30 staff, which complements the elite focus of the OSG (RYA 1999: Appendix 19); an organisational framework that is far removed from the situation before the 1988 Seoul Olympics. As one senior RYA racing manager related, 'we've gone from having people in blazers wandering around trying to decide who should go to the Olympic Games, to coming up with systems that have the ability to send people to the Games who are most likely to win medals' (Interviewee EE, 25 March 2002). Clearly, the coalition of actors grouped around the OSG and the Performance Directorate has one primary focus: to win Olympic/World Championship medals, a focus in line with that of UK Sport and Sport England. Yet, on the question of whether these organisations are 'too directive' in their relationships with NGBs, the senior racing manager argued that this is not the case and that 'with UK Sport, in particular, we work really closely with them to ensure that they have a good understanding of what we are trying to achieve and how we want to achieve it, and that has offset any directives' (Interviewee EE, 25 March 2002); an organisational complementarity that has yet to emerge to the same degree in swimming and athletics.

7   Conclusion

At first sight, it would seem that each of the countries under consideration arrived at a policy emphasis on elite sport by very different routes. For Canada, the primary catalyst was the urgent domestic concern with national identity and the challenge posed by the growing influence of Québec separatism on national politics. The desire to utilise international sporting success as both a symbol of Canadian unity and as a stimulus to a common identity was certainly important in generating federal funding for elite sport. The enthusiasm of Canadian cities to host major international sports events and the willingness of the federal government to provide some support for facility development may be traced back to the same motive of enhancing national (or, in the case of Montreal, Québécois) identity through a high international profile. As regards Australia, it is possible to argue that the increasing priority, in terms of resource allocation for example, of elite achievement was a natural extension of the country's long history of sporting involvement at the international level and the crucial role played by innovative coaches, such as Forbes Carlile in swimming and Herb Elliot in track and field. By contrast, the progress of the UK towards a greater emphasis on elite sport was hampered by a deeply-rooted disdain for a professional approach to sport and the consequent support for high quality coaching, full-time training and first class facilities. For the UK, reference to Corinthian ideals was used as a diversion from the inadequacies of the sports system that prevailed into the late twentieth century. This institutionalised complacency was only gradually undermined by repeated failure in international competition.

Although the particular circumstances under which each country gave greater priority to elite achievement vary, the general context is remarkably similar. In all three countries the exogenous factor of poor performance either in international sport generally or, more usually, at the Olympic level precipitated or strengthened state intervention which was often encouraged by media criticism of the national performance. For Australia, the defining Games were those in 1976, for Canada the country's poor performance at the 1960 Rome Olympics where it won just a single (Silver) medal and, probably more importantly defeat by the Soviet Union in the national game of ice hockey, and for the UK a more generalised sense of decline that built up during the 1990s, which was confirmed by the exceptionally poor performance at the Atlanta Olympic Games in 1996.

The general context within which the prioritisation of elite sport emerged was also similar in relation to the increasing recognition of the powerful symbolism of international sporting success (and failure). All three countries had an acute awareness of the success with which the GDR, the Soviet Union and the United States had used their considerable Olympic achievements to promote their political objectives. There was also an acceptance that prominence at the Olympic Games either through hosting a successful Games or by virtue of a high medal count was a powerfully positive metaphor for the nation. More importantly there was a casual assumption that the symbolism of international sport was malleable and could be defined and managed by governments. Even when there was clear evidence that the symbolic properties of international sport were unstable governments frequently persisted in their prioritisation of elite sport. Australia brushed aside doping scandals at the Australian Institute of Sport (AIS) in the late 1980s and proceeded to bid successfully for the 2000 Olympics and invest substantial sums of public money from the mid-1990s to ensure that it maximised the chances of success of its athletes. Of the three countries in this study, Canada is the one that has shown the most prolonged disillusion with elite sport. The coincidence of the lengthy period of intro-spection prompted by the Ben Johnson drugs scandal in 1988 with the election of a budget cutting government has made the revival of public investment in elite sport a slow process. However, for all three countries the attraction of Olympic success has proved difficult to resist for long.

The common features of the experience of Australia, Canada and the UK in their engagement with elite sport are paralleled at the national governing body level. Before examining their experience in detail, it is worth emphasising the four broad common tensions which were rarely far from the surface and which provided an almost constant context for their work with high performance athletes. The first tension was between elite development and club development. All three countries and all three sports were addressing the apparent incompatibility between the needs of the elite athlete for a concentration of expertise, financial resources and management time, and their requirement for non-transferable resources (for example, specialist competitions and sports science support) and the needs of the club infrastructure and the grass roots participant for access to adequate facilities, a competition calendar that reinforced the value of club membership and provided a supportive pattern to the club member's season. The second tension overlaps substantially with the first and was that between the highly individual needs of the elite athlete, the value placed on individual achievement and the progressive isolation of the elite athlete from her/his club origins on the one hand and the collective needs of club members, the value placed on sport as a socially valuable undertaking and sports participation as a social activity on the other. Third, there was the tension between an aspiration towards a professionalised rational-bureaucratic model of management and the voluntaristic and more sectional/political model of decision-making found in many sports. In the former, success is more likely to be equated with change or modernisation, while in the latter success is more likely to be measured in terms of stability, continuity and longevity. Finally, all six cases involving swimming and athletics were affected by the tension between a pressure to centralise and resistance from the peripheral regions, states, territories and provinces.

Four areas of elite sport development

Facility development

It is rare and perhaps unheard of for a sport to claim that all its elite development facility needs have been met. Certainly among the three sports considered here the inadequacy of facilities for elite training was a recurring theme. For swimming in all three countries, a major constraint on elite development was the lack of ownership and control over pools. In Australia, the weaknesses in the network of pools were, to a substantial extent, addressed by the allocation of funds to ensure maximum success at the 2000 Olympics. Of particular importance was the establishment of the AIS at Canberra and the network of State/Territory institutes which provided competition quality facilities in the major centres of population. However, the size of the country and its relatively sparse population meant that access to suitable pools was always uneven. The problem was compounded by the limitations on access to pools based in the country's extensive private school network. Nevertheless, it is clear that Australia has a broadly appropriate geographical distribution of pools and that issues of access are not of major significance.

Much the same conclusion can be drawn regarding facility provision for athletics. As with swimming, the investment in State/Territory and federal elite institutes ensured a minimum distribution of elite level competition and training facilities. However, it was also clear that planning a national strategic distribution of centres of expertise was hampered by the determination of the State/Territory authorities to identify their own priorities. Consequently, Australia has not been able to optimise the use of scarce facility resources (and also coaching and sports science expertise). More importantly, it was repeatedly argued that the concentration on meeting the extensive needs of elite athletes had a significant opportunity cost for the club level participant. Not only did the NSOs for both swimming and athletics skew resources in favour of elite competitors but federal government attempts to sharpen the focus on participation seemed half-hearted. The cynical response of Athletics Australia Incorporated (AAI) to the federal government's drive to increase participation was, as noted, to redefine its remit to encompass activities such as fun running and jogging which will do little for the development of the club infrastructure. More surprising was the apparent willingness of the government to accept this strategy as constituting compliance with its policy. Facility provision for Australian sailors followed a broadly similar pattern to the other two sports insofar as the provision of specialist training facilities was dependent on federal funding which was provided to support the preparations for the Sydney Games. Similar to swimming and athletics, membership of the elite squad usually involved transferring from club to specialist facility.

In contrast to Australia, the three Canadian sports faced considerable problems in meeting the facility needs of their elite athletes. All three sports had great difficulty in developing a national facility strategy to suit the particular needs of their sport, partly due to a lack of resources and partly due to the dispersal of power between the various jurisdictions within the sport. All three sports were obliged to adapt their strategic preferences to fit with the location of Canadian Sport Centres (CSCs). Swimming/Natation Canada (SNC) worked within the CSC network to a greater degree than either Athletics Canada (AC) or the Canadian Yachting Association (CYA), arguing that a close alignment with CSCs was supportive of its recent re-emphasis on high performance objectives, most clearly stated in its 'COMMIT TO WIN!' philosophy in 2002 (SNC 2002a: 4). Indeed, SNC established seven dedicated swimming centres, six of which are aligned to the CSCs. AC, although embracing the CSC concept to a certain degree, has yet to formulate a coherent policy position in relation to this element of high performance sport, as revealed by the somewhat ambiguous statements on this issue in recent Annual General Meeting and Semi-Annual General Meeting reports (cf. AC 2001a). That AC has yet to formulate coherent policy direction on this issue is perhaps not surprising as the organisation struggles to come to terms with the ramifications of the damning assessment of its organisational capabilities in the internal audit in 2001.

For sailing, the CYA has established three sailing centres aligned to CSCs close to water in Halifax, Toronto and Vancouver. Senior officials at the CYA and Sport Canada made it clear that utilisation of the CSCs is not just about elite sailor development, it is also about long-term sailor development, and thus for those sailors below the high performance level who have suffered from variable commitment to high performance sport at provincial/territorial levels. However, one area where the CYA does not appear to have maximised opportunities for facility use is at provincial and/or club levels. Unlike the Australian experience and, as we will see, that of the UK, the involvement of sports in the CSC network did little to enhance the lobbying capacity of the elite interests within the sport. The AIS in Canberra with its close links with the ASC provided an organisational focus for the activities of the network of centres and also for the NSOs that used them and a voice close to the centre of decision-making within the federal government. In Canada, the CSCs had no similarly effective federal level focus for advocacy.

In the UK, the issue of facility development cannot easily be separated from the internal organisational tensions found in both swimming and athletics. With regard to the sport of swimming, for example, it is important to recall that for many years the dominant organisational force for policy direction was the Amateur Swimming Association (ASA). However, the establishment of the Amateur Swimming Federation of Great Britain (ASFGB) as a constitutionally distinct limited company in 2002, together with the creation of a wholly-owned subsidiary company, High Performance Swimming Ltd, radically shifted the balance of power at the elite level of swimming and effectively insulated elite interests from others within the sport. One consequence of this internal reorganisation was to increase the confidence within UK Sport that swimming was in a position to use its organisational resources to complement the investment in facilities. The ASFGB has witnessed unprecedented investment in 50 metre swimming pools rather than the traditional construction of short-course 25 metre pools. Although these 50 metre pools are clearly aimed at providing training conditions tailored towards elite swimmers, contractual agreements under National Lottery rules extend access to the general public. Policy for facility development/use has thus been turned on its head. In the past, elite level swimmers trained, in large part, in pools owned by local authorities and/or educational institutions where lane hire was costly and access times were most usually restricted to early mornings and/or late at night. Today, the UK's elite swimmers are the primary 'customers' of many of these new 50 metre pools and the general public's access is incorporated around training times for the elite swimmer.

As with swimming, access to National Lottery funding has been central to the increased availability of suitable facilities, especially indoor facilities, for elite track and field athletes. The improvement has been largely due to the continuing investment of Lottery funds in the network of facilities/support services aligned to the United Kingdom Sports Institute (UKSI). However, substantial concerns remain regarding a lack of core funding for the development of facilities at grass roots levels (O'Connor 2003; UKA 2002b). Unlike swimming and athletics, which are both increasingly locked into a resource dependency relationship with their public funding agencies, sailing has largely avoided the necessity of developing a close relationship with government agencies and has also been remarkably successful in delivering medals. Part of the explanation for the greater autonomy of sailing was undoubtedly the reluctance of the then GB Sports Council to offer funding support to a sport perceived as socially exclusive. However, part of the explanation was that the sport's socio-economic profile, and the capacity of many water sports participants to pursue their activity with few financial concerns, reduced significantly the need for financial aid. Finally, the nature of the sport, which requires a substantial variety of sailing conditions, made the argument for a single national sailing centre less compelling, and explained why the closure, in 1987, of Cowes as a primary sailing centre caused so little concern. Nevertheless, in recent years a much closer relationship has developed between the RYA and Sport England (RYA and Sport England 2001), though prompted more by the RYA's capacity to deliver Olympic medals on a regular basis and less on the Association's enthusiastic embrace of social inclusion. As a result there is currently a strategy to develop nine sailing academies in the UK within which the development of sailors for high performance competitions will take place.

There is also an increasingly close relationship between the RYA and UK Sport, which has been made possible because the Association has not had to deal with the debilitating internal factionalism that has dogged both swimming and athletics and also because the Association had anticipated much of the current modernisation agenda promoted by UK Sport. Because of the relative lack of internal tensions the Association was better placed to embrace the values of elite achievement and, more importantly, the organisational consequences that followed. The establishment of the Olympic Steering Group in the early 1990s and the more recent creation of a 30–strong Performance Directorate were largely uncontroversial within the organisation. Thus, the RYA has embraced the increasingly contractual agreements set out by funding agencies such as Sport England and, more significantly, UK Sport, in relation to the elite level with far greater enthusiasm and success than was evident in swimming and athletics. 'Success' here for both the RYA and Sport England/UK Sport is, primarily, Olympic and World Championship medals. However, there is another, and perhaps equally important, aspect of this positive-sum relationship, namely the support it provides for UK Sport's drive to 'modernise' national governing bodies of sport. In short, UK Sport cites the RYA as an exemplar of organisational and administrative effectiveness, thereby, in turn helping to legitimise its own programme of modern-isation in a policy sector that has traditionally valued autonomy, voluntarism and independence.

Not surprisingly, in the two sports in all three countries which were the most dependent on public resources for facility development, namely swimming and athletics, there was little evidence of an emerging consensus over the prioritisation of elite achievement. Both sports were characterised by value conflict which was often managed by the isolation of elite facilities from mass access, for example, through the establishment of CSCs in Canada and the network of elite sport institutes (UKSI) in the UK, and thus the creation of separate administrative and financial arrangements to ensure that no elite level funding can be siphoned off for grass roots use. Where high performance advocacy coalitions have emerged in swimming and athletics, they have done so, in most cases, only with the sustained sponsorship of the state. In other words, states have frequently con-structed a supporting coalition within NSOs/NGBs to serve their own objectives. Sailing was an exception largely because its well-established club structure and the financial independence of its membership left it insulated from the competition for scarce resources that featured so significantly in the other two sports. If the resource dependency relationship between the advocates of elite sport and the state was a major factor shaping elite policy development, a second factor of equal significance was the jurisdictional complexity that most NSOs/NGBs had to cope with. On the one hand, jurisdictional rivalry overlaid, and often subsumed, debates on the preferred pattern of values in the sport: on the other hand, jurisdictional rivalry presented government agencies, especially in the UK, with a legitimation of their strategies to modernise and professionalise the management and decision-making within these bodies.

The emergence of 'full-time' competitors

Canada began to provide a direct financial subsidy to its elite athletes in the 1970s followed some time later by both Australia and the UK. In none of the countries, even the UK where National Lottery funding was the most generous, was the subsidy sufficient to enable elite competitors to be financially independent with the consequence that many relied on parental support or commercial sponsorship. This was perhaps most noticeable for Australian sailors who suffered not only from a lack of sustained direct assistance from the ASC, at least until the introduction of Olympic Athlete Programme (OAP) funding, but also because sailing had not been able to obtain corporate sponsorship at a level enjoyed by more high profile Olympic sports, such as swimming. For most subsidised competitors direct funding was often linked to their transfer from their local clubs to national or regional high performance training centres frequently exacerbating tensions between the NSO/NGB and the constituent clubs who saw 'their' athletes being poached, thus further undermining the club infrastructure. An additional problem that arose as a consequence of public subsidy was the tendency of elite athletes to seek to maximise their personal commercial income at the expense of the commercial success of their NSO/NGB. In both swimming and athletics, competitors frequently gave priority to the commercial Grand Prix circuit and the personal income it generated, and to preparing for Olympic competition, rather than participate in competitions organised by their NSO/NGB and from which their NSO/NGB would derive income. For example, almost all the UK's potential medallists failed to compete at the 2003 World Indoor Athletics Championships trials in Birmingham, prompting UKA's High Performance Director to argue that 'The sport's lottery funding is judged on how many medals we win at major championships ... My job is to achieve that and everything is subservient to it. It's not my job to get people to compete at the trials' (quoted in Mackay 2003: 33) or apparently to support the commercial strategy of the parent organisation. This has led to the bizarre situation in the UK where publicly subsidised athletes 'are to be offered financial incentives for the first time in an attempt to ensure they turn out for Britain' (Mackay 2003: 33) and protect the lucrative sponsorship deals that UKA has recently negotiated.

A second key comparison across the three countries, and across the three sports, concerns the involvement of the corporate/business sector in supporting NSOs/NGBs. Although all sports were to keen to maximise corporate sponsorship, Canada had perhaps the greatest need due to the severity of federal funding reductions in the 1990s. Both the 1998 National Conference on Sport and the Corporate Sector (Nieuwenhuis 1999) and the discussions surrounding the new Canadian Sport Policy (Canadian Heritage 2001) emphasised the need for corporate support. However, corporate sponsorship of individual athletes, especially in swimming and athletics, encouraged elite swimmers and athletes to compete abroad for prize monies often to the detriment of their long-term development and consequently to Canada's medal-winning potential at the Olympic Games. As Slack observed, these athletes 'no longer represent their club, their country, or themselves, they represent the corporations who provide the money for their sport' (1998: 3). In a climate of variable federal and provincial/territorial funding for amateur sport, Canadian NSOs are thus hamstrung on the one hand by the need to seek corporate monies, while on the other having to contend with the dilemmas such corporate support creates.

The calls for corporate support from those charged with shaping (elite) sport policy in the UK have been somewhat less urgent. Indeed, as recently as 2001, the DCMS-sponsored *Elite Sports Funding Review* paid scant attention to this issue. Where the issue was raised, it was couched in the language of searching for 'other sources of support … to help maximise the Lottery investment in elite sport (e.g. sponsorship)' (DCMS 2001: 5). At the elite level at least, and for all three UK sports considered here, the urgency in seeking corporate support has been reduced by the present levels of World Class Performance funding. However, although the availability of Lottery funding helps UK NGBs avoid the pressures of corporate sponsorship, it is clear that Lottery funding is provided with substantial conditions attached.

Coaching, and sports science and medicine

In all sports covered in this study and across all three countries acceptance of coaching as an important, if not essential, ingredient in elite success and, more importantly, an ingredient that required status and investment was slow in developing. Until the advent of substantial public subsidy of both swimming and athletics investment in coaching was not possible in the volume that would encourage talented amateur coaches to see the occupation as a full-time career. However, even when public funds became available, the initial focus for investment was on facilities followed by athletes: the supporting services of coaching, sports science and medicine were generally an afterthought.

Up until the mid-1990s, coaching was of extremely variable quality and uneven in its distribution within the sports considered here. The systematic planning of coaching services and coach development is therefore a very recent consideration. Part of the explanation of the slow pace of the development of coaching services lay in the legacy of the ethos of amateurism, while part of the explanation, especially in Australia, lay in the concern of established, often volunteer, interests in the sports that coaches might usurp their control. What is clear in all the cases in this study, but especially in Australia, is that investment in coaching tended to mean investment in elite coaching with investment in coaching for the mass of participants receiving a much lower priority. In Australia, this was most notable, somewhat paradoxically given their history of innovative and esteemed coaches, in swimming and athletics (cf. Phillips 2000). In swimming, a key concern was that ASI had failed to establish effective grass roots relationships between swimming coaches and schools. However, perhaps the most damning critique of coaching was evident in athletics, where Roe (2002) argued that, across the elite sport-mass participation spectrum, AAI had neglected the development of coaches and that a radical shake-up of coaching education and development was required if both the decline in the popularity of the sport at the grass roots levels and the lack of success on the international stage were to be reversed.

The emphasis on elite coaching was also notable in Canada. For example, although SNC has embraced recent coaching developments, such as the coaching-based education and training (CBET) programme and the sports science services provided through the CSC network, concerns persist in Canadian swimming circles regarding the distribution of benefits across the sport. Jean Tihanyi (2001a) maintains that coaching is not regarded as a profession and that at grass roots levels little is being done to support the large numbers of volunteer coaches.

Indeed, elsewhere Tihanyi (2001b) has argued that SNC's current emphasis on the CSC support services, and thus elite level swimmers, fails to address the nurturing of swimmers at levels below the elite. However, of the three Canadian NSOs investigated, AC stands out for the damning criticism of its coaching structures in the 2001 audit, with *The Globe and Mail* reporting that 'Athletics Canada gets flayed for "failing to deliver coaching education programmes, failing to compensate coaches adequately and failing to develop coaches through appointment to national teams"' (quoted in Christie 2001a).

With regard to the CYA, although changes to coaching education and development inherent in the CBET initiative have been embraced, this is a recent phenomenon; until recently the CYA employed no full-time sailing coaches (five full-time coaches are now in place) and high performance sailors were left to develop their own training programmes. Only recently, at the Association's Strategic Pursuits Planning Workshop in 2001, was the need for greater investment in coaches acknowledged (CYA 2001). The 2001 Workshop also highlighted a somewhat sceptical attitude to sports science/medicine disciplines and a lack of awareness as to how they might be applied to high performance sailing. What is evident here, though, is a form of policy transfer. One senior CYA official clearly stated that the Association had looked to the success of the UK sailing team in recent years (Interviewee T, 17 June 2002) and an internal CYA paper revealed the value now placed on closely mirroring the techniques adopted by the Royal Yachting Association's (RYA) elite sailing team's sports science based approach to training and competition (CYA 2002c).

Turning to the three UK NGBs, the appointment in 2000 of former Australian swimming coach, Bill Sweetenham, as National Performance Director for swimming is instructive. Sweetenham is credited as the driving force behind recent changes in approaches to coaching techniques in swimming, with much more emphasis now placed on linking aspects of coaching certification with performance and the assessment of the quality of swimmers produced (ASA 2002a). There are also comparisons with SNC's high performance philosophy in Sweetenham's comments that 'Our team motto [now] is that winning is the only option. We don't want to know about anything else' (quoted in Dryden 2002: 13). In sailing, the requirement for elite coaching expertise has been far less contested than in either swimming or athletics. From the early 1990s, the RYA facilitated a gradual evolution towards the creation of a pool of coaches with expertise in the different yacht Classes that allowed for a more effective targeting of resources, the success of which was manifest in both the Atlanta and Sydney Olympics. A similar picture of organisational effectiveness with regard to coaching was not apparent in athletics, one key indicator of which was UKA's failure to integrate sports science and medicine expertise within structures for coach education and development. There are undoubtedly excellent individual track and field coaches in the UK. However, part of the explanation for UKA's difficulties in constructing a coherent structure for coaching development throughout the sport lies in the embedded factionalism that has blighted athletics for many years (cf. Foster 2004).

As regards the acceptance and exploitation of sports science and medicine, all sports have been fairly slow to explore the potential of sports science in relation to competitors. In all three sports, but sailing in particular, the early engagement with sports science has been with equipment and apparel rather than science focused on the preparation and training of competitors. Part of the explanation is that there is profit to be made from boat design and the sale of sports clothing, but little profit to be made from scientific research into training, nutrition and psychological preparation for competition. Athlete-centred sports science and medicine only became more readily available when governments decided to invest public money in its development. However, public investment has been erratic and often mediated by universities with the result that the impact has been variable. What tended to make a difference was the establishment of an elite level organisational focus, such as the AIS or the UKSI, which could, to some degree at least, give direction to sports science research and, more importantly, facilitate its dissemination, acceptance and application. However, especially in the case of the UK, the effective utilisation of sports science and medicine is clearly some way off. For example, as one former senior official at the British Athletic Federation (BAF) explained, the Genesis Report into athletics was highly critical of the absence of significant sports science research in the sport (Interviewee AA, 30 April 2002).

Competition opportunities

The establishment of a competition calendar that met the needs of elite athletes was surprisingly hard to achieve in almost all nine cases. Five factors help to account for the slow emergence of an appropriate elite competition schedule. First, this was the issue which crystallised the conflicting interests of clubs/grass roots members and elite performers. For many clubs, regular regattas, galas or inter-club track and field competitions are, on the one hand, the organisational rationale for the club's existence and, on the other, important opportunities for the social contact that helps to bind members together. Second, the establishment of a competition schedule suitable for elite athletes was difficult because many high performance athletes were content to put their own financial interests (or those of their sponsor) ahead of those of their country. In athletics and swimming in particular, it was often the case that athletes would prefer to compete on the commercial Grand Prix circuit rather than in domestic club competitions or international representative events. Third, it must also be admitted that some NSOs/NGBs have not been very successful in constructing an appropriate calendar which balanced their need to generate income with the needs of their elite athletes to prepare systematically for major international competitions. Fourth, both Australia and Canada had to overcome the problems associated with the size of their countries and the consequent problems of arranging national events and competitions. Australia faced the further problem of its relative isolation from the main international competition circuits in all three sports. Finally, Canada faced the additional problem of having a number of their track and field athletes and swimmers obliged to compete for United States colleges in NCAA competitions.

With regard to the Australian NSOs, the targeting of swimming and athletics by the ASC in the early to mid-1990s as two of the sports that were expected to contribute significantly to a successful Sydney Olympics, was part of the explanation for ASI and AAI establishing national domestic elite-focused competition opportunities. However, little thought was given to the implications for sub-elite and grass roots competition. These sports are thus currently in a position of facing both internal and external criticism of their elite emphasis in the 1990s and consequently face substantial problems in re-building competition structures for the developmental levels of their sports. The 2000 Olympic Games was also the prompt for the AYFI (with financial backing eventually from the ASC) to develop a more coherent set of competition opportunities for its sailors. It remains to be seen whether the AYFI's recent attempts to establish a coherent competition calendar in sailing will provide not only continued success at the elite level, but also, and perhaps more importantly, an embedded structure of competition opportunities for its future elite sailors.

Of the three Canadian NSOs only the CYA had managed to establish, albeit only very recently, a coherent developmental competition calendar. In contrast to the recent past, when sailors were left to devise their own competitive programmes, a more structured, cost-efficient and locally-based North American programme has now been put in place, and one which, crucially, takes account of the current resource conditions within which the Association operates. This is not to argue that the CYA has been free from the type of difficulties faced by SNC and AC in respect of a complex competitive calendar and jurisdictional divisions. Rather, it is to highlight the capacity of the CYA to adapt to the shifting resource conditions that have emerged within the Canadian sport delivery system with greater flexibility and clarity of purpose than was evident in either swimming or athletics. In short, the CYA has acknowledged that within the current climate of variable commitment at federal level to high performance objectives and the Canadian Olympic Committee's (COC) policy of targeting funds only to NSOs capable of winning Olympic medals (and the CYA is not yet in this category) it has been prudent to adopt a policy approach whereby its competitive calendar is tightly-resourced, well-structured and North American-based.

With regard to the three UK NGBs, the appointment of Bill Sweetenham as the sport's National Performance Director led to fundamental changes to the philosophy underlying the sport's training and competition opportunities and structures. In the past, elite level training/competition revolved around short-course competitions (which had much to do with the tradition of building 25 metre rather than 50 metre swimming pools). In just over three years, Sweetenham and the Performance Directorate team at the ASFGB have restructured policy for training/competition such that it has been turned on its head. There is now far less time spent attending 'non-useful' competitions and far more time spent training to peak at the Olympic Games and World Championships. Yet, this calculated drive to achieve Olympic success has not been welcomed by all in the sport, especially by those with a primary interest in club development (cf. Ballard 2002; Lodewyke 2002). A similar picture is evident within athletics where the competition calendar was subject to very little debate until recently (UKA 2000) when the focus was sharply placed on the needs of the elite athlete (Ward 2002a). As a former senior BAF official argued, 'The sport's competition structure is about the drive for medals. That's what the government wants. That's what Sport England wants' (Interviewee AA, 30 April 2002). In all cases, when NSOs/NGBs in each of the three countries identified the need to restructure their competition calendar, they were almost always referring to the elite competition calendar.

Common themes in elite sport development

The review of the four areas of elite sport development policy reveals five common themes and tendencies. The first is the extent and scope of intervention in influencing the policy of NSOs/NGBs towards elite sport. All three countries provide evidence of the determination of federal/central government to shape policy to suit its own agenda and Canada also illustrates the vulnerability of NSOs when government priorities change. Even though sailing is a partial exception, in the UK more than in either Canada or Australia, due to its substantial financial independence from governments, the sport was still reliant to an increasing extent on the provision of public subsidy to support its elite ambitions. When governments seek to achieve their policy objective through the offering of substantial inducements it is difficult to justify refusal especially when the policy objective is wrapped in the national flag and resonates so clearly with some, at least, of the objectives of the NSO/NGB. Not surprisingly, in no country did any sport reject the gift-laden intervention of government. To date, perhaps only Canadian NSOs, with hindsight produced by painful experience, are aware that the provision of public funding comes at a price and that once an organisation has adjusted to high public subsidy the extent of resource dependence can leave little option but to follow the shifts in government priorities. Canadian NSOs suffered a double blow when the government cut their subsidy and also downgraded the emphasis on elite development and international success. At present, the Australian NSOs and the UK NGBs are still enjoying considerable government financial support but should the government change its priorities or determine that its strategy for elite success is not giving value for money then they too will face a period of traumatic readjustment.

The second common theme is the insulation of elite resources and services from grass roots members. Most of the NSOs/NGBs established separate internal structures (for example, the RYA's Olympic Steering Group and Performance Directorate) and most also adopted separate financial and accounting procedures as a way of ring-fencing elite funding from those responsible for meeting the needs of clubs and grass roots members. Although few went as far as UKA and the ASFGB in establishing legally separate organisations to manage their elite income there was a clear concern to prevent government subsidy being reallocated. In essence, traditional top-down lines of accountability which enabled the membership of the NSO/NGB to exercise significant control over the actions of the leadership was replaced by a horizontal line of accountability between the

NSO/NGB leadership and national governmental agencies such as the ASC or UK Sport. Such horizontal lines of accountability were reinforced by the establishment, by most NSOs/NGBs, of management posts, such as performance director, with clearly identified, limited and specialist responsibilities.

The third theme to emerge from the cases is the increasing tension between grass roots members and clubs on the one hand and elite athletes and training centres on the other. Even in sailing there were some expressions of unease at the apparent diversion of resources away from the development of the club infrastructure. In all three countries, grass roots versus elite tensions were over-laid with (and confused by) jurisdictional friction between states/territories/provinces/regions on the one hand and the NSO/NGB on the other. However, swimming and athletics in particular faced substantial problems in reassuring the generality of members and clubs that they constituted a high priority for the national leadership. Only in sailing, where competition for public resources was far less intense was the tension muted. In swimming and athletics, there was the frequently expressed view that the interests of clubs and grass roots members were, at best, being marginalised and, at worst, were being sacrificed for the benefit of the elite.

The fourth theme was the tension between the personal ambitions and obligations of elite athletes, particularly in swimming and athletics, and the ambitions of their NSOs/NGBs for international competition medals. Although the interests of elite athletes and their NSOs/NGBs often coincided, as they did, for example, over participation in the Olympic Games, there were many occasions when elite athletes were either content to place their own personal financial gain ahead of representing effectively their country or were required to give priority to representing their United States college sponsors over participation in NSO-organised events. Although elite athletes were best able to maximise their income by using Olympic success to demand high appearance fees from the organisers of commercial Grand Prix events, their NSO/NGB maximised income (both public funding and commercial sponsorship) by sustained international success and organising domestic national competitions in which their elite athletes were guaranteed to participate.

The final theme is the increasing difficulty that NSOs/NGBs face in trying to balance elite achievement objectives with those associated with mass participation. As mentioned above, the concentration on elite development has usually resulted in the relative neglect of the development and maintenance of the club infra-structure, perhaps best illustrated by the skewing of coaching development towards the needs of the elite rather than the generality of members. However, part of the problem facing NSOs/NGBs is the result of the lack of integration between government allocation of resources and government policy objectives. At various times in all three countries the central/federal government has raised the status of mass participation objectives and encouraged or required the support of NSOs/NGBs. Unfortunately, such shifts in policy priorities have rarely been accompanied by adequate changes in funding often because central/federal governments assume that the resources for mass participation will or should be provided by levels of sub-national government. What is very clear from all three countries is the absence of a voice of any significant volume for the mass participant.

As the foregoing discussion suggests, the maintenance of an emphasis on elite sport and achievement has not always been easy for the NSOs/NGBs concerned and has been far from cost or risk free. As is nearly always the case with public policy, it is rare for the objectives of policy to be clear and unequivocal. In the three countries in this study, there has clearly been a concern to improve international sporting success, but this objective has sat alongside other more complex objectives. In Canada, for example, the process of collectively striving for Canadian international success has been almost as important as the success itself. Indeed, national unity can probably be enhanced as much through the collective experience of failure and disappointment as through success. However, governments clearly prefer to see their investment in elite sport rewarded by medals and trophies even if success of the policy can be measured in other ways. Consequently, the questions must be asked regarding how much success governments expect, how long after their initial investment they expect to witness that success and how long lasting they expect the success to be.

Canada is a valuable study of the risks of high dependence on public funding and the fragility of that funding commitment. The disillusionment with elite sport that followed the Ben Johnson case produced a radical reassessment of the commitment of public resources, the consequences of which are still affecting the activities of many NSOs, including swimming, athletics and sailing. In many ways the NSOs/NGBs in Australia and the UK have embarked on an extremely risky path which has led them to neglect their club infrastructure, alienate many of their volunteers and foster the development of an increasingly self-centred cadre of rich elite athletes. Should government decide that elite sport was no longer a priority, because of the embarrassment of a positive doping case, or the lack of rapid high level success, or because objectives such as national unity can be better achieved through other means for example, the consequences for national sports infrastructure would be serious and long-lasting.

Advocacy coalitions and elite sport policy change

In Chapter 2, the advocacy coalition framework (ACF) was identified as a useful analytic framework for understanding the rise in the political priority given to elite sport. As explained, the ACF is based on five assumptions:

- a time perspective of at least 10 years is required for the analysis of policy change;
- a focus on policy subsystems which, for Sabatier, 'consist of actors from a variety of public and private organisations who are actively concerned with a policy problem or issue ... and who regularly seek to influence public policy in that domain' (1998: 99);
- subsystems involve actors from different levels of government and increasingly from international organisations and other countries;

- the possession and use of technical information is important; and
- public policy incorporates implicit 'sets of value priorities and causal assumptions about how to realise them' (Jenkins-Smith and Sabatier 1994: 178).

Policy subsystems normally comprise between two and four coalitions which would be competing for influence, although one might be a dominant coalition. Belief systems provide the source of cohesion within coalitions, with beliefs being disaggregated into three levels: first, 'deep core' beliefs which cover basic values regarding gender relations and individual property rights for example; second, 'policy core' beliefs which are the basic normative commitments within the sub-system; and third, secondary policy core beliefs which are narrower beliefs regarding, for example, the seriousness of particular issues and the details of resource allocation within the subsystem.

Conflict between coalitions, often mediated by a 'policy broker', is a source of policy outputs and policy change, although change can occur as a result of medium- to long-term 'policy-oriented learning' (Sabatier 1998: 104). Policy-oriented learning describes relatively long term changes in beliefs that result from 'experience and/or new information' (1998: 104). Although Sabatier accepts that coalitions will resist the acceptance of information that challenges core beliefs, he argues for the essential rationality of coalition behaviour. Further sources of policy change include exogenous developments such as economic recession and war, and also changes in personnel, both of which constitute examples of 'non-cognitive source[s] of change that can substantially alter the political resources of various coalitions and thus policy decisions' (1998: 105).

The key question for consideration is whether the recent priority given to elite sport is the consequence of the effective exercise of power over an extended period by an elite sport advocacy coalition. Analysis at the macro-level focuses attention on issues of power manifest within the pattern of structure and agency relations found within sport public policy (cf. Hay 2002; Layder 1985). Of particular interest for our study is Hay's notion of 'context-shaping' – an indirect form of power. Power thus conceived, centres on the capacity of actors to redefine the parameters of what is socially, politically and economically possible for others. To define power in this way emphasises power relations whereby actors shape structures, organisations and institutions such that the parameters of subsequent action are altered. In short, this is 'an *indirect* form of power in which power is mediated by, and instantiated in, structures' (Hay 1997: 51).

This view of power is useful in answering two important questions: 'Why are certain actors in a privileged position in the policy-making process?' and 'In whose interest do they rule, and how does their rule result in that interest being served?' (Marsh and Stoker 1995: 293). In Australia, Canada and the UK there is persuasive evidence of power embodied in and mediated by the structure of elite sport development. In Australia, the establishment of the AIS in 1981, the ASC in 1985 and the formulation of the state funding framework (the OAP) as well as that of the AOC were structures that expressed and consolidated the priorities of elite sport interests. Similarly, in Canada, the establishment of the Quadrennial Planning Process in the 1980s and the implementation of the Sport Funding and Accountability Framework in the 1990s are clear embodiments of such planning priorities in relation to NSOs and high performance sport. In the UK, the requirement for NGBs to produce planning documents in relation to elite sport has emerged more recently, most notably, with the requirement for NGBs to publish World Class Performance plans in order to access National Lottery funding. The distinctive feature of this type of bureaucratic form at the level of elite sport policy-making in Australia, Canada and the UK is that control becomes embedded in the social and organisational structure of the NSOs/NGBs and reflects the values of their paymasters – in Australia, the ASC, in Canada, the federal sport agency, Sport Canada and in the UK, primarily the DCMS, Sport England and UK Sport.

Taking Canada as an illustration, it is argued that the 'philosophy of excellence' that has pervaded the sport delivery system for the past three decades became a 'powerful ideology' in the sense of an unobservable structure within which the interests of particular groups have been/are sidelined (Kidd 1988b; 1995). Kidd, referring to Canada, talks of the 'glacial weight of dominant structures' (1995: 9), which reproduce asymmetries of power between elite and mass interests through a system of incentives for appropriate behaviour (funding for medal-winning success) and also impose penalties for inappropriate behaviour (funding reductions for the failure to win medals). Similar conclusions can be drawn from our analysis of Australia where, in 1993, the winning bid to host the 2000 Olympic Games provided substantial political legitimation to decisions taken in the 1980s to create the AIS and ASC as institutional focal points for developing medal-winning elites. Such was the dominance of elite sport interests during the years leading up to the 2000 Games that, as the swimming and athletics cases reveal, scant consideration was given to developing structures at the sports' developmental levels. These examples reveal the extent to which both ASI and AAI became enveloped within structures largely beyond their control as resource dependency deepened under the weight of federal pressure to succeed at the Sydney 2000 Olympics. In short, ASI and AAI had little option but to comply with their status as two of the eight targeted sports expected to contribute to success in Sydney (cf. Commonwealth of Australia 1999). The broader ramifications of this dominance of elite interests in the two sports only emerged post-2000. Although swimming has been and remains successful at the elite level, ASI has undergone a painful restructuring of its governance structures and reassessed its contribution to developing policies that embrace all levels of the sport. Unfortunately, athletics' performance at the elite level has been poor, and such is the internal and external criticism of AAI that the organisation will be subject to a similarly painful audit of its governance structures by the ASC following the 2004 Athens Olympic Games (DCITA 2004).

Similar patterns of structural change were evident in the UK with the most important being the introduction of National Lottery funding in the mid- to late 1990s, and the subsequent requirement for NGBs to produce World Class Performance, Potential and Start plans in order to access Lottery funding. As regards the implications of these developments, McDonald argues that we are witnessing 'a qualitative shift in the sports-participation culture away from the egalitarian and empowering aspirations of community-based sporting activity to an hierarchical and alienating culture of high-performance sport' (2000: 84). In the words of one interviewee, 'The way athletics, and sport generally, is going, [what] we're all trying to do is find talent and hothouse it to the top … We don't believe that any experience is, in a sense, intrinsically worthwhile anymore. Anything is only worthwhile if there is a big pay-off at the end' (Interviewee Y, 28 May 2002). As McDonald (2000: 86) notes, 'policy commitments do not exist in a political vacuum, but emerge out of a deeper structure of norms, values and belief systems' and, in the UK sport policy sector, the actions of those involved in shaping sport policy are increasingly shaped by the requirements of elite sport and, specifically, the requirement to construct 'pathways to the podium' that serve to subdue other voices within the sporting community – voices, for example, that might argue for sport's intrinsic qualities in respect of fun, play, and the enjoyment of sport without the over-riding desire to succeed at the highest level. As Lewis maintains, in this sense, 'the state [here, the DCMS/UK Sport/Sport England] is able to set limits on people's interpretative activities which ensure that public discourse is dominated by narratives and meanings which serve its own ends' (2000: 262).

It is clear in all three countries that state agencies have been crucial in specifying, constructing and maintaining through resource control and dependency the pattern of values and beliefs supportive of elite achievement. While in each sport in the three countries there has been a lobby on behalf of greater priority for elite development it has often been marginal and has had to compete with other internal sets of interests that prioritised, for example, club development, regional development, or mass participation. Shared values and belief systems that link NSOs/ NGBs and state agencies have been built upon and maintained by substantial resource dependency of the NSOs/NGBs. Indeed, even in Australia, where elite sport interests have been least contested, it is difficult to argue for the effectiveness of high performance sport advocacy coalitions such was the strength of the state (i.e. federal government) in steering and regulating policy direction for NSOs towards elite sport objectives. The dominance of the state in relation to elite sport policy was further confirmed by the successful bid to host the 2000 Olympic Games. Even though the award of the Games to Sydney could be considered a significant event exogenous to the elite sport subsystem (Sabatier and Jenkins-Smith 1999), it simply served to reinforce government policy priorities. Given the strong complementarity between government policy and elite sport interests there was little need for advocacy to promote elite values by the latter, while competing interests found themselves increasingly confined to the margins of policy debate. However, the complementarity between government objectives and elite sport interests was sometimes slow to be recognised, as was the case regarding Australian sailing where, until the mid- to late 1990s, there was neither sustained advocacy by the NSO nor active interest from government. As one senior AYFI official explained, sailing had been relatively ignored by the AIS and the ASC, but in a climate of federal munificence towards elite sport objectives, in 1996–7 the AYFI finally presented a case to the ASC for strengthening support for elite sailor development (Interviewee L, 28 May 2003). However, one consequence of the subsequent success of the Australian sailing team in Sydney 2000 was a rapid deepening of the extent of the NSO's dependency on AIS/ASC resources.

Canada not only provides a further example of the extent of resource dependency, but also highlights the serious consequences of the withdrawal of resources. In Canada, the state clearly engineered a radical shift in values from kitchen-table type organisations to those more akin to corporate-professional bodies: from organisations based around the traditional values of voluntarism and amateurism to organisations that were much more corporate, professional and technocratic in outlook. However, just as the state can promote particular values it can also abandon them (or at least the associated resource commitments) for, as an experienced Canadian sports analyst argued, 'we've gone from kitchen-table to professional organisation and administration and back to kitchen-table, and what neo-conservative governments are doing, is pushing it back to the kitchen-table administrator, the volunteer official …' (Interviewee O, 19 June 2002). But as another long-standing Canadian sports analyst emphasised, 'They [the federal government] haven't given up control … it's state direction and control without any money. In the early 1970s and 1980s, at least the state direction and control came with some money' (Interviewee Q, 11 June 2002). In Canada, as in Australia throughout the 1990s and more recently in the UK, the picture was of substantial value imposition by the state on NSOs which muted the more usual values present in most NSOs.

The experience of NSOs in Canada provides an example of change in beliefs at the policy core and secondary policy core levels. While beliefs supportive of high performance sport have dominated Canadian amateur sport policy for the past 30 years (cf. Kidd 1988a, 1988b, 1995; Macintosh and Whitson 1990), recent shifts in 'policy core policy preferences' (Sabatier and Jenkins-Smith 1999: 133) at federal level towards a lessened emphasis on high performance sport suggest that we are witnessing a significant moment, if not major policy change, in Canadian amateur sport policy. As Sabatier and Jenkins-Smith comment, 'significant perturbations external to the subsystem (e.g. changes in socio-economic conditions, public opinion, system wide governing coalitions, or policy outputs from other systems) are a *necessary, but not sufficient,* cause of change in the *policy core* attributes of a governmental programme' (1999: 147). What is clear from the analysis of Canadian sport policy is that the cluster of policy actors favouring the prioritisation of elite sport is heavily dependent on government sponsorship and once that sponsorship was removed it lacked any significant capacity to defend its resource allocation or to recover lost political support. Although part of the explanation for the weakness of elite sport interests rests with the heavy dependency of NSOs on federal resources, part also rests with the absence of an organisational focus for effective advocacy. While the COC clearly has an interest in lobbying for continued public support, there is no effective advocate within the federal government, Sport Canada notwithstanding, on behalf of elite sport. Whereas UK Sport and the ASC fulfil important internal advocacy functions on behalf of UK and Australian elite sport, in Canada, it must be concluded that the cluster of policy actors favouring elite sport do not constitute an advocacy coalition and are better described as the participants in the process of the implementation of federal government policy.

If an effective advocacy coalition is not present in Canada or Australia, is a similar conclusion appropriate for the UK? The first point of note is that the resource dependency between NGBs and the government bodies funding elite sport programmes deepened steadily following the establishment of the National Lottery. All three UK NGBs investigated have revealed, to a greater or lesser extent, policy initiatives that now place elite sport development as a prominent policy priority within their respective organisational strategic plans. For all three sports, current policy direction is framed, in large part, by the contingencies of developing elite swimmers, athletes and sailors such that other policy initiatives e.g. youth development and club modernisation, often serve to support the policy framework for developing elite and potential elite level performers and certainly do not provide a challenge to the elite focus. In essence, there is now a set of conditions in place within which a coalition of actors/organisations, centring on a set of shared values/belief systems, has the potential to emerge in the UK. Most importantly, at the policy core level a series of values have been identified and promoted by recent governments, which are highly supportive of an emphasis on elite sport. Included in these values would be the high political priority given to elite sport achievement, the provision of public resources, organisational modernisation, strategic planning and corporate accountability. These values were reflected in the Conservative and Labour Government sport policy documents, *Sport: Raising the Game* and *A Sporting Future for All* respectively, the introduction of Lottery funding and the requirement for NGBs to produce objectives-related strategic plans.

Flowing from changes at the policy core level, there is also evidence of change at the level of secondary aspects. Here, the ACF is concerned with, for example, decisions regarding specific 'budgetary allocations' (e.g. ring-fenced Lottery funding), 'administrative rules' (the requirement to publish World Class Performance, Potential and Start plans) and information with respect to the 'performance of specific programmes' (e.g. the monitoring of these plans). Thus, from the mid-1990s onwards, we have witnessed what the ACF might term 'major policy change', through the dynamic interaction of exogenous and endogenous factors and a process of systematic policy learning and transfer especially from Australia, but also from Canada. From Australia came the proposal for a national elite development academy and the systematic identification of talent, and from Canada came the business model for re-establishing the relationship between federal funding agencies and NSOs. Key actors/organisations in the process of change are the Performance Directorates in the ASFGB, UKA and the RYA, the Sport and Recreation Division of the DCMS, UK Sport, the BOA, Sport England and those actors/organisations within the other three Home Country Sports Councils concerned with developing elite performers.

The argument that this elite sport-focused coalition is currently dominating the sport development policy subsystem is supported by Houlihan and White's (2002) recent research into sport development in the UK. Houlihan and White argue that there are four potential advocacy coalitions evident in the sport development policy subsystem, 'with one of the strongest being that focused on high performance achievement in Olympic and major team sports' (2002: 220). Less prominent, or in Houlihan and White's terms, 'not yet quite so coherent and cohesive', is a cluster of organisations centring on school/youth sport – the Youth Sport Trust, Sport England, the central government Department for Education and Skills and the growing number of Specialist Sports Colleges are important organisational actors in this respect. Two rather weaker clusters of interest are those around community sport/Sport for All and the 'provision of opportunities to play sport at the performance or routine competitive level' (Houlihan and White 2002: 221).

While acknowledging the general strength of elite sport interests, there are pockets of opposition. There was evidence of resistance to the prioritisation of elite sport interests in all three sports although it was most evident in athletics. However, even in athletics, there was a willingness to embrace the changing conditions of action within which sport policy in the UK operated. Although the 1995 review of athletics – *Athletics 21* (BAF 1995) – revealed considerable disquiet at grass roots levels over the increasing emphasis on, and monetary rewards available to, elite athletes, policy developments over the ensuing seven to eight years merely served to reinforce the argument that there is now a discernible coalition of actors focused on elite sport and underpinned by a set of values/belief systems centring on professionalism, commercialism, corporate organisational structures and the drive for medal-winning success at major international sporting events. Resistance to this shift in emphasis towards the elite level was amorphous as the underlying resource conditions for the sport, in effect, legitimise policy decisions emphasising elite athlete success. However, while it is possible to argue for the existence of an active advocacy coalition in the UK there is a need for caution as the true test of the influence and effectiveness of a coalition is when the socio-political environment is less benign.

While advocacy coalitions can be identified by the exercise of influence within the policy subsystem, Sabatier also suggests that one important basis for influence is the practice of policy-oriented learning. It is through the practice of policy-oriented learning and the accumulation of evidence that it produces that results in policy change. However, policy-oriented learning is more likely to take place in relation to the effective achievement of particular goals rather than in relation to the selection of those goals. Thus in the case studies there were many examples of NSOs/NGBs, coaches and performance directors transferring ideas about talent development, the application of sports science and the refinement of training regimes from other countries, but far fewer examples of the learning which would result in a higher or lower valuation being given to elite sport.

In the UK, one of the most significant examples of policy-oriented learning was the visit by the Sports Minister, Iain Sproat, to the AIS, which resulted in the Conservative Government proposal to build a British academy of sport. In

Canada, the CYA's emulation of its UK counterpart's approach to sports science based training and development of elite sailors was another clear example of policy-oriented learning and policy transfer. In addition, policy-oriented learning and transfer can be facilitated in other ways, for example, through the biennial International Forum on Elite Sport where the exchange of ideas, methods, experiences and future directions for elite level sport was at the centre of proceedings amongst actors from a wide range of countries. Furthermore, Australia has been an important influence on the emerging policy framework for elite sport development in the UK through the appointment to pivotal coaching posts of Australians including Bill Sweetenham, National Performance Director for *British Swimming*, Deidre Anderson, UKSI Programme Manager, and Wilma Shakespear, National Director of the English Institute of Sport. These and other international appointments bring ideas, methods, and experiences from Australia and other leading countries and have been very influential in shaping elite sport in the UK.

In summary, the evidence for the existence of effective advocacy coalitions in the three countries is mixed. In the UK, although there is clear evidence of a cluster of policy actors for whom elite sport is a priority, there is little evidence that it was their effective advocacy that resulted in the increased commitment of successive governments to elite sport and the allocation of resources that now underpins that commitment. Until this cluster of interests can demonstrate its influence in a less supportive policy climate, it is safest to view them as a network for the implementation of government determined policy. There is little to contradict this conclusion from the Canadian cases. Indeed, the experience of the three sports in Canada highlights the vulnerability of elite sport interests to the changes in federal government priorities. The cluster of interests around elite sport (Olympic NSOs and the COC) demonstrated little capacity to direct federal policy after it began to drift following the outcome of the Dubin Inquiry into the Ben Johnson doping scandal in 1988. Finally, the presence of an effective advocacy coalition in Australia is difficult to specify with any confidence as sport policy generally was profoundly distorted from the time the 2000 Olympic Games were awarded to Sydney. From the early 1990s to 2000, elite sport received lavish resources, which resulted from federal commitment to hosting a successful Games rather than a commitment to ensure the construction of an effective and sustainable sport development system. Indeed, it is possible to argue that the distorting effect of hosting the Games was such that non-elite sport suffered significant neglect during the mid- to late 1990s. The successful Sydney Olympic Games were followed by a period of uncertainty over funding levels which lasted about 18 months, after which the federal government broadly renewed its commitment to funding elite sport. In short, the cases examined here illustrate the dependence of elite sport on public resources and its vulnerability to the shifting priorities of government.

There must also be a question mark over the depth and extent of the value change underpinning the prioritisation of elite sport within NSOs/NGBs. On the one hand, the embrace by governments of achievement values gave powerful support (in the form of legitimation and material resources) to those within the various NSOs/NGBs concerned with elite development, which was sufficient to marginalise other competing internal interests. In part, this has been achieved by the use of funding to bring into NSOs/NGBs senior administrators and coaches who are supportive of the prioritisation of elite sport and of professionalisation and modernisation. Not surprisingly, this government sponsored group acts as an internal lobby for the elite agenda. While this group of professionals has, at various times, constituted a vocal and well resourced group within NSOs/NGBs they have, at best, merely subsumed the long-standing tensions between the supporters of values associated with elite achievement and those supportive of club/grass roots development, and, at worst, have exacerbated those tensions. Overall, it is hard to avoid the conclusion that elite sport development and achievement on the one hand and mass participation and club development on the other are deeply incompatible functions within the policy frameworks current in Australia, Canada and the UK.

Notes

1 Investigating elite sport policy processes and policy change

1 The terms sailing and yachting are used interchangeably. The study does not include elite level Paralympic or Special Olympic sport and we use the terms 'elite sport', or 'high performance sport' (the Australian and Canadian terminology) interchangeably to denote 'a competition sport at the highest international level with a priority placed on sports in the Olympic Games programme and on those sports with regular world championships' (Semotiuk 1996: 7).

2 The focus of the study is on three sports that compete at the summer Olympic Games. However, it should be borne in mind that Canada puts greater emphasis (than does either Australia or the UK) on supporting sports that send teams to the winter Games. Therefore, (cross-national) observations in subsequent chapters, in respect of medal-winning performances at the summer Games, should be tempered by Canadian performances in the winter Olympic events.

3 In addition to the World Class Performance programme funding distributed by UK Sport, the four Home Country Sports Councils (in England, Scotland, Wales and Northern Ireland) award Lottery funding through their own 'talented athlete' programmes (for more detail, see UK Sport 2002c).

4 Some clarification is required with regard to the use of the terms United Kingdom (UK) and Great Britain (GB) in the study. First, no other country competes internationally at two different levels: sometimes as UK/GB, and sometimes as the Home Countries (see also note 3 above). This means that there are five Sports Councils in the UK, four of which deal with elite sport and grass roots sport (the four Home Country Sports Councils) and one of which deals with elite sport at a UK level (UK Sports Council, known as UK Sport). All five both fund and provide services. Second, the term GB refers to England, Scotland and Wales, while UK refers to the same three countries plus Northern Ireland (NI). Just to confuse matters further, when the UK competes in the Olympic Games it is referred to as GB and NI. Thirdly, space precludes an in-depth analysis of elite sport development specific to Scotland, Wales and Northern Ireland. Therefore, while this study has a UK/English focus, much of the discussion in respect of elite sport policy also pertains to the other three Home Countries.

5 For an in-depth analysis of Lukes' three dimensions of power, see Lukes (1974, 1986), and for an influential critique of classic pluralism linked to its failure to adequately characterise power relations in Western politics, see Bachrach and Baratz (1962, 1970).

4 Australia

1 The Targeted Sports Participation Growth Programme (TSPGP) is one aspect of the federal government's sport policy published in 2001 – *Backing Australia's Sporting Ability: A More Active Australia*. The initiative currently involves 21 sports with funding provided for three years, in response to concerns that participation levels in sport are falling in Australia (cf. Commonwealth of Australia 1999). The swimming TSPGP, known as *Go Swim*, involves a three-way partnership between ASI, the ASC and a commercial partner, *Uncle Toby's*. The programme has a goal of involving 300 swim centres and recruiting 12,000 new members in 2003, rising to 40,000 over the three years (DCITA 2003). However, whether the aim of increasing *participation* levels can be met by what is essentially a programme to increase *club memberships* is questionable.

5 Canada

1 The Team Elite programme is over and above SNC's 'International High Performance Swimmer Incentive' programme which rewards outstanding performances in Olympic events at major international competitions. The latter programme awards points for Gold, Silver and Bronze medals as well as lifetime best times. As stated in SNC's 2000–1 Annual Report, 'The more significant the achievement, the greater the point score. The greater the point score, the greater the financial award' (SNC 2001: 72).

2 It should be noted that AC did not release the contents of the full audit.

6 United Kingdom

1 From 1997 until March 2002, PAS was the elite-focused subsidiary company within UKA responsible for administering Lottery monies. However, a senior UK Sport official explained that PAS has now merged with UKA into one organisation due, in large part, to UKA's organisational and administrative restructuring under UK Sport's modernisation programme (Interviewee Z, 28 October 2002; see also UKA 2003).

References

Abbott, A., Collins, D., Martindale, R. and Sowerby, K. (2002) *Talent Identification and Development: An Academic Review*, Edinburgh: Sport Scotland.

ABC Online (2004) *Athletics Not up to Scratch, Minister Told*, Online. Available: http://www.abc.net.au/sport/content/s1055447.htm (accessed 2 March 2004).

Adair, D. and Vamplew, W. (1997) *Sport in Australian History*, Oxford: Oxford University Press.

Allison, L. (2001) *Amateurism in Sport*, London: Frank Cass.

Altheide, D. (1996) *Qualitative Media Analysis*, London: Sage.

Amateur Swimming Association (ASA) (1970) *Report and Recommendations of the ASA Special Committee on Competitive Swimming* (Martin Report – Part One), Loughborough: ASA.

—— (1971) *Annual Report 1970*, Loughborough: ASA.

—— (1973) *Annual Report 1972*, Loughborough: ASA.

—— (1974) *Annual Report 1973*, Loughborough: ASA.

—— (1977) *Annual Report 1976*, Loughborough: ASA.

—— (1979) *Annual Report 1978*, Loughborough: ASA.

—— (1980) *Annual Report 1979*, Loughborough: ASA.

—— (1987) *Which Way Forward?* (ASA Working Party), Loughborough: ASA.

—— (1988) *Annual Report 1987*, Loughborough: ASA.

—— (1989) *Annual Report 1988*, Loughborough: ASA.

—— (1990) *Annual Report 1989*, Loughborough: ASA.

—— (1992) *Annual Report 1991*, Loughborough: ASA.

—— (1993) *Annual Report 1992*, Loughborough: ASA.

—— (1994) *Annual Report 1993*, Loughborough: ASA.

—— (1995) *Annual Report 1994*, Loughborough: ASA.

—— (1997) *Annual Report 1996*, Loughborough: ASA.

—— (1998) *Past Presidents' Commission*, Loughborough: ASA.

—— (1999) *Annual Report 1998*, Loughborough: ASA.

—— (2001) *Business Plan 2001–2005*, Online. Available: http://www.britishswimming.org/about/businessplan.asp (accessed 12 February 2002).

—— (2002a) *Annual Report 2001*, Loughborough: ASA.

—— (2002b) *National Facilities Strategy for Swimming*, Loughborough: ASA.

Amateur Swimming Federation of Great Britain (ASFGB) (1998) *Annual Report 1997*, Loughborough: ASFGB.

—— (2001) *Annual Report 2000*, Loughborough: ASFGB.

—— (2002) *Annual Report 2001*, Loughborough: ASFGB.

Antal, A.B. (1987) 'Comparing notes and learning from experience', in M. Dierkes, H.N. Weiler and A.B. Antal (eds), *Comparative Policy Research: Learning from Experience* (pp. 498–515), Aldershot: Gower.

Anthony, D. (1978) 'Introduction', in J. Riordan (ed.), *Sport Under Communism* (pp. 1–11), London: C. Hurst.

Archer, M., Bhaskar, R., Collier, A., Lawson, T. and Norrie, A. (eds) (1998) *Critical Realism: Essential Readings*, London: Routledge.

Armstrong, T. (1997) 'Government policy', in W. Vamplew, K. Moore, J. O'Hara, R. Cashman and I.F. Jobling (eds), *The Oxford Companion to Australian Sport* (2nd Revised edn, pp. 188–90), Oxford: Oxford University Press.

Athletes Canada (2002) *A Declaration by Canadian Athletes* (10th Annual Athletes Canada Forum), Quebec: Athletes Canada.

Athletics Australia Incorporated (AAI) (1990) *Annual Report 1989–1990*, Melbourne: AAI.

—— (1991) *Annual Report 1990–1991*, Melbourne: AAI.

—— (1992) *Annual Report 1991–1992*, Melbourne: AAI.

—— (1993) *Annual Report 1992–1993*, Melbourne: AAI.

—— (1994) *Annual Report 1993–1994*, Melbourne: AAI.

—— (1995) *Annual Report 1994–1995*, Melbourne: AAI.

—— (1996) *Annual Report 1995–1996*, Melbourne: AAI.

—— (2002) *Annual Report 2001–2002*, Melbourne: AAI.

—— (2003a) *About Athletics Australia*, Online. Available: http://www.athletics.org.au/ insideaa/federation.cfm (accessed 12 May 2003).

—— (2003b) *Australian Athletics Federation*, Online. Available: http://www.athletics. org.au/insideaa/federation.cfm (accessed 12 May 2003).

Athletics Canada (2001a) *Annual General Meeting Report*, Toronto: Athletics Canada.

—— (2001b) *Athletics Canada Looking to Turn the Corner*, Online. Available: http://www. canoe.ca/AthcanNews/011030_ath.html (accessed 11 December 2002).

—— (2002a) *2001/2002 Athlete Assistance Programme*, Online. Available: http://www. athleticscanada.com/athcan/news/020117_noms.html (accessed 13 November 2002).

—— (2002b) *2002/2003 Athlete Assistance Programme Draft Nomination List* (Bulletin XXX), Online. Available HTTP: http://www.otfa.ca (accessed 9 March 2003).

—— (2002c) *Semi-annual General Meeting Report*, Ottawa: Athletics Canada.

Australian Institute of Sport (2001) *Talent Search: About the National Talent Search MILO Programme*, Online. Available: http://www.ais.org.au/talent/index.htm (accessed 12 July 2001).

Australian Labor Party (2001a) *Kelly Scraps Community-based Sport Programme* (Media Statement, 6 June), Online. Available: http://www.alp.org.au/print.html?link=/media/ 0601/klmssdgs060601.html (accessed 26 September 2001).

—— (2001b) *Restoration of Sport Funding Welcomed* (Media Statement, 24 April), Online. Available: http://www.alp.org.au/print.html?link=/media/0401/klmsfund240401.html (accessed 26 September 2001).

Australian Sports Commission (ASC) (1993a) *Evaluation of the Australian Sports Commission's Impact on Sports Performances and Participation in Australia*, Canberra: ASC.

—— (1993b) *Evaluation of the Australian Sports Commission's Impact on Sports Performances and Participation in Australia: An Overview*, Canberra: ASC.

—— (1994) *Olympic Athlete Programme: Making Great Australians*, Canberra: ASC.

—— (1998) *Excellence: The Australian Institute of Sport*, Canberra: ASC.

—— (1999) *The Australian Sports Commission – Beyond 2000*, Canberra: ASC.

—— (2003) *Annual Report 2002–2003*, Canberra: ASC.

—— (2004) *Business Improvement: Targeted Sports Participation Growth*, Online. Available: http://www.activeaustralia.org/business/tspgpswim.htm (accessed 17 February 2004).

Australian Sports Commission/Australian Institute of Sport (AIS) (1988) *Commonwealth Assistance to Australian Sport 1987–88*, Canberra: ASC/AIS.

Australian Swimming Incorporated (ASI) (1988) *Annual Report 1987–1988*, Canberra: ASI.

—— (1991) *Annual Report 1990–1991*, Canberra: ASI.

—— (1992) *Annual Report 1991–1992*, Canberra: ASI.

—— (1996) *Annual Report 1995–1996*, Canberra: ASI.

—— (2000) *Australian Swimming Incorporated Governance Review*, Canberra: ASI.

—— (2003) *Annual Report 2002–2003*, Canberra: ASI.

Australian Yachting Federation Incorporated (AYFI) (1992) *Annual Report 1991–1992*, Sydney: AYFI.

—— (1993) *Annual Report 1992–1993*, Sydney: AYFI.

—— (1996) *Annual Report 1995–1996*, Sydney: AYFI.

—— (1997) *Annual Report 1996–1997*, Sydney: AYFI.

—— (1998) *Annual Report 1997–1998*, Sydney: AYFI.

—— (1999) *Annual Report 1998–1999*, Sydney: AYFI.

—— (2000) *Annual Report 1999–2000*, Sydney: AYFI.

—— (2001a) *Annual Report 2000–2001*, Sydney: AYFI.

—— (2001b) *Strategic Plan for Australian Yachting 2001–2004*, Sydney: AYFI.

—— (2001c) *Strategic Plan Summary*, Online. Available: http://www.yachting.org.au/default.asp?Page=1154&MenuID=Download%2F1063%2F0S (accessed 2 February 2004).

—— (2002a) *Annual Report 2001–2002*, Sydney: AYFI.

—— (2002b) *A Presentation to the Australian Sports Commission*, Sydney: AYFI.

—— (2002c) *Yacht Club Briefing Paper*, Sydney: AYFI.

—— (2003a) *Annual Report 2002–2003*, Sydney: AYFI.

—— (2003b) *Board Minutes 19 January*, Sydney: AYFI.

—— (2003c) *A Proposal for Corporate Sponsorship of the Australian Yachting Federation 'OnBoard' Sailing Participation Programme*, Sydney: AYFI.

Aversa, J.A. (1986) 'Notes on entry routes into a sport/recreational role: the case of sailing', *Journal of Sport and Social Issues*, 10: 49–59.

Bachrach, P.S. and Baratz, M.S. (1962) 'Two faces of power', *American Political Science Review*, 56: 947–52.

Bachrach, P.S. and Baratz, M.S. (1970) *Power and Poverty: Theory and Practice*, New York: Oxford University Press.

Baka, R.S. (1986) 'Australian government involvement in sport: a delayed, eclectic approach', in G. Redmond (ed.), *Sport and Politics*, 7: 27–32, Champaign, IL: Human Kinetics.

Bales, J. (1996) 'The Canadian sports schools', *Coaching Focus* (Spring), pp. 7–8.

Ballard, B. (2002) 'Atkinson starts off Potential', *Swimming* (January), pp. 22–3.

Baumann, A. (2002) 'Developing sustained high performance services and systems that have quality outcomes', paper presented at the Commonwealth Games Conference, Manchester.

Beamish, R. and Borowy, J. (1987) 'High performance athletes in Canada: from status to contract', in T. Slack and C.R. Hinings (eds), *The Organisation and Administration of Sport* (pp. 1–33), London, Ontario: Sports Dynamics.

Betts, K. (1986) 'The conditions of action, power, and the problem of interests', *Sociological Review*, 34(1): 39–64.

Bhaskar, R. (1975) *A Realist Theory of Science*, Brighton: Harvester-Wheatsheaf.

Blackhurst, M., Schneider, A. and Strachan, D. (1991) *Values and Ethics in Amateur Sport: Morality, Leadership, Education* (Prepared for Fitness and Amateur Sport, Government of Canada), London, Ontario: Fitness and Amateur Sport.

Bloomfield, J. (1973) *The Role, Scope and Development of Recreation in Australia*, Canberra: Department of Tourism and Recreation.

Bloomfield, J. (2003) *Australia's Sporting Success: The Inside Story*, Sydney: University of New South Wales Press.

Boating Alliance (2002) *About the Boating Alliance*, Online. Available: http://www.boating alliance.org.uk/ (accessed 16 October 2002).

Boating Industry Association of New South Wales (2001) *Olympic Marina to be Demolished*, Online. Available: http://www.bia.org.au/Press/030401.html (accessed 16 March 2004).

Booth, D. (1995) 'Sports policy in Australia: right, just and rational?', *Australian Quarterly*, 67(1): 1–10.

Boudreau, F. and Konzak, B. (1991) 'Ben Johnson and the use of steroids in sport: sociological and ethical considerations, *Canadian Journal of Sport Sciences*, 16(2): 88–98.

British Amateur Athletic Board (BAAB) (1984) *Report on the National Coaching Strategy 1980–1984 and Proposals for the National Performance Strategy 1984–1988*, Birmingham: BAAB.

—— (1986) *Money and Athletes* (Internal Paper), Birmingham: BAAB.

British Athletic Federation (BAF) (1995) *Athletics 21: Strategic Planning for British Athletics in the 21st Century*, Birmingham: BAF.

Broom, E. F. (1996) 'Principles in organisation and administration of sport for the pursuit of medals', in K. Hardman (ed.), *Sport for All: Issues and Perspectives in International Context* (pp. 1–6), Manchester: Centre for Physical Education and Leisure Studies.

Bryceson, S. and Herbert, P. (1992) *The Making of Champions*, Melbourne: Victoria Press.

Buffery, S. (2000) *A Bitter Exit for Track CEO* (First Posted in *Toronto Sun*, 16 November), Online. Available: http://www.canoe.ca/Slam001116/trk_abi-sun.html (accessed 5 November 2002).

—— (2001) *No Medals is No Big Deal* (First Posted in *Toronto Sun*, 13 August), Online. Available: http://www.canoe.ca/Slam010813/col_buffery-sun.html (accessed 5 November 2002).

Bulkeley, H. (2000) 'Discourse coalitions and the Australian climate change policy network', *Environment and Planning C: Government and Policy*, 18: 727–48.

Byers Report (1968) *Report of the Committee of Enquiry into the Development of Athletics Under the Instruction of the AAA and the BAAB*, London: AAA/BAAB.

Campagnolo, I. (1979) *Partners in Pursuit of Excellence: A National Policy on Amateur Sport* (White Paper), Ottawa: Fitness and Amateur Sport.

Canada (1969) *Report of the Task Force on Sports for Canadians*, Ottawa: Department of National Health and Welfare.

—— (1970) *A Proposed Sports Policy for Canadians* (White Paper), Ottawa: Fitness and Amateur Sport.

—— (1981) *A Challenge to the Nation: Fitness and Amateur Sport in the '80s* (White Paper), Ottawa: Fitness and Amateur Sport.

—— (1988) *Toward 2000: Building Canada's Sport System* (Report of the Task Force on National Sport Policy), Ottawa: Fitness and Amateur Sport.

—— (1992) *Sport: The Way Ahead* (Report of the Minister's Task Force on Federal Sport Policy, Chairman, J. C. Best), Ottawa: Fitness and Amateur Sport.

—— (1998) *Sport in Canada: Everybody's Business – Leadership, Partnership and Account-ability* (Sub-committee on the Study of Sport in Canada – Mills Report), Ottawa: Public Works and Government Services.

Canadian Heritage (1998) *Sport Canada Strategic Plan 1998–2001*, Online. Available: http://www.pch.gc.ca/sportcanada/SC_E/strate.htm (accessed 15 August 2000).

—— (1999a) *Athlete Assistance Programme: Policies, Procedures and Guidelines* (Sport Canada Report), Ottawa: Canadian Heritage.

—— (1999b) *National Sport Centres Position Paper*, Online. Available: http://www.pch. gc.ca/sportcanada/SC_E/nsce.htm (accessed 27 July 2001).

—— (2000a) *The Government of Canada Announces Additional Funding for Amateur Sport* (News Release), Online. Available: http://www.pch.gc.ca/bin/News.d11/View?Lang= EandCode=9NR179E (accessed 14 August 2001).

—— (2000b) *Sport Funding and Accountability Framework for National Sport Organisations: How it Works!* Ottawa: Canadian Heritage.

—— (2001) *Towards a Canadian Sport Policy: Report on the National Summit on Sport*, Online. Available: http://www.pch.gc.ca/Sportcanada/Sc_e/ncs-1–e.htm (accessed 27 November 2001).

—— (2002) *The Canadian Sport Policy*, Online. Available: http://www.canadianheritage. gc.ca/progs/sc/pol/pcs-csp/index_e.cfm#ca (accessed 20 March 2003).

Canadian Olympic Committee (COC) (2002) *Canadian Olympic Association – Major Shift in NSF Funding Philosophy Underlines Commitment to High Performance Sport Excellence* (Media Release), Online. Available: http://www.micro.newswire.ca/860–0.html?Start=80 (accessed 29 April 2004).

Canadian Yachting Association (CYA) (1997) *Action Plan 1997–98*, Kingston, Ontario: CYA.

—— (2000) *Action Plan 2000–2001*, Kingston, Ontario: CYA.

—— (2001) *Strategic Pursuits Planning Workshop*, Kingston, Ontario: CYA.

—— (2002a) *Executive Committee Minutes, 18–19 January*, Kingston, Ontario: CYA.

—— (2002b) *The 3M National Coaching Certification Programme: Programme Structure in a CBET System* (Internal Paper), Kingston, Ontario: CYA.

—— (2002c) *Long Term Athlete Development* (Internal Paper), Kingston, Ontario: CYA.

—— (2002d) *Operations Plan for Canadian Yachting Association*, Kingston, Ontario: CYA.

—— (2002e) *Priorities and Goal Statement for 2002 and Beyond* (Internal Paper), Kingston, Ontario: CYA.

Cansport (2000) *Clarke Retires After Finishing 17th*, Online. Available: http://www. canoe.ca/2000GamesSailing/sep30_cla-cp.html (accessed 5 November 2002).

Cashman, R. (1995) *Paradise of Sport: The Rise of Organised Sport in Australia*, Melbourne: Oxford University Press.

Cavanagh, R.C. (1988) 'State policy, ideology and the formal organisation of sport', *Arena Review*, 12(2): 128–39.

Childs, D. (1978) 'The German Democratic Republic', in J. Riordan (ed.), *Sport Under Communism* (pp. 67–101), London: C. Hurst.

Christie, J. (2001a) *Athletics Canada Chastised* (From *The Globe and Mail*, 30 October), Online. Available: http://www.cansport.com/cgi-bin/search?lang=e&pg=list&keys= track+and+field&bool=AND&limit=99999&types (accessed 10 July 2002).

—— (2001b) *Top Swimmers Will Splash for Cash* (From *The Globe and Mail*, 28 June), Online. Available: http://www.cansport.com/cgi-bin/search?lang=e&p g=list&types=2 &keys=swimming&bool=AND&limit=99999 (accessed 10 July 2002).

Coaching Association of Canada (CAC) (1977) *1976 Post-Olympic Games Symposium* (Proceedings), Ottawa: CAC.

—— (1996) *Results of the NCCP Evaluation Project: A Blueprint for Change* (Preliminary Report), Ottawa: CAC.

—— (2002) *A Competency-based Approach*, Online. Available: http://www.coach.ca/e/ 3m_nccp/index.htm (accessed 24 October 2002).

Coalter, F., with Long, J. and Duffield, B. (1988) *Recreational Welfare*, Aldershot: Gower.

Cobham Report. (1973) *Second Report of the Select Committee of the House of Lords on Sport and Leisure* (Select Committee Report), London: HMSO.

Coe, P. (1994, 20 November) 'Why athletics has missed the coach', *Observer*, p. 9.

Coghlan, J. with Webb, I. M. (1990) *Sport and British Politics Since 1960*, London: Falmer Press.

Coleman, W.D. and Perl, A. (1999) 'Internationalised policy environments and policy network analysis', *Political Studies*, XLVII: 691–709.

Coles, A. (1975) *Report of the Australian Sports Institute Study Group*, Canberra: Australian Government Publishing Service.

Collier, D. (1993) 'The comparative method', in A. Finifter (ed.), *Political Science: The State of the Discipline*, Washington, DC: American Political Science Association.

Colwin, C.M. (1996) 'The changing face of swimming', *Swim Canada* (March), pp. 12–13.

—— (1997) 'Dave Johnson on national sports centres', *SwimNews* (January), pp. 6–8.

—— (1998) 'A puzzle with two few clues: even skilled analysts can't see where the sport is heading', *SwimNews* (July), pp. 10–12.

Commonwealth of Australia (1999) *Shaping Up: A Review of Commonwealth Involvement in Sport and Recreation in Australia* (Sport 2000 Task Force), Canberra: Commonwealth of Australia.

Connell, R.W. (1990) 'The state, gender and sexual politics: theory and appraisal', *Theory and Society*, 19(5): 507–44.

Court, J. (1997) *In Pursuit of Excellence: The Australian Institute of Sport* (Report of a study visit to the Australian Institute of Sport and the New South Wales Institute of Sport, January 1997), Stafford: Recreational Services, Staffordshire University.

Crenson, M.A. (1971) *The Un-politics of Air Pollution: A Study of Non-Decision Making in the Cities*, Baltimore, MD: John Hopkins University Press.

Cunningham, D., Slack, T. and Hinings, B. (1987) 'Changing design archetypes in amateur sport organisations', in T. Slack and C.R. Hinings (eds), *The Organisation and Administration of Sport* (pp. 59–81), London, Ontario: Sports Dynamics.

D'Alpuget, L. (1980) *Yachting in Australia*, Melbourne: Hutchinson Group.

Dalton, T., Draper, M., Weeks, W. and Wiseman, J. (1996) *Making Social Policy in Australia: An Introduction*, St Leonard's, Australia: Allen and Unwin.

Daly, J. (1994) 'Track and field', in W. Vamplew and B. Stoddart (eds), *Sport in Australia: A Social History*, Cambridge: University Press.

Daugbjerg, C. and Marsh, D. (1998) 'Explaining policy outcomes: integrating the policy network approach with macro-level and micro-level analysis', in D. Marsh (ed.), *Comparing Policy Networks* (pp. 52–71), Buckingham: Open University Press.

de Castella, R. (1994) *The Contenders: part 5*, BBC Videos.

de Leon, P. (1999) 'The stages approach to the policy process: what has it done? where is it going?', in P.A. Sabatier (ed.), *Theories of the Policy Process: Theoretical Lenses on Public Policy* (pp. 19–32), Boulder, CO: Westview Press.

Department for the Arts, Sport, the Environment and Territories (DASET) (1992) *Maintain the Momentum* (Australian Government Sports Policy 1992 to 1996), Canberra: DASET.

Department for the Arts, Sport, the Environment, Tourism and Territories (DASETT) (1989) *The Australian Sports Kit* (The Next Step), Canberra: DASETT.

Department of Communications, Information Technology and the Arts (DCITA) (2003) *Go Swim Programme to Boost Numbers of Young Swimmers* (Media Release), Online. Available: http://www.dcita.gov.au/Article/0,,0_5–2_4009–4_113178,00.html (accessed 17 February 2003).

—— (2004) *Wide-ranging Review into Athletics* (Media Release), Online. Available: http://www.dcita.gov.au/Article/0,,0_5–2_4009–4_117978,00.html (accessed 3 March 2004)

Department for Culture, Media and Sport (DCMS) (2000) *A Sporting Future for All*, London: DCMS.

—— (2001) *Elite Sports Funding Review* (Report of the Review Group, Chaired by the Rt Hon Dr Jack Cunningham MP), London: DCMS.

—— (2002) *The Coaching Task Force – Final Report*, London: DCMS.

Department for Culture, Media and Sport/Strategy Unit (2002) *Game Plan: A Strategy for Delivering Government's Sport and Physical Activity Objectives*, London: DCMS/Strategy Unit.

Department for Education and Employment (DfEE) (1998) *Specialist Schools: Education Partnerships for the Twenty-First Century*, London: DfEE.

Department for Education and Skills/Department for Culture, Media and Sport (2003) *Learning Through PE and Sport: A Guide to the Physical Education, School Sport and Club Links Strategy*, London: Department for Education and Skills/DCMS.

Department of the Environment (1975) *Sport and Recreation* (White Paper, Cmnd. 6200), London: HMSO.

Department for the Environment, Sport and Territories (DEST) (1994) *Olympic Athlete Programme: Making Great Australians* (Australian Government Sports Policy), Canberra: Author.

Department of Industry Science and Resources (2001) *Backing Australia's Sporting Ability: A More Active Australia*, Online. Available: http://www.isr.gov.au/sport-tourism/publications/Active.pdf (accessed 3 August 2001).

Department of National Heritage (DNH) (1995) *Sport: Raising the Game*. London: DNH.

Dick, F. (1990) 'Learning from East Germany', *Coaching Focus* (Autumn), pp. 8–9.

Digel, H. (2002) *Organisation of High-Performance Athletics in Selected Countries* (Final Report for the International Athletics Foundation), Tübingen, Germany: University of Tübingen.

Dogan, M. and Pelassy, D. (1990) *How to Compare Nations: Strategies in Comparative Analysis*, 2nd edn, Chatham, NJ: Chatham House.

Dolowitz, D. and Marsh, D. (2000) 'Learning from abroad: the role of policy transfer in contemporary policy-making', *Governance: An International Journal of Policy and Administration*, 13(1): 5–24.

Dryden, N. (2002, July/August) 'Winning is the only option: Bill Sweetenham takes British swimming to the edge of success', *SwimNews*, p. 13.

Dubin, C. (1990) *Commission of Inquiry Into the Use of Drugs and Banned Practices Intended to Increase Athletic Performance* (Charles Dubin, Commissioner), Ottawa: Ministry of Supply and Services.

Dunleavy, P. and O'Leary, B. (1987) *Theories of the State: The Politics of Liberal Democracy*, London: Macmillan.

English Sports Council (1998) *The Development of Sporting Talent 1997*, London: English Sports Council.

Evans, M. and Davies, J. (1999) 'Understanding policy transfer: a multi-level, multi-disciplinary perspective', *Public Administration*, 77(2): 361–85.

Fairley, G. (1983) *Minute by Minute: The Story of the Royal Yachting Association (1875–1982)*, Woking: Royal Yachting Association.

Fischer, F. (2003) *Reframing Public Policy: Discursive Politics and Deliberative Practices*, New York: Oxford University Press.

Fisher, R.J. and Borms, J. (1990) *The Search for Sporting Excellence*, Schorndorf: Verlag Karl Hofmann.

Foster, A. (2004) *Moving On: A Review of the Need for Change in Athletics in the UK*, London: UK Sport and Sport England.

Franks, C.E.S., Hawes, M. and Macintosh, D. (1988) 'Sport and Canadian diplomacy', *International Journal*, XLIII: 665–82.

Frecknall, T., Henderson, J. and Dunn, E. (1997, 22 October) 'Athletes lead BAF battle for survival', *Athletics Weekly*, pp. 12–13.

Gains, C. (2002, 23 January) 'Another Birmingham black hole', *Athletics Weekly*, p. 50.

Giddens, A. (1998) *The Third Way: The Renewal of Social Democracy*, Cambridge: Polity Press.

Gillingham, M. (1991, 20 March) 'Long wait is over as the BAF is born', *Athletics Weekly*, p. 3.

Godfrey, J. and Holtham, G. (1999) *Sporting Lives: A Vision for Sport in the UK*, London: Institute for Public Policy Research.

Goldman, B. and Katz, R. (1992) *Death in the Locker Room II: Drugs and Sport*, Chicago, IL: Elite Sports Medicine Publications.

Goverde, H. and Tatenhove, J. van. (2000) 'Power and policy networks', in H. Goverde, P.G. Cerny, M. Haugaard and H. Lentner (eds), *Power in Contemporary Politics: Theories, Practices and Globalisations* (pp. 96–111), London: Sage.

Green, M. (2003) 'An analysis of elite sport policy change in three sports in Canada and the United Kingdom', unpublished PhD thesis, Loughborough University, UK.

Green, M. and Houlihan, B. (2004) 'Advocacy coalitions and elite sport policy change in Canada and the United Kingdom', *International Review for the Sociology of Sport*, 39(4): 387–403.

Green, M. and Oakley, B. (2001a) 'Elite sport development systems and playing to win: uniformity and diversity in international approaches', *Leisure Studies*, 20(4): 247–67.

—— (2001b) 'Lesson-drawing: international perspectives on elite sport development systems in established nations', paper presented at the Nation and Sport Conference, Brunel University, London, June.

Grix, J. (2002) 'Introducing students to the generic terminology of social research', *Politics*, 22(3): 175–86.

Guesdon, C. (2001) *Swimming in Crisis: Australian Open Water falls by the wayside*, Online. Available: http://www.oceanswims.com/WORLDCUP/ausow.html (accessed 19 February 2004).

Gullan, S. (2004) *Athletics Runs into Dead End*, Online. Available: http://www.foxsports.news.com.au/print/0,8668,8785989–23218,00.html (accessed 2 March 2004).

Haas, P.M. (1992) 'Introduction: epistemic communities and international policy coordination', *International Organisation*, 46(1): 1–35.

Habermas, J. (1971) *Toward a Rational Society*, London: Heinemann.

Hague, R., Harrop, M. and Breslin, S. (1998) *Comparative Government and Politics: An Introduction*, 4th edn, Basingstoke: Macmillan.

Ham, C. and Hill, M. (1993) *The Policy Process in the Modern Capitalist State*, 2nd edn, New York: Harvester-Wheatsheaf.

Harvey, J. (1999) 'Sport and Québec nationalism: ethnic or civil identity?', in J. Sugden and A. Bairner (eds), *Sport in Divided Societies* (pp. 31–50), Aachen: Meyer and Meyer.

Hassall, P. (2001) 'Action Man', *Swimming Times* (October), pp. 26–7.

Hay, C. (1995) 'Structure and agency', in D. Marsh and G. Stoker (eds), *Theory and Methods in Political Science* (pp. 189–206), Basingstoke: Macmillan.

—— (1996) *Re-stating Social and Political Change*, Buckingham: Open University Press.

—— (1997) 'Divided by a common language: political theory and the concept of power', *Politics*, 17(1): 45–52.

—— (2002) *Political Analysis: A Critical Introduction*, Basingstoke: Palgrave.

Heclo, H. (1972) 'Review article: policy analysis', *British Journal of Political Science*, 2: 83–108.

—— (1974) *Modern Social Politics in Britain and Sweden: From Relief to Income Maintenance*, New Haven and London: Yale University Press.

Heidenheimer, A.J., Heclo, H. and Adams, C.T. (1990) *Comparative Public Policy: The Politics of Social Choice in America, Europe, and Japan*, 3rd edn, New York: St Martin's Press.

Held, D. (1996) *Models of Democracy*, 2nd edn, Cambridge: Polity Press.

Helmstaedt, K. (1995) 'Swimming: cluttered calendar', *Swim Canada* (January), p. 19.

Henry, I.P. (1993) *The Politics of Leisure Policy*, Basingstoke: Macmillan.

—— (2001) *The Politics of Leisure Policy*, 2nd edn, Basingstoke: Palgrave.

Hill, M. (1997a) *The Policy Process in the Modern State*, 3rd edn, London: Prentice Hall/Harvester-Wheatsheaf.

—— (1997b) *The Policy Process: A Reader*, 2nd edn, London: Prentice Hall/Harvester-Wheatsheaf.

Hinings, C.R., Thibault, L., Slack, T. and Kikulis, L.M. (1996) 'Values and organisational structure', *Human Relations*, 49(7): 885–916.

Hoare, D. (1996) 'The Australian national talent search programme', *Coaching Focus* (Spring), pp. 3–4.

Hoberman, J.M. (1984) *Sport and Political Ideology*, London: Heinemann.

—— (1992) *Mortal Engines: The Science of Performance and the Dehumanisation of Sport*, New York: The Free Press.

Hoey, K. (2000) 'A sporting future for all: the government's new sports strategy', *FHS*, 8, pp. 13–15.

Hogan, K. and Norton, K. (2000) 'The "price" of Olympic gold', *Journal of Science and Medicine in Sport*, 3(2): 203–18.

Hopkin, J. (2002) 'Comparative methods', in D. Marsh and G. Stoker (eds), *Theory and Methods in Political Science* (2nd edn, pp. 249–67), Basingstoke: Palgrave Macmillan.

Horne, J., Tomlinson, A. and Whannel, G. (1999) *Understanding Sport: An Introduction to the Sociological and Cultural Analysis of Sport*, London and New York: E&FN Spon.

Houlihan, B. (1991) *The Government and Politics of Sport*, London: Routledge.

—— (1997) *Sport, Policy and Politics: A Comparative Analysis*, London and New York: Routledge.

—— (2000a) 'Sporting excellence, schools and sports development: the politics of crowded policy spaces', *European Physical Education Review*, 6(2): 171–93.

—— (2000b) 'Theorising sport policy-making: problems of globalisation and marginalisation', paper presented at the pre-Olympic Congress, Brisbane, September.

—— (2002) *Dying to Win: Doping in Sport and the Development of Anti-Doping Policy*, 2nd edn, Strasbourg: Council of Europe Publishing.

Houlihan, B. and White, A. (2002) *The Politics of Sport Development: Development of Sport or Development through Sport?*, London and New York: Routledge.

House of Commons (2002) *Testing the Waters: The Sport of Swimming* (Culture, Media and Sport Select Committee – Second Report), London: House of Commons.

House of Commons of Canada (2002) *An Act to Promote Physical Activity and Sport: Bill C-12*, Ottawa: House of Commons of Canada.

Howarth, D. (1995) 'Discourse theory', in D. Marsh and G. Stoker (eds), *Theory and Methods in Political Science* (pp. 115–33), Basingstoke: Macmillan.

Howell, M.L. and Howell, R.A. (1985) 'Canadian sport in perspective', in M.L. Howell and R.A. Howell (eds), *History of Sport in Canada* (pp. 396–417), Champaign: IL: Stipes Publishing.

Howell, R. Howell, M. and Norton, P. (1997) 'Swimming', in W. Vamplew, K. Moore, J. O'Hara, R. Cashman and I.F. Jobling (eds), *The Oxford Companion to Australian Sport* (2nd Revised edn, pp. 416–19), Oxford: Oxford University Press.

Hubbard, A., Liston, R. and Mackay, D. (1994, 24 April) 'Athletics a running sore', *Observer*, p. 11.

Humber Sailing and Powerboat Centre (2002) *Our Facilities and Location*, Online. Available: http://sailing.humberc.on.ca/facilities.shtml (accessed 5 December 2002).

Hurst, M. (2004) *Athletics a Rabble Says Games Bigwig*, Online. Available: http://dailytelegraph.news.com.au/index.jsp (accessed 10 March 2004).

Irons, K. (1983) 'Canadian Track and Field Association', *Track and Field Journal*, (June), pp. 23–6.

Jacques, T.D. and Pavia, G.R. (1976) 'The Australian government and sport', in T.D. Jacques and G.R. Pavia (eds), *Sport in Australia: Selected Readings in Physical Activity* (pp. 148–57), Sydney: McGraw-Hill.

Jarver, J. (1981) 'Procedures of talent identification in the USSR' *Modern Athlete and Coach*, 19(1): 3–6.

Jenkins, B. (1997) 'Policy analysis: models and approaches', in M. Hill (ed.), *The Policy Process: A Reader* (2nd edn, pp. 30–8), London: Prentice Hall/Harvester-Wheatsheaf.

Jenkins-Smith, H.C. and Sabatier, P.A. (1993a). 'The dynamics of policy-oriented learning', in P.A. Sabatier and H.C. Jenkins-Smith (eds), *Policy Change and Learning: An Advocacy Coalition Approach* (pp. 41–56), Boulder, CO: Westview Press.

—— (1993b) 'The study of public policy processes', in P.A. Sabatier and H.C. Jenkins-Smith (eds), *Policy Change and Learning: An Advocacy Coalition Approach* (pp. 1–9), Boulder, CO: Westview Press.

—— (1994) 'Evaluating the advocacy coalition framework', *Journal of Public Policy*, 14: 175–203.

Jewes, P. and Jobling, I.F. (1997) 'Athletics Australia', in W. Vamplew, K. Moore, J. O'Hara, R. Cashman and I.F. Jobling (eds), *The Oxford Companion to Australian Sport* (2nd Revised edn, p. 26), Oxford: Oxford University Press.

John, P. (1998) *Analysing Public Policy*, London: Pinter.

Johnson, D. (1995) 'In reference to Ken McKinnon's letter in the January Swim Canada', *Swim Canada*, (March), pp. 22–3.

Kane, J. E. (1986) 'Giftedness in sport', in G. Gleeson (ed.), *The Growing Child in Competitive Sport* (pp. 184–204), London: Hodder and Stoughton.

Keil, I. and Wix, D. (1996) *In the Swim: The Amateur Swimming Association From 1869 to 1994*, Loughborough: Swimming Times Ltd.

Kidd, B. (1988a) 'The elite athlete', in J. Harvey and H. Cantelon (eds), *Not Just a Game: Essays in Canadian Sport Sociology* (pp. 287–307), Ottawa: University of Ottawa Press.

—— (1988b) 'The philosophy of excellence: Olympic performances, class power, and the Canadian state', in P.J. Galasso (ed.), *Philosophy of Sport and Physical Activity: Issues and Concepts* (pp. 11–31), Toronto: Canadian Scholars' Press.

—— (1995) 'Confronting inequality in sport and physical activity', *Avante*, 1(1): 3–19.

Kikulis, L.M. and Slack, T. (1995) 'Toward an understanding of the role of agency and choice in the changing structure of Canada's national sport organisations', *Journal of Sport Management*, 9(2): 135–52.

Kingdon, J.W. (1995) *Agendas, Alternatives and Public Policies*, 2nd edn, New York: Harper Collins.

Kondratyeva, M. and Taborko, V. (1979) *Children and Sport in the USSR*, trans. C. English, Moscow: Progress Publishers.

Kozel, J. (1996) 'Talent identification and development in Germany', *Coaching Focus*, (Spring), pp. 5–6.

Krüger, A. (1999) 'Breeding, rearing and preparing the Aryan body: creating superman the Nazi way', in J.A. Mangan (ed.), *Shaping the Superman: Fascist Body as Political Icon – Aryan Fascism* (pp. 42–68), London: Frank Cass.

Kübler, D. (2001) 'Understanding policy change with the advocacy coalition framework: an application to Swiss drug policy', *Journal of European Public Policy*, 8(4): 623–41.

Lahmy, E. (1985) 'GDR: mass or elite, sport remains a high priority', *Olympic Review* (May/June), pp. 309–13.

Layder, D. (1985) 'Power, structure and agency', *Journal for the Theory of Social Behaviour*, 15(2): 131–49.

Lentell, B. (1993) 'Sports development: goodbye to community recreation?' in C. Brackenridge (ed.), *Body Matters: Leisure Images and Lifestyles* (pp. 141–9), Eastbourne: Leisure Studies Association.

Lewis, P.A. (2000) 'Realism, causality and the problem of social structure', *Journal for the Theory of Social Behaviour*, 30(3): 249–68.

Lindblom, C.E. (1977) *Politics and Markets*, New York: Basic Books.

Lipset, S. (1990) *Continental Divide: The Values and Institutions of the United States and Canada*, New York and London: Routledge.

Lodewyke, J. (2002) 'The great debate', *Swimming* (July), pp. 24–5.

Lovesey, P. (1979) *The Official Centenary History of the AAA*, Enfield: Guinness Superlatives.

Lowry, M. (2000) 'Now they tell us', *SwimNews* (September/October), p. 44.

—— (2001) *Canadian High Performance Sport Council*, Online. Available: http://www.sportmatters.ca/index.php3?Action=Item-View-17–2 (accessed 12 November 2002).

Lukes, S. (1974) *Power: A Radical View*, London: Macmillan.

—— (1986) 'Introduction', in S. Lukes (ed.), *Power* (pp. 1–18), Oxford: Blackwell.

Lundy, K. (1999) *Community vs Elite Sport – The Elusive Balance*, Online. Available: http://www.katelundy.com.au/access&.htm (accessed 11 February 2004).

McAsey, J. (2004) *Athletics In-Fighting Threatens Games*, Online. Available:http://www.theaustralian.news.com.au/printpage/0,5942,8829687,00.html (accessed 4 March 2004).

MacDonald, B. (1998) 'Dinosaur age is over, swimming stuck in the past', *SwimNews* (February), p. 37.

McDonald, I. (2000) 'Excellence and expedience? Olympism, power and contemporary sports policy in England', in M. Keech and G. McFee (eds), *Issues and Values in Sport and Leisure Cultures* (pp. 83–100), Oxford: Meyer and Meyer.

Mach, G. (1980) 'Towards developing a strong club system in Canada', *Track and Field Journal* (August), p. 3.

Macintosh, D. (1991) 'Sport and the state: the case of Canada', in F. Landry, M. Landry and M. Yerle (eds), *Sport, … The Third Millennium* (pp. 269–75), Sainte-Foy: Les Presses de l'Université de Laval.

—— (1996) 'Sport and government in Canada', in L. Chalip, A. Johnson and L. Stachura (eds), *National Sports Policies: An International Handbook* (pp. 39–66), London: Greenwood Press.

Macintosh, D., Bedecki, T. and Franks, C.E.S. (1987) *Sport and Politics in Canada: Federal Government Involvement since 1961*, Montreal: McGill-Queen's University Press.

Macintosh, D. and Whitson, D. (1990) *The Game Planners: Transforming Canada's Sport System*, Montreal: McGill-Queen's University Press.

McIntyre, M. (2000) *Report on the 2000 Olympic Sailing Campaign* (Internal Paper), Eastleigh: Royal Yachting Association.

Mackay, D. (1994a, 20 March) 'Athletics shake-up', *Observer*, p. 7.

—— (1994b, 17 April) 'Brasher: athletics in a mess', *Observer*, p. 3.

—— (1995, 9 July) 'Sprinter of our discontent', *Observer*, p. 11.

—— (1997, 9 November) 'Brave new world beckons Moorcroft after bedlam', *Observer*, p. 9.

—— (1998a, 22 December) 'Athletics 1998: the defining moments – a golden glimpse of the future', *Guardian*, p. 24.

—— (1998b) 'United Kingdom's serious intentions for sport and coaching', *Coaching Focus* (Spring), pp. 4–5.

—— (2001, 22 February) 'Blood on the tracks as athletics fights for its future', *Guardian*, p. 30.

—— (2003, 4 March) 'New pot of gold for medallists', *Guardian*, p. 33.

McKinsey and Company (2002) *Strategic Priorities for the RYA* (Findings Presented to RYA Council, June 12). London: McKinsey and Company.

McLennan, G. (1990) *Marxism, Pluralism and Beyond: Classic Debates and New Departures*, Cambridge: Polity Press.

McWha, M. (1998) 'Going south: the exodus of Canadian swimmers to American universities', *SwimNews* (May), pp. 32–3.

MacWilliam, T. (1982) 'IAAF one step forward – Canadian athletes mark time', *Track and Field Journal* (October), p. 2.

Magdalinski, T. (2000) 'The reinvention of Australia for the Sydney 2000 Olympic Games', in J.A. Mangan and J. Nauright (eds), *Sport in Australasian Society: Past and Present* (pp. 305–22), London: Frank Cass.

Marsh, D. (1998) 'The utility and future of policy network analysis', in D. Marsh (ed.), *Comparing Policy Networks* (pp. 185–97), Buckingham: Open University Press.

Marsh, D., Buller, J., Hay, C., Johnston, J., Kerr, P., McAnulla, S. and Watson, M. (1999) *Postwar British Politics in Perspective*, Cambridge: Polity Press.

Marsh, D. and Rhodes, R.A.W. (1992a) 'Policy communities and issue networks: beyond typology', in D. Marsh and R.A.W. Rhodes (eds), *Policy Networks in British Government* (pp. 249–68), Oxford: Clarendon.

—— (eds) (1992b) *Policy Networks in British Government*, Oxford: Clarendon.

Marsh, D. and Smith, M. (2000) 'Understanding policy networks: towards a dialectical approach', *Political Studies*, 48: 4–21.

—— (2001) 'There is more than one way to do political science: on different ways to study policy networks', *Political Studies*, 49: 528–41.

Marsh, D. and Stoker, G. (1995) 'Conclusions', in D. Marsh and G. Stoker (eds), *Theory and Methods in Political Science* (pp. 288–97), Basingstoke: Macmillan.

Mathieson, S. (2004) *Action Urged on Athletics Worries*, Online. Available: http://www.foxsports.news.com.au/print/0,8668,8815060-23218,00.html (accessed 2 March 2004).

Mawhinney, H.B. (1993) 'An advocacy coalition approach to change in Canadian education', in P.A. Sabatier and H.C. Jenkins-Smith (eds), *Policy Change and Learning: An Advocacy Coalition Approach* (pp. 59–82), Boulder, CO: Westview Press.

May, T. (1992, 11 July) 'Britain's challenge: race for funds to get our team to the starting line', *Guardian*, p. 36.

—— (1997) *Social Research: Issues, Methods and Process*, 2nd edn, Buckingham: Open University Press.

Maynard, J. (1976) *The 1977–1980 Olympic Effort* (Internal Paper), Woking: Royal Yachting Association.

Merkel, U. (1995) 'The German government and the politics of sport and leisure in the 1990s: an interim report', in S. Fleming, M. Talbot and A. Tomlinson (eds), *Policy and Politics in Sport, Physical Education and Leisure* (pp. 95–108), Eastbourne: Leisure Studies Association.

Mintrom, M. and Vergari, S. (1996) 'Advocacy coalitions, policy entrepreneurs and policy change', *Policy Studies Journal*, 24(3): 420–34.

Morrow, D., Keyes, M., Simpson, W., Consentino, F. and Lappage, R. (1989) *A Concise History of Sport in Canada*, Toronto: Oxford University Press.

Morse, E. (2002) *Investment in Canadian Athletes is an Investment in Ourselves*, Online. Available: http://www.cansport.com/cgi-bin/articles.pl?lang=eandtpl=andtype=viewpointandrec_id=2540 (accessed 10 July 2002).

Morton, H.W. (1982) 'Soviet sport reassessed', in H. Cantelon and R. Gruneau (eds), *Sport, Culture and the Modern State* (pp. 209–19), Toronto: University of Toronto Press.

Murray, V. (1997) *Australian Swimming Incorporated Letter to SCORS Working Party on Management Improvement*, Canberra: ASI.

Nauright, J. (1996) 'Money, methods and medals: the Australian elite sports system in the 1990s', in K. Hardman (ed.), *Sport for All: Issues and Perspectives in International Context* (pp. 18–22), Manchester: Centre for Physical Education and Leisure Studies.

Nieuwenhuis, J. (1999) *National Conference on Sport and the Corporate Sector: Summary Report* (Prepared for the Department of Canadian Heritage [Sport Canada] by the Canadian Centre for Business in the Community), Ottawa: The Conference Board of Canada.

Noah, H. (1984) 'Uses and abuses of comparative education', *Comparative Education Review*, 28(4): 550–62.

Oakley, B. and Green, M. (2001a) 'The production of Olympic champions: international perspectives on elite sport development systems', *European Journal for Sport Management*, 8(Special Issue): 83–105.

—— (2001b) 'Still playing the game at arm's length? The selective re-investment in British sport, 1995–2000', *Managing Leisure*, 6: 74–94.

O'Connor, A. (2003, 26 March) 'Cashflow problems could hit UKA track projects', *The Times* (Business), p. 40.

Ontario Sailing Association (2002) *Notice of Race: Canadian Olympic Classes Queensway Audi Icebreaker Regatta, May 18–19, 2002*, Online. Available: http://www.sailon.org/Racing/race_02_a_nrOCR.htm (accessed 5 December 2002).

Ontario Track and Field Association (2002) *Minutes of the OTFA Board Meeting*, Online. Available: http://home.eol.ca/~ontrack/board_minutes_jan_25_2002.htm (accessed 5 November 2002).

Ostrom, E. (1999) 'Institutional rational choice: an assessment of the institutional analysis and development framework', in P. Sabatier (ed.), *Theories of the Policy Process: Theoretical Lenses on Public Policy* (pp. 35–71), Boulder, CO: Westview Press.

Paddick, R.J. (1997) 'Amateurism', in W. Vamplew, K. Moore, J. O'Hara, R. Cashman and I.F. Jobling (eds), *The Oxford Companion to Australian Sport* (2nd Revised edn, pp. 11–15), Oxford: Oxford University Press.

Paish, W. (1983) 'Athletics in Canada – an outsider's view', *Track and Field Journal* (October), pp.14–15.

Parliament of the Commonwealth of Australia (1983) *The Way We P(l)ay: Commonwealth Assistance for Sport and Recreation* (Report From the House of Representatives Standing Committee on Expenditure), Canberra: Parliament of the Commonwealth of Australia.

—— (1989) *Going for Gold: The First Report on an Inquiry into Sports Funding and Administration* (The House of Representatives Standing Committee on Finance and Public Administration), Canberra: Parliament of the Commonwealth of Australia.

—— (1990) *Can Sport be Bought? The Second Report on an Inquiry into Sports Funding and Administration* (The House of Representatives Standing Committee on Finance and Public Administration), Canberra: Parliament of the Commonwealth of Australia.

Parrack, J. (2001) 'What price gold?', *Swimming* (September), pp. 24–5.

Parrish, R. (2003) 'The politics of sports regulation in the European Union', *Journal of European Public Policy*, 10(2): 246–62.

Parsons, W. (1995) *Public Policy: An Introduction to the Theory and Practice of Policy Analysis*, Cheltenham: Edward Elgar.

Peppard, V. and Riordan, J. (1993) *Playing Politics: Soviet Sport Diplomacy to 1992*, London: Jai Press.

Pera, M. (1989) *The Yacht Racing Rules: A Complete Guide*, London: Nautical Books.

Peters, B.G. (1998) *Comparative Politics: Theory and Methods*, Basingstoke: Macmillan.

Phillips, M. (2000) *From Sidelines to Centrefield: A History of Sports Coaching in Australia*, Sydney: University of New South Wales Press.

Pickup, D. (1996) *Not Another Messiah: An Account of the Sports Council, 1988–93*, Edinburgh: Pentland Press.

Pinaud, Y. L. (1971) *Sailing From Start to Finish*, trans. J. Moore and I. Moore, London: Adlard Coles.

Powell, D. (2001, 13 August) 'Britain's tale of woe runs the full course', *The Times (Sport Daily)*, p. 2.

Proctor, I. (1962) *Racing Dinghy Handling: A Complete Guide*, 6th edn, London: Adlard Coles.

Przeworski, A. and Teune, H. (1970) *The Logic of Comparative Social Inquiry*, New York: Wiley.

Pyke, F. and Norris, K. (2001) 'Australia from Montreal to Sydney: a history of a change in model', paper presented at the 2nd International Forum on Elite Sport, San Cugat, Catalonia, September.

Radford, P., Hemery, D. and Biddle, J. (1989) *Independent Review of Coaching*, London: Sports Council.

Redmond, G. (1985) 'Developments in sport from 1939 to 1976', in M.L. Howell and R.H. Howell (eds), *History of Sport in Canada* (pp. 303–83), Champaign: IL: Stipes Publishing Co.

Riley, R. (2002) 'The future of swimming?', *Recreation* (January/February), pp. 6–10.

Riordan, J. (1978) 'The USSR', in J. Riordan (ed.), *Sport Under Communism* (pp. 13–53), London: C. Hurst.

—— (1986a) 'Elite sport policy in East and West', in L. Allison (ed.), *The Politics of Sport* (pp. 66–89), Manchester: Manchester University Press.

—— (1986b) 'The selection of top performers in East European sport', in G. Gleeson (ed.), *The Growing Child in Competitive Sport* (pp. 220–38), London: Hodder and Stoughton.

—— (1991) *Sport, Politics and Communism*, Manchester: Manchester University Press.

—— (1993) 'The rise and fall of Soviet Olympic champions', *Olympika: The International Journal of Olympic Studies*, II: 25–44.

—— (1999) 'The impact of communism on sport', in J. Riordan and A. Krüger (eds), *The International Politics of Sport in the 20th Century* (pp. 48–66), London: E&FN Spon.

Roche, M. (1993) 'Sport and community: rhetoric and reality in the development of British sport policy', in J.C. Binfield and J. Stevenson (eds), *Sport, Culture and Politics* (pp. 72–112), Sheffield: Sheffield Academic Press.

Rodda, J. (1994, 12 December) 'Athletics: time for cross-country to grasp the nettle', *Guardian*, p. 17.

Roe, B. (2002) *The State of Domestic Athletics Competition in Australia*, Melbourne: AAI.

Rose, R. (1991) 'What is lesson-drawing?', *Journal of Public Policy*, 11(1): 3–30.

Royal Yachting Association (RYA) (1970) *Olympic Committee Minutes, 3 February: The Olympic Training Coach*, London: RYA.

—— (1972) *A National Yacht Racing Centre*, London: RYA.

—— (1973a) *National Yacht Racing Centre* (February), London: RYA.

—— (1973b) *National Yacht Racing Centre* (October), London: RYA.

—— (1985) *Grant Application and Rolling Four Year Plan 1985–1988*, Woking: RYA.

—— (1986) *Yacht Racing Divisional Committee Minutes, 14 January: Sports Council*, Woking: RYA.

—— (1990) *Race Training Committee Minutes, 1 May: Olympic Selection Procedures 1992*, Woking: RYA.

—— (1992a) *Race Training Committee Minutes, 1 December*, Eastleigh: RYA.

—— (1992b) *Race Training Committee Minutes, 6 October*, Eastleigh: RYA.

—— (1994) *Yacht Racing Divisional Committee Minutes, 8 February: Commonwealth Games*, Eastleigh: RYA.

—— (1998a) *National Junior/Youth Sailing Strategy*, Eastleigh: RYA.

—— (1998b) *Report and Accounts 1997–1998*, Eastleigh: RYA.

—— (1998c) *World Class Performance Plan 1998–2001*, Eastleigh: RYA.

—— (1999) *World Class Start and Potential Plan 1999–2008*, Eastleigh: RYA.

—— (2000) *Report and Accounts 1999–2000*, Eastleigh: RYA.

—— (2001a) *Development Plan 2002–2006*, Eastleigh: RYA.

—— (2001b) 'New chairman starts work', *RYA Magazine* (Winter), pp. 18–19.

—— (2002a) *About the RYA*, Online. Available: http://www.rya.org.uk/HQ/default.asp?contentID=569107 (accessed 30 August 2002).

—— (2002b) *Why Should I Join the RYA and What Are the Benefits?*, Online. Available: http://www.rya.org.uk/faqs.asp?contentId=1323808 (accessed 11 September 2002).

Royal Yachting Association and Sport England (2001) *Facilities Strategy for Sailing*, Eastleigh: RYA.

Sabatier, P.A. (1998) 'The advocacy coalition framework: revisions and relevance for Europe', *Journal of European Public Policy*, 5(March): 98–130.

Sabatier, P.A. and Jenkins-Smith, H.C. (1993a) 'The advocacy coalition framework: assessment, revisions, and implications for scholars and practitioners', in P.A. Sabatier and H.C. Jenkins-Smith (eds), *Policy Change and Learning: An Advocacy Coalition Approach* (pp. 211–35), Boulder, CO: Westview Press.

—— (eds) (1993b) *Policy Change and Learning: An Advocacy Coalition Approach*, Boulder, CO: Westview Press.

—— (1999) 'The advocacy coalition framework: an assessment', in P.A. Sabatier (ed.), *Theories of the Policy Process: Theoretical Lenses on Public Policy* (pp. 117–66), Boulder, CO: Westview Press.

Sayer, A. (1992) *Method in Social Science: A Realist Approach*, 2nd edn, London: Routledge.

Scammell, R. (2000a) *Going for Gold With Richard Clarke*, Online. Available: http://www.cansport.com/cgi-bin/articles.pl?lang=eandtpl=andtype=viewpointandrec_id=10 (accessed 5 November 2002).

—— (2000b) *Pound Misses the Mark on Sport Funding*, Online. Available: http://www.cansport.com/cgi-bin/articles.pl?lang=eandtpl=andtype=viewpointandrec_id =800 (accessed 5 November 2002).

—— (2001) *Funding Boost Must Go Hand in Hand With New Canadian Sport System*, Online. Available: http://www.cansport.com/cgi-bin/articles.pl?lang=eandtpl=and type=viewpointandrec_id=1728 (accessed 5 November 2002).

Schembri, G. (2000) 'Coach education in Australia', paper presented at the Pre-Olympic Study Seminar, Rome, May.

Semotiuk, D.M. (1986) 'National government involvement in amateur sport in Australia 1972–1981', in M.L. Krotee and E.M. Jaeger (eds), *Comparative Physical Education and Sport* (Vol. 3, pp. 159–71), Champaign, IL: Human Kinetics.

—— (1996) 'High performance sport in Canada', in K. Hardman (ed.), *Sport for All: Issues and Perspectives in International Context* (pp. 7–17), Manchester: Centre for Physical Education and Leisure Studies.

Shneidman, N.N. (1978) *The Soviet Road to Olympus: Theory and Practice of Soviet Physical Culture and Sport*, Toronto: The Ontario Institute for Studies in Education.

Sibeon, R. (1997) *Contemporary Sociology and Policy Analysis: The New Sociology of Public Policy*, London: Kogan Page & Tudor.

—— (1999) 'Agency, structure, and social chance as cross-disciplinary concepts', *Politics*, 19(3): 139–44.

Slack, T. (1998) *Studying the Commercialisation of Sport: The Need for Critical Analysis*, Online. Available: http://www.physed.otago.ac.nz/sosol/home.htm (accessed 4 December 2001).

Slack, T., Berrett, T. and Mistry, K. (1994) 'Rational planning systems as a source of organisational conflict', *International Review for the Sociology of Sport*, 29(3): 317–28.

Smith, M.J. (1993) *Pressure, Power and Policy: State Autonomy and Policy Networks in Britain and the United States*, Hemel Hempstead: Harvester-Wheatsheaf.

—— (1995) 'Pluralism', in D. Marsh and G. Stoker (eds), *Theory and Methods in Political Science* (pp. 209–27), Basingstoke: Macmillan.

Sport England (1999a) *Best Value Through Sport*, London: Sport England.

—— (1999b) *Investing for Our Sporting Future: Sport England Lottery Fund Strategy 1999–2009*, London: Sport England.

—— (2001) *Planning for Water Sports* (Planning Bulletin), London: Sport England.

Sports Council (1978) *Facilities for Yachting*, London: Sports Council.

—— (1982) *Sport in the Community: The Next Ten Years*, London: Sports Council.

—— (1987a) *Athletics: On the Right Track* (A Report of a National Working Party, Vol. 1), London: Sports Council.

—— (1987b) *Athletics: On the Right Track* (Workshop Report from the Sports Council's National Seminar and Exhibition), London: Sports Council.

—— (1988) *Sport in the Community: Into the '90s*, London: Sports Council.

—— (1991) *Coaching Matters: A Review of Coaching and Coach Education in the United Kingdom*, London: Sports Council.

Sport Industry Research Centre (2002) *European Sporting Success: A Study of the Development of Medal Winning Elites in Five European Countries*, Sheffield: Sheffield Hallam University.

Stamm, H. and Lamprecht, M. (2001) 'Sydney 2000 – The best Games ever? World sport and relationships of structural dependency', in Proceedings, 1st World Congress of Sociology of Sport (pp. 129–36), Seoul, Korea.

St-Aubin, M. (1994) 'Talent identification in Canada', *Swim Canada* (February), p. 7.

Sutcliffe, P. (1988) 'Sport in the German Democratic Republic', *Coaching Focus*, 8, pp. 8–11.

Swimming/Natation Canada (SNC) (1993) *Strategic Plan 1993–1998*, Ottawa: SNC.

—— (1997) *Annual Report 1996–1997*, Ottawa: SNC.

—— (1998) *Annual Report 1997–1998*, Ottawa: SNC.

—— (2001) *Annual Report 2000–2001*, Ottawa: SNC.

—— (2002a) *Annual Report 2001–2002*, Ottawa: SNC.

—— (2002b) *President's Report* (E-News), Online. Available: http://www.swimming.ca/ pdf/enews_volume3.pdf (accessed 23 October 2002).

The Sweeney Sports Report 2001/2002 (2002) *Australians' Sporting Interests* (Vol. 1), Albert Park, Victoria: Sweeney Sports Pty Ltd.

Theodoraki, E. (1999) 'The making of the UK sports institute', *Managing Leisure*, 4(4): 187–200.

Thibault, L. and Harvey, J. (1997) 'Fostering interorganisational linkages in the Canadian sport delivery system', *Journal of Sport Management*, 11: 45–68.

Thomas, G. (2002) *Track and Field Athletics Australia: Rick Mitchell's Letter*, Online. Available: http://www.geocities.com/geetee/rick_letter.html (accessed 9 March 2004).

Tihanyi, J. (2001a) 'Discontent on deck', *SwimNews* (May/June), pp. 6–9.

—— (2001b) 'A plea for a critical review', *SwimNews* (April), p. 29.

Toohey, K.M. (1990) 'The politics of Australian elite sport: 1949–1983', unpublished PhD thesis, The Pennsylvania State University.

Treadwell, P. (1987) 'Giftedness and sport in schools: a comparative perspective', *British Journal of Physical Education*, 18(2): 63–5.

True, J.L., Jones, B.D. and Baumgartner, F.R. (1999) 'Punctuated-equilibrium theory: explaining stability and change in American policymaking', in Sabatier, P.A. (ed.) *Theories of the Policy Process: Theoretical Lenses on Public Policy* (pp. 97–115), Boulder CO: Westview Press.

UK Athletics (UKA) (1998) *National Athletics Facilities Strategy 1998–2004*, Online. Available: www.ukathletics.net/default.asp?page=7C3356243A3F743B5E2D7232 andarticle_id=CE6DC66AD267CE67 (accessed 21 May 2002).

—— (2000) *Competition Review*, Birmingham: UKA.

—— (2001) *UK Athletics News: Annual Review*, Birmingham: UKA.

—— (2002a) *About UK Athletics*, Online. Available: http://www.ukathletics.net/default.asp?page=78234E352A3F743B7E2F7A3D (accessed 23 April 2002).

—— (2002b) *Interviewee: David Moorcroft*, Online. Available: http://www.ukathletics.net/vsite/vcontent/page/custom/0,8510,4854–132351–133659–21233–79782–custom-item,00.html (accessed 12 March 2003).

—— (2003) *UK Athletics News: Annual Review*, Birmingham: UKA.

UK Sport (1999) *The Development of Coaching in the United Kingdom*, London: UK Sport.

—— (2000a) *Annual Report 1999–2000*, London: UK Sport.

—— (2000b) *Great Britain's Sporting Preferences*, London: UK Sport.

—— (2001) *Annual Report 2000–2001*, London: UK Sport.

—— (2002a) *Lottery Funding: Facts and Figures*, Online. Available: http://www.uksport.gov.uk/lotteryfacts/ (accessed 18 September 2002).

—— (2002b) *UK Athletics Welcomes £40m Award*, Online. Available: http://www.uksport.gov.uk/template.asp?id=996 (accessed 24 May 2002).

—— (2002c) *UK Sport Lottery Strategy 2002–2005*, London: UK Sport.

—— (2002d) *United Kingdom's Sporting Preferences*, London: UK Sport.

Vamplew, W. (1997) 'Sports medicine', in W. Vamplew, K. Moore, J. O'Hara, R. Cashman and I.F. Jobling (eds), *The Oxford Companion to Australian Sport* (2nd Revised edn, pp. 396–7), Oxford: Oxford University Press.

Vamplew, W., Moore, K., O'Hara, J., Cashman, R. and Jobling, I.F. (eds) (1997) *The Oxford Companion to Australian Sport* (2nd Revised edn), Melbourne: Oxford University Press.

Verkhoshansky, Y. (1998) 'Main features of a modern scientific sports training theory', *New Studies in Athletics*, 13(3): 9–20.

Volkwein, K.A.E. and Haag, H.R. (1994) 'Sport in unified Germany: the merging of two different sport systems', *Journal of Sport and Social Issues*, 18(2): 183–93.

Wallechinsky, D. (1996) *The Complete Book of the Olympics*, London: Aurum.

—— (2000) *The Complete Book of the Olympics*, 2000 edn, London: Aurum.

Ward, T. (2002a, 15 May) 'Follow the sun', *Athletics Weekly*, p. 50.

—— (2002b, 2 January) 'Future investment', *Athletics Weekly*, pp. 20–1.

—— (2002c, 9 January) 'Unfinished odyssey', *Athletics Weekly*, pp. 20–3.

Watman, M. (2002, 30 January) 'The glittering eighties', *Athletics Weekly*, pp. 24–5.

Weiss, C.H. (1977) 'Research for policy's sake: the enlightenment function of social research', *Policy Analysis*, 3(Fall): 531–45.

Westerbeek, H. (1995) 'How they do it down under', *Recreation* (October), pp. 39–46.

Whitson, D. (1998) 'Olympic sport, global media and cultural diversity', in R.K. Barney, K.B. Wamsley, S.G. Martyn and G.H. MacDonald (eds), *Global and Cultural Critique: Problematising the Olympic Games* (pp. 1–9), London, Ontario: University of Western Ontario.

Whitson, D. and Macintosh, D. (1988) 'The professionalisation of Canadian amateur sport: questions of power and purpose', *Arena Review*, 12(2): 81–96.

—— (1989) 'Rational planning vs regional interests: the professionalisation of Canadian amateur sport', *Canadian Public Policy*, XV(4): 436–49.

Woodman, L. (1989) 'The development of coach education in Australia', *The Journal of the Australian Society for Sports History*, 5(2): 204–24.

—— (1997) 'Coaching', in W. Vamplew, K. Moore, J. O'Hara, R. Cashman and I.F. Jobling (eds), *The Oxford Companion to Australian Sport* (2nd Revised edn, pp. 102–4), Oxford: Oxford University Press.

Yachting Association of New South Wales (2001) *National Sailing Centre* (Media Release), Online. Available: http://www.boatingoz.com.au/news01/010423.htm (accessed 15 March 2004).

Yin, R.K. (1994) *Case Study Research: Design and Methods* (2nd edn), London: Sage.

Young, K. (1977) '"Values" in the policy process', *Policy and Politics*, 5: 1–22.

Index

eBooks – at www.eBookstore.tandf.co.uk

A library at your fingertips!

eBooks are electronic versions of printed books. You can store them on your PC/laptop or browse them online.

They have advantages for anyone needing rapid access to a wide variety of published, copyright information.

eBooks can help your research by enabling you to bookmark chapters, annotate text and use instant searches to find specific words or phrases. Several eBook files would fit on even a small laptop or PDA.

NEW: Save money by eSubscribing: cheap, online access to any eBook for as long as you need it.

Annual subscription packages

We now offer special low-cost bulk subscriptions to packages of eBooks in certain subject areas. These are available to libraries or to individuals.

For more information please contact webmaster.ebooks@tandf.co.uk

We're continually developing the eBook concept, so keep up to date by visiting the website.

www.eBookstore.tandf.co.uk